CHRISTIAN FAITH
IN DARK TIMES

CHRISTIAN FAITH IN DARK TIMES

THEOLOGICAL CONFLICTS IN THE SHADOW OF HITLER

JACK FORSTMAN

WESTMINSTER / JOHN KNOX PRESS
LOUISVILLE, KENTUCKY

© 1992 H. Jackson Forstman

Book design by Christine Leonard Raquepaw

First edition

This book is printed on acid-free paper that meets the American National Standards Institute Z39.48 standard. ∞

Published by Westminster/John Knox Press
Louisville, Kentucky

PRINTED IN THE UNITED STATES OF AMERICA
9 8 7 6 5 4 3 2 1

Library of Congress Cataloging-in-Publication Data

Forstman, Jack, 1929–
   Christian faith in dark times : theological conflicts in the shadow of Hitler
/ Jack Forstman. — 1st ed.
      p.   cm.
   ISBN 0-664-21974-8 (alk. paper)

   1. Theology, Doctrinal—Germany—History—20th century. 2. Germany—
Religion—20th century. 3. Protestant churches—Germany—History—20th
century. I. Title.
BT30.G3F67 1992
230′.0943′09041—dc20   91-45744

IN MEMORY OF

my brother-in-law

Paul Cronk (1925–1945)

who died in the Battle of the Bulge

and

DEDICATED TO

my grandchildren of two nations

Jackson and Ryan (U.S.A.)

Gabriel, Nathalie, and Isabel (Germany)

and to their generation

CONTENTS

ACKNOWLEDGMENTS

For the title of this book, I have drawn on a phrase in Bertolt Brecht's striking and sobering poem *"An den Nachgeborenen"* (To Those Born Later). The poem begins, "Truly, I live in dark times." In twelve short stanzas, Brecht describes, starkly and poignantly, those dark times. He wrote the poem from exile in the early years of the Third Reich.

With the exception of the quotation of Heinrich Heine, the quotations at the beginning of the major sections of this volume are from nontheological writers who came to prominence in the Weimar years. These remarkable authors, Hans Fallada excepted, were, as the Nazis determined it, "non-Aryan" or "not purely Aryan." To think about those dark times is necessarily to think as well about the Holocaust. I hope the citations will serve as an indirect reminder.

I am grateful to the German Fulbright Commission, the Association of Theological Schools in the United States and Canada, the Lilly Endowment, and the Graduate Research Council of Vanderbilt University for generous grants that made possible a number of visits to Germany for long and short periods in order for me to work on German culture and theology of the late nineteenth and early twentieth centuries, and to professors and librarians at the universities in Tübingen and Marburg, who made my work pleasant and easy.

I am also grateful to Davidson College, whose invitation to present the Ott Lectures provided an impetus to conceive this volume more or less in the form it has taken. The discussions with students and faculty at Davidson were both a stimulant and an encouragement. I offer special thanks to Professor Karl Plank for his hospitality and friendship, which I treasure. A further impetus came from my close friend, Judy Thompson. In the spring of 1990, when she was Senior Warden of St. Mark's in the Valley, Los Olivos, California, she arranged for me to rehearse the main themes of my work with thoughtful nonprofessional theologians, and she and Bill Killingsworth provided an unforgettable long weekend of stimulating conversation and sheer pleasure.

This book includes a number of quotations from German books, essays, and letters. I have used available English translations in most cases, citing the translators in the notes. Where no translator is cited in the notes the translation is my own.

J.F.

Grateful acknowledgment is made for permission to reprint the following copyrighted material.

Excerpts from *The Beginnings of Dialectical Theology,* ed. James M. Robinson, are used by permission of Christian Kaiser Verlag.

Excerpts from *Deutschlands Schicksal,* by Emanuel Hirsch (Göttingen: Vandenhoeck & Ruprecht, 1920) are used by permission of Vandenhoeck & Ruprecht.

Excerpts from *Existence and Faith: Shorter Writings,* by Rudolf Bultmann, intro. and trans. Schubert Ogden, translation copyright 1960 by Meridian Books Inc., are used by permission of New American Library, a division of Penguin Books USA Inc.

Excerpts from *The Epistle to the Romans,* by Karl Barth, trans. Edwyn C. Hoskyns (London: Oxford University Press, 1933) are used by permission of Oxford University Press.

Excerpts from *Faith and Understanding,* by Rudolf Bultmann, trans. Louise Pettibone Smith, ed. Robert W. Funk, are copyright © 1987 SCM Press Ltd. Used by permission of Augsburg Fortress.

Excerpts from *The Word of God and the Word of Man,* by Karl Barth, trans. Douglas Horton, are copyright 1928, © 1956, 1957 by Douglas Horton. Reprinted by permission of HarperCollins Publishers.

INTRODUCTION

A THEOLOGICAL QUESTION
FOR TODAY

Nichts ist schwerer und nichts erfordert mehr Charakter, als sich in offenem Gegensatz zu seiner Zeit zu befinden und laut zu sagen: Nein.

Nothing is more difficult and nothing requires more character than to find oneself in open opposition to one's time and to say loudly: No.—KURT TUCHOLSKY[1]

Kurt Tucholsky wrote this powerful aphorism not long before Adolf Hitler was named Chancellor of Germany on January 30, 1933. Tucholsky was German, and he was Jewish—one of a throng of German Jews, masters of the German language, who were given, I am convinced, from the heartbeat of the Jewish tradition, the perceptiveness to recognize tyranny, oppression, and the demonic, and the power to name it for what it was before it stood naked, complete with horns, cleft feet, and trident.

Three months after Hitler was given absolute power by the German parliament in March of 1933, Tucholsky was deprived of his German citizenship, and his writings were forbidden and burned. He found asylum in Sweden. One might think he was lucky. But from his exile he poignantly wrote to a friend: "I will never be able to write in another language. . . . The world for which we have worked and to which we belong no longer exists.—The world to which we have belonged is dead. One has to learn to bear it with propriety."[2] Tucholsky found he could bear it in no way at all. In 1935 he committed suicide.

---

1. Kurt Tucholsky, *Schnipsel,* ed. Mary Gerold-Tucholsky and Fritz J. Raddaz (Reinbeck bei Hamburg: Rowohlt Taschenbuch Verlag, 1973), p. 67.
2. Klaus-Peter Schulz, *Kurt Tucholsky* (Reinbeck bei Hamburg: Rowohlt Taschenbuch Verlag, 1959), p. 165.

This astonishingly perceptive wit and the cloud of witnesses with him are now, I believe, in the company of the saints; but their voices were abruptly silenced, and their books, along with many other books, burned. Those were dark times in what will surely be remembered as a dark century in which there has been more human oppression, more violation of basic human rights, more killing of people by leaders or hackneys of regimes or would-be regimes, more terror and deprivation, than in any other set of similarly linked years.

But we must remember that darkness almost never descends in an instant. It almost always comes after imperceptible changes of twilight. The storm almost always begins as a small cloud on the horizon, like a person's hand, as the story in 1 Kings 18 describes it; but rare indeed is the prophet Elijah who can see from the speck in the distance the storm that is coming.

Actually, it is easy to say "no." Every time and place limps and exposes its Achilles tendon. Thus every time has its naysayers who by the constancy of their objections abstract themselves from the common life, with its necessity to build and to plant. Tucholsky wrote about the difficult "no," the "no" by the one who wants above all else to say "yes." I know no more poignant illustration of what this means than Tucholsky himself. Although he had good reason to shake the dust of Germany from his feet and to be grateful for finding haven in a country that was and would remain neutral, he was too much the German, wedded to the German language and culture, to be at ease in a friendly but alien land.

In a sharp list of his hates and loves, he listed under his hates "Deutschland" (Germany), putting the name purposefully in quotation marks. This "Deutschland" conjured up rabble-rousing appeals to false patriotism and the perversion of the name of his country by Nazi rhetoric. Under his loves he listed Deutschland without quotation marks. It was the "yes" behind the "no," and it is what makes his aphorism so potent. Indeed, "Nothing is more difficult and nothing requires more character than to find oneself in open opposition to one's time and to say loudly: No."

Kurt Tucholsky is not the subject of this book, but his aphorism serves well as a superscription of the whole. The subject matter is Christian faith—more specifically, the understanding of Christian faith and its implications for human life in the world; more specifically still, the serious question whether Christian faith, properly understood, has within it the foundation for recognizing the demonic and the strength of character to say "no."

The effort to comprehend the meaning of Christian faith and its implications for the lives of women and men is called Christian theology. Theology is the science or knowledge of God. The definition is short; the object is incomparably weighty. To state the definition with a straight face and without a stammer seems light-minded, and to presume that the undertaking is not impossible or ridiculous seems pretentious.

Christian theology, however, like any other particular form of theology related to a discrete and discernible tradition, is, at least in some respects, manageable. It does not start from nothing. Rather, it begins with the disciplined and reflective effort to gain clarity about God as faith in God emerged and has been received and developed in the Christian tradition. This undertaking is more manageable in the sense that it can deal with the description and analysis of what persons who were or are apparently Christian have said about God and the many topics that follow. But the description and analysis of what others have said is not yet properly theology; rather, it is the history of theology or the interpretation of theology. One comes closer to theology as such if one ventures, in one's description and analysis of what others have said, to make judgments about the adequacy or inadequacy, the rightness or wrongness of a particular exposition of the meaning and implications of Christian faith in God. This venture requires the establishment of norms on the basis of which such judgments can be made; and if one wants to avoid provincialism—in this case, claiming something for oneself on an arbitrary basis while not granting what another claims on a similarly arbitrary basis—one must be prepared to defend in a public arena not only the movement from the foundation to the norms of judgment but the foundation as well. One becomes, by vocation or avocation, a theologian.

As a theologian, one wants to move beyond the description and analysis of what others have said about Christian faith together with one's judgments about these varied expressions. One wants to be able to express for oneself the meaning and implications of faith. If one takes the subject matter (God) seriously, one recognizes that it is fraught with unbounded significance. One wants to get it right—or, to be properly modest, more nearly right. That is, the question of truth looms before one, even if one acknowledges that an absolute statement of the truth in full and final form is impossible in our conditioned and limited human sphere. That impossibility, however, never manages to set aside the question of truth.

Raising that question by no means implies that there is one and only one true expression of the meaning and implications of Christian faith available to humankind. One gladly and rightly affirms the famous saying of Gotthold Ephraim Lessing in the late eighteenth century:

> If God held all truth in his right hand and in his left the never-ending struggle for truth—with the proviso that I would always and eternally err—and said to me, "Choose!" I would fall before his left hand with humility and say, "Father, give! The pure truth is for you alone!"[3]

Everlastingly to be mistaken in the context of striving after truth does not mean that one is always simply and without remainder wrong. It does mean that one hazards to think that some advancement in comprehension and understanding is possible. If it comes at all, it must, of course, come by exercising critical judgment of one's past and present comprehensions and understandings. In short, one is in critical dialogue with oneself, just as one is in critical dialogue with others who have tried and continue to try to give expression to Christian faith.

The variety of expressions of Christian faith is immense. Although none gives a final statement of absolute truth, it would be foolhardy to suppose that all are equally right or equally wrong. If one is serious, then, about the work of theology, about its object—God as God is believed to be disclosed in Jesus Christ and in the traditions of faith in ancient Israel and Christianity—one must make judgments. That is, one must find a basis and a way for

---

3. Gotthold Ephraim Lessing, "Eine Duplik," in *Gesammelte Werke in zwei Bänden,* ed. Otto Mann (Gütersloh: Sigbert Mohn Verlag, 1966), vol. 2, p. 771.

saying "no" and for saying "yes," with whatever modulation of volume and whatever qualification are appropriate. When the stakes are particularly high, when what one reflectively and critically judges to be in serious error, and when the times are dark such that the effects of error are especially acute, one must summon the strength of character and be prepared to say loudly: "No!"

There is another way in which the work of theology leads one to say not only "yes" but "no" as well (with however many decibels). If theology tries to gain clarity about its subject matter (God as God is believed to be disclosed in Jesus Christ and in the traditions of ancient Israel and Christianity) and about the implications of that subject matter for human life, the church, and the world, then it also tries to achieve clarity about what is not God, about what confuses the difference between God and what is not God, and about what is opposed to God. To the degree that one finds responsible clarity about the "yes" (what one must affirm), one ought also to find clarity about the "no" (what one must deny). This task is always difficult. Even so, one cannot resist the force of the conviction that the darker the times, the more ominous and terrible the fruit of serious error and the more difficult it is to say clearly and definitely both "no" and "yes."

It was under such a gathering cloud of darkness that Tucholsky wrote the maxim cited at the beginning of this Introduction: "Nothing is more difficult and nothing requires more character than to find oneself in open opposition to one's time and to say loudly: No."

Germany under the shadow of Hitler was a particularly dark and demonic time in a century that will surely be remembered as one of the darkest and most demonic.[4] Looking back on the Third Reich, we have no problem with clarity. We see the lies, the perversion of the language, the oppression, the tyranny, the inhumanity, and above all, the Holocaust. In short, we look back as historians. But we must recall and ponder Friedrich Schlegel's

---

4. I use the term "demonic" here and elsewhere rather than "evil" because it not only is stronger but also suggests the deceptive, seductive, and finally unfathomable character of inhumanity and oppression. By it I do not mean that those who perpetrate, approve, or passively acquiesce in acts of inhumanity and oppression are possessed by powers beyond their control.

early nineteenth-century description of the historian as "a backward turned prophet," and we must understand that the definition is a sound warning.[5] It is considerably easier to "predict" after everything has already happened!

That warning should be especially heeded with respect to the years of the Weimar Republic in Germany (1918–1933) and the beginning of Hitler's rule precisely because from where we stand everything is clear. But we presume to our own peril that from the other side of 1933 everything was clear. Such a view guarantees that we will not see the demonic in our own time until it stands boldly before us without disguise, displaying its horns, cleft feet, and trident. It all but assures that we will not realize that it is dark until we are deep into the moonless night.

From the other side of 1933, during the fateful fourteen years of the Weimar Republic, almost everything was fuzzy. There were not many Kurt Tucholskys.[6] One could see only the tiny cloud on the horizon or perhaps sense the first dimming of the twilight. Moreover, the cloud could be taken as harbinger of the drought's end, and the twilight dimness as the first sign of the new dawn.

When Hitler was named Chancellor of the Weimar Republic on January 30, 1933, the head of a coalition because the Nazi party did not hold a majority of the seats in the parliament, and then on March 23 was granted dictatorial powers, many hailed the change as *die große Wende,* "the great turning point," in German history. (We need to note that in March Hitler managed the two thirds vote necessary to alter the constitution to give himself total power only because his brown shirt thugs bodily prevented 107 Communist and Socialist deputies from attending the session and because he lied to the leader of the Center Party in order to gain his support. But this fact, too, was not widely known at the time.) The Hitler enthusiasts believed their *Führer* ("leader") would bring an end to the political instability of the Weimar Republic, reestablish freedom for the German people, rectify the unjust and oppressive

---

5. Friedrich Schlegel, *Kritische Schriften,* ed. Wolfdietrich Rasch (München: Carl Hanser Verlag, 1964), p. 34.

6. Here is one of Tucholsky's pointed quips from the time before Hitler: "Satire has its limits from above: Buddha shuns it. Satire also has its limits from below. In Germany, for example, the existing fascist powers. It doesn't work—you simply can't shoot that low." Tucholsky, *Schnipsel,* p. 119.

terms of surrender in 1918, and make it possible once again to be proud to be a German. In its first few months, the Nazi state solved a number of serious problems and showed promise of solving others. The Weimar Republic had had to contend with economic exhaustion, heavy reparations, and unimaginable inflation followed by severe depression, with their attending chaos and deprivation. The Third Reich brought a new sense of unity and purpose as a people, social order, work, good bread, Volkswagens, and four-lane highways to drive them on.

To be sure, the darker side was not entirely hidden. Demagoguery, in order to embed itself more firmly, inflame passions, and induce the people to overlook or excuse its excesses, will create enemies. International capitalism was one, but it was an evasive target. Moreover, Hitler needed its money and capacity. Communism was another enemy, and it was less evasive. Before noon on February 28, the day after the Reichstag fire, which Hitler blamed on the Communists, four thousand Communists and suspected Communists were under arrest—the beginning of the obliteration of that party. Most ominous of all, the Jews were declared enemies. Hitler and his supporters claimed that the Jews were the leading force behind both international capitalism and communism. Equally damning was the claim that the Jews were an alien people, or *Volk,* that they were not and could never be true Germans, part of the blood and soil of the German *Volk.*

This darker side was evident in speeches, placards, and demonstrations. It was available for all to read in Hitler's rambling, not widely read book *Mein Kampf.* But it was not difficult to overlook the darker side or not take it seriously. It seems that many Germans in the 1920s and early 1930s took their politicians less seriously even than Americans take theirs today. It was easier to take instances of violence in the streets and offensive statements in speeches as the excessive enthusiasm of a few or as harmless rhetoric, rather than be alarmed. Hans-Georg Gadamer, later a philosopher of world renown and never a supporter of the Nazi regime, was a student in Marburg at the time of the change in government. He reports that he and his friends were unprepared for what happened. They had not read *Mein Kampf,* and the liberal press, which they did read, did not greatly alarm them. Anti-Semitism was repugnant to them, but they could not believe anything would come of the offensive rhetoric. "Until June 30, 1934, we all basically believed that the spook would soon disappear."[7] By that time there was no liberal press, and the Nazi regime controlled the news.

The tendency not to take Hitler seriously was a widespread condition. Papen, the former Chancellor and the one who persuaded a reluctant President Hindenberg to ask Hitler to form a government, boasted, "Within two months we will have pushed Hitler so far into the corner that he'll squeak!"[8] Even such a savant as the Nobel Prize-winning novelist Thomas Mann, who had the good sense and the means to leave Germany, insisted that Hitler could not possibly maintain power more than six months.[9]

Given the fuzziness of the situation at the end of the Weimar Republic and the ease with which people could take Hitler lightly and discount his potential for endurance, those who are concerned for Christian faith must be grateful that some theologians managed to gain a measure of clarity at the beginning and to resist at least at some points. Actually, there were a good many, but in this book I will deal with the three Protestant theologians who were most gifted and best known: Karl Barth, Paul Tillich, and Rudolf Bultmann.[10]

There were also a good many theologians who hailed the advent of the Third Reich and tried to justify it theologically. The most

---

7. Hans-Georg Gadamer, *Philosophische Lehrjahre: Eine Ruckschau* (Frankfurt am Main: Vittorio Klostermann, 1977), p. 51. June 30, 1934, was "The Night of Long Knives." On that night, the Nazis brutally purged the SA (*Sturmabteilung*), murdering its chief of staff, Ernst Röhm, and dozens of his senior aides. The Nazis used the occasion to murder a good many others as well: former associates, suspected dissidents, army generals. Some were murdered because of mistaken identity, mistakes that apparently did not bother the murderers.

8. Quoted by Gordon A. Craig in *Germany: 1866–1945* (New York: Oxford University Press, 1978), p. 570.

9. According to an account by George Grosz of a luncheon with Mann in New York City, in Grosz, *Ein kleines Ja und ein Großes Nein: Sein Leben von ihm selbst erzählt* (Reinbeck bei Hamburg: Rowohlt Taschenbuch Verlag, 1974), p. 266.

10. I omit consideration of Dietrich Bonhöffer, who was executed for his complicity in the attempt on Hitler's life. Bonhöffer was just beginning his theological work in 1933, and his most important work came later. In 1933, he was 27.

gifted and best known among the Protestant theologians were Friedrich Gogarten, Paul Althaus, and Emanuel Hirsch. Gogarten and Althaus apparently realized their mistake a couple of years before the beginning of the war in 1939. Gogarten, who was a prodigious writer, fell silent after 1937 and published nothing again until 1948. After 1937, Althaus also published nothing of a political nature. Hirsch, arguably the most brilliant theologian in that time, remained a supporter of the Third Reich to the end and never publicly renounced his position.

These six Protestant theologians were approximately the same age (mid- to late forties in 1933).[11] All of them established themselves as leading theologians during the years of the Weimar Republic and were voices to whom people listened in 1933. The more important consideration in focusing primarily on these six is their interconnectedness; the easy, uneasy, and shifting alliances among them, and the controversies they had with each other beginning in the early years of the Weimar Republic and becoming acute in the critical years of 1933 and 1934. No two of these theologians stood on the same side of every fence.

Christian theology, I have said, begins with hazarding judgments about statements on the meaning and implications of Christian faith by others (whether it be the authors or editors of books of the Christian scriptures, Augustine, Thomas Aquinas, Luther, Calvin, or whoever). Although one of the central figures in this book argued in 1931 that Christian faith is always and everywhere in crisis,[12] I have also said that the judgments people concerned for Christian faith and its implications make about other theologians are more instructive and helpful in those times of special crisis, when the stakes are higher.

As we look back on the 1920s and early 1930s in Germany, there can be no doubt that the stakes were high indeed. Thus an evaluation of theology in that time and place should be particularly instructive and helpful. But it can become acutely unsettling and thus all the more potentially helpful if we can bring ourselves

---

11. In 1933, Althaus and Hirsch were 45, Gogarten 46, Barth and Tillich 47, and Bultmann 49.

12. Rudolf Bultmann, "The Crisis in Belief," in *Essays Philosophical and Theological,* trans. James C. G. Greig (New York: Macmillan, 1955), pp. 1–21.

to realize that the players, as they sat down at the table, could not see the pot. They were not aware that the stakes were so high, just as it is not possible in our own situation at any given time to know whether we are playing for copper or for gold.

The analogy is severely limited. The struggle to gain clarity about Christian faith, about its "yes" and its "no," is not a game. Even so, the analogy helps us to realize that Christian faith, indeed, is always in crisis and that its implications for human life in this world may at any time be in severe crisis. We cannot know with certainty, just as we cannot know the future.

Here is where the "prophetic" powers of the historian—that is, the historian's ability to look backward knowing already what happened later—can be useful. But using those powers is a fatal mistake if the historian assumes that the transcendent vantage point should have been available to the persons under study. Then both the struggles of the others in the past and one's own effort to be theological in the present are rendered trivial. Judgments about both the "yes" and the "no" of Christian faith become a matter of "of course."

Hopeful at least of mitigating the danger of that pitfall, I have chosen here to give special attention to the alliances—easy, uneasy, and changing—and to the controversies among and between these six remarkably gifted and eloquent Protestant theologians. My purpose is theological: to achieve a better understanding of the substance or meaning of Christian faith and its implications for human life, the church, and the world; to see a bit more clearly the "yes" of Christian faith and consequently its "no."

The theological question for today is, Are there in Christian faith understandings of God, self, and the world that can help one recognize the demonic *before* it shows itself boldly? That question is the seed of this book. There is a related and equally crucial question: Does Christian faith provide the courage publicly to name the demonic and to say "No"? That question, however, is unanswerable in advance. It has to do, as Tucholsky recognized, with character; and in dark times, strength of character, from whatever source, cannot be predicted.

PART I

THE END OF A WORLD: 1918

NEW ALTERNATIVES FOR THEOLOGY

The old faith has become a superstition. I do not say: Let the new faith come. One does not wish into being or expedite things of this sort; they spring forth from creative distress. Our task can be only to provide clarity and purity. Then the ground is prepared for things that are ready to come. . . .

But too many hands busy themselves with skills. Too few with life. . . . Too few people in the life of the spirit. Too many in science, too many in the million little studies strewn about through the academies. . . . Back to the springs, to the meaning of life, to religion. Find the center. Purify it. Make it known.—ALFRED DÖBLIN[1]

One of the most telling testimonies to the end of the world that was the Second German Empire, with its patterns of thought and attitudes, comes from Carl Zuckmayer in his excellent book of memoirs, *Als wär's ein Stuck von mir* (As If It Were a Piece of Myself). Zuckmayer is one of the best-known German writers of this century. He won the Kleist prize in 1925 and the Büchner prize in 1929, the most coveted awards for drama in Germany. The Nazis did not like his work. In 1933 they burned his books.

However, in the summer of 1914, Zuckmayer was a 17-year-old high school student on vacation with his family in The Netherlands. He was a passionate pacifist. A cycle of pacifist poems he wrote had been accepted for publication by the *Frankfurter Zeitung,* one of Germany's leading newspapers. Although the Grand Duke Franz Ferdinand of the Austro-Hungarian Empire had been assassinated in Sarajevo on June 28 and Austria was rattling its swords, there was no thought of war among the Germans enjoying the North Sea beaches in Holland. Carl

---

1. "Jenseits von Gott!" in *Die Erhebung: Jahrbuch für neue Dichtung und Wertung,* ed. Alfred Wolfenstein (Berlin: S. Fischer Verlag, 1919), p. 395.

Zuckmayer's world was intact, and he enjoyed the leisure of his youthful idealism.

On July 28, Austria declared war on Serbia, Russia began to mobilize against Austria, and the European cauldron began to boil. Germany was not yet at war, but Zuckmayer's father learned that the Kaiser had called for a partial mobilization. He decided the family should return to Germany. They were on the last train before the border closed.

Once their train crossed the border into Germany, signs of mobilization were everywhere. Soldiers in jubilant moods crowded the train, and the stations swarmed with men in uniform and people who had come to see them off. Zuckmayer described the transformation that took place within him:

> I can register what I experienced exactly. With every kilome-
> ter we traveled through the German countryside, something
> came upon me—not like an infection, rather like a radiation,
> like an unperceived, prickling surge, as if one, with hand on
> the vital parts of a machine, were charged with electricity.[2]

As if in a trance he found himself wanting, even lusting, to share the experiences of these men in uniform and to be side by side with them. The fate of these soldiers and that of all his people became, in this electrifying experience, his destiny. Before the train reached Mainz, his home city, he was eager to go to war and to sacrifice himself for his people.

Kaiser Wilhelm II proclaimed August 2 as the first full mobiliza-tion day. On that morning, Zuckmayer and eight classmates marched to the city square, arms locked to avoid being separated in the mass of people. Together they enlisted in the army. They wanted to defend their Kaiser, their *Volk,* and their way of life. They wanted to crush Germany's enemies as the army had done so quickly and decisively in 1870, when Bismarck brought the Second German Empire into being. Over the course of the next four years, all of these teenage enlistees except Zuckmayer were killed.

Zuckmayer fought four years on the western front. As injury

---

2. Carl Zuckmayer, *Als wär's ein Stuck von mir* (Frankfurt am Main: Fischer Taschenbuch Verlag, 1969), p. 164.

and death diminished the officer corps, he rose to the rank of lieutenant. Along the way, he lost every trace of his youthful idealism. In October of 1918, after partial recovery from a severe grenade wound above an eye, he was reassigned to the western front. His regiment consisted of men as severely wounded and exhausted as he. They all knew each other. As he arrived, they were in the process of forming a soldiers' council, in spite of threats of execution from their officers. The next morning, however, the officers, apparently most concerned for their own safety, abandoned the men. The soldiers chose Lieutenant Zuckmayer as their leader. He stole a horse and led the bedraggled company eastward—away from the front. It was days before armistice was declared. "We knew we had been defeated. . . . Starved, beaten, but with our weapons, we marched homeward."[3] For them the war was over. Their world had come to an end.

What the soldiers found at home confirmed the end of that world. Kaiser Wilhelm II had abdicated and with his family had fled to The Netherlands. There was talk that a revolution had taken place, but, although there had been some uprisings as the war came to an end, what happened had none of the trappings of a revolution. Prince Max von Baden, the Kaiser's last Chancellor, had asked Friedrich Ebert, head of the largest political party (the SPD, moderate Socialists) to convene a constituent assembly to determine a new form of government. Ebert accepted the request from Prince Max, though he still felt loyal to the Kaiser, in whose service two of his sons had lost their lives in battle. The country was on its way toward becoming a republic, more by default than by design. But many people did not like the idea, and the country was so politically fragmented, with parties covering the entire spectrum from far right to far left, that it was certain no single party could ever win a majority. Worse still, there would be parties participating in government that wanted nothing more than to subvert and destroy the democracy. Uprisings were in the offing, and other signs of unrest were everywhere. The country was further crippled by debt, because the Kaiser had financed the war by borrowing rather than by raising taxes, and the indications of reprisals on the part of the victorious neighboring powers were

---

3. Ibid., p. 217.

omens of further economic hardship. At home, the people, for the most part, had believed in victory until the end. Defeat was bitter and abrupt. It left a vacuum—nothing.

Whether suddenly, as for many at home, or gradually, as for many on the front, the old world, the world of the Second German Empire, died.

In Protestant theology, the effects of the collapse were dramatic. For generations, there had been two major types of Protestant theology, each, of course, with variations. On the one side, the "Positive Christians" were conservative, basing their work on a strict doctrine of biblical authority, the ancient creeds, and the classic confessions of the Protestant Reformation. They saw it as their vocation to preserve the old truths of the faith, especially against modern currents of thought. On the other side were the "Liberal Christians." Liberal theologians attuned themselves to the currents of modern thought and investigation, in some cases leading them. They engaged in the critical historical study of the Bible and documents of Christian history, and reinterpreted Christian faith in ways they thought would be more accessible to people in a world quite different from that of antiquity. For a growing number of ministers and theologians, neither of these ways was adequate any longer to the situation at hand or, of more importance, to the faith itself. They wanted to close the old arena, and they did.

In the Weimar years, leadership in Protestant theology shifted downward a full generation. The character of the discussion had almost nothing to do with the older parties, and no major creative work was produced by any who had acted in one of the old rings. The old understandings of the faith were dead. A new search for the center and efforts to clarify it and make it known burst upon the scene with startling discontinuity. New understandings did not spring forth full-grown like Athena from the head of Zeus, but like her, they were fully armed from the beginning.

Two books in particular sounded clarion calls that created new formations. They were utterly different from one another, sharing only a transcendence of and inattention to the old debate between the Positives and Liberals. What did spring forth fully formed was a new arena. The two new rings, though imperfectly formed and allowing for tangential circles and leaps from one ring to another, set the course for the discussion in the years of the Republic and for the responses to Adolf Hitler and the policies of his totalitarian regime.

The two books were *Der Römerbrief* (The Epistle to the Romans) by Karl Barth (first edition in 1919, important second edition in 1922) and *Deutschlands Schicksal* (Germany's Destiny) by Emanuel Hirsch (1920).[4]

---

4. Two other books from the same time had enormous impact, both of which also transcended the old lines between the Positives and the Liberals. One was *Das Heilige* (The Idea of the Holy) by Rudolf Otto, Professor of Theology at Marburg. This book appeared in 1917 and went through twenty-five editions by 1936. Otto attempted to set forth the unity of all religions in the experience of the awe-inspiring, overwhelming power and fascination of the "Wholly Other" (God), and to show the congruence of Christianity and eastern religions in this experience. The experience is beyond reason (nonrational or irrational), and it has nothing to do with ethics. It is impossible to trace the effects of this position in the Weimar years and into the Third Reich, though a preoccupation with the mystery beyond (and perhaps in) all tangible things, a yearning, as it were, to move beyond the limits of human life, was characteristic of many who supported the heroic measures of the Third Reich. Otto has points of contact with the poetry of Rilke and Stefan George, the novels of Hermann Hesse, the depth psychology of Carl Jung, and the anthroposophy of Rudolf Steiner, all of whom had considerable followings in the 1920s.

The other book was a stunningly brilliant piece of historical work by Professor Karl Holl in Berlin, an essay on what Luther understood by "religion." Holl first presented this piece as a lecture on the four hundredth anniversary of the Reformation in 1917. He published it in a book of essays on Luther in 1921. Holl's essay and his other work on Luther revolutionized the understanding of the German Reformer and has rightly continued to have a positive effect on Luther research to the present. I will allude to Holl's essay in my discussion of the work of Emanuel Hirsch, one of Holl's students.

KARL BARTH

1

KARL BARTH AND
THE EPISTLE TO THE ROMANS

Karl Barth's household upbringing was in the tradition of Positive Christianity. His father was a teacher at the *Predigerschule* ("Preacher School") in Basel, Switzerland, when Karl was born and later was Professor of Ancient Church History and New Testament on the theological faculty of the University of Bern. He easily identified with the Preacher School, which had been founded in opposition to Liberal theology in order to train "Bible-bound" preachers.[1] When he moved to Bern, he sided with the Positive camp on that mixed faculty. However, as committed as he was to the conservative cause, he was open to honest discussion with Liberals and to the problems of the day. (As a matter of fact, he was ahead of his time on some social issues, such as women's rights.)

When Karl declared for theological study, it was his father who guided and counseled him. The son studied for two years at Bern, a safe place, by the father's canons of judgment. Most of the lectures he heard from that faculty did not engage him, and his father's courses, to all of which Barth listened with genuine respect, did not stimulate him theologically. He was weaning himself from his upbringing, though he was not a rebellious son.

---

1. Eberhard Busch, *Karl Barths Lebenslauf* (München: Christian Kaiser Verlag, 1975), p. 13.

However, he also was not a docile one. Barth later observed, "I could not appropriate his . . . (more or less) 'Positive' . . . theological orientation and view."[2] With caution from his father, he received permission to study in Germany, first in Berlin, where the most famous Liberal, a church historian, Adolf von Harnack, taught, and to whom Barth became devoted. He would continue imbibing Liberal theology at Marburg, after an interim in Tübingen.

Barth's father did not want him to study at Marburg. It was the place of Wilhelm Herrmann, the most prominent Liberal systematic theologian of the day, and of Martin Rade, a somewhat more moderate colleague of Herrmann and the editor of the major Liberal magazine in German-speaking Protestantism, *Die christliche Welt* (The Christian World). Rade and Barth grew quite attached to each other, and Barth was Rade's editorial assistant for a year. Although there are signs that Barth, from his earliest years, was singularly distinctive, both personally and theologically, in his own fashion he became a committed Liberal.

Barth tells us that for him the world of Liberal theology came to an abrupt end at the beginning of the war in 1914. At that time, Barth was a pastor in Safenwil, a small agricultural and industrial town in the Aar valley of Switzerland. He thought Wilhelm II was ridiculous, the war an offense against humankind, and the German army guilty of violating long-standing rules for the conduct of war.

In 1957 he recalled—but not very precisely—the moment at which the bottom of Liberal theology fell out for him.[3]

> For me personally, a day at the beginning of August in that year [1914] branded itself upon me as the *dies ater* ["dark day"]. Ninety-three German intellectuals signed a public declaration in support of the war politics of Kaiser Wilhelm II

---

2. Quoted in ibid., p. 46.

3. It is important to note that Barth was also thoroughly disillusioned by the Socialist Party of Germany (SPD). He had become a member of the Socialist Party of Switzerland and placed a good deal of hope in the programs of democratic socialism. When the party in Germany voted in favor of granting Wilhelm II the war credits for which he asked, Barth lost his confidence in the party.

and his advisors. To my horror, the list included the names of almost all of my theological teachers, whom, until that time, I held in faithful respect. Having lost my confidence in their character, it occurred to me that I would no longer be able to follow their interpretation of the Bible or their representations of history and that the theology of the nineteenth century, at least for me, no longer had a future.[4]

An entire world of theological exegesis, ethics, dogmatics, and preaching therewith [that is, with the declaration] . . . became root and branch a farce.[5]

The declaration was ill-advised and badly informed, but, remembering Zuckmayer's experience, it was characteristic of the patriotism that infected all engaged countries in 1914 and the United States in 1917. Even so, Barth's recollection is faulty on at least two scores. First, the declaration was not made until October 1914. Second, of the ninety-three signatories, only twelve were theologians (both Protestant and Catholic), and of the twelve, only two were teachers whom Barth mentions as having been important to him. But they were leading lights: Adolf von Harnack and Wilhelm Herrmann. (Barth could not know that Harnack had not seen the text of the declaration before it was published or that Herrmann would later want to retract his signature from it because it denied that the German army had done in Belgium what in fact it had done.) There have been impressive efforts to disqualify Barth's typically firm statement,[6] but Barth's recollection of his break with Liberal theology, though imprecise, is essentially sound. For him, the war brought the Bismarck-Biedermeyer-Wilhelm II world to an end, and that crisis also brought to an end the era of Liberal theology.

The most difficult part of this experience for Barth personally had to do with his disillusionment with Martin Rade. Rade was

---

4. Karl Barth, "Evangelische Theologie im 19. Jahrhundert," in *Theologische Studien,* no. 49, ed. Karl Barth and Max Geiger (Zollikon-Zürich: Evangelischer Verlag, 1957), p. 6.

5. Karl Barth, "Nachwort" to *Schleiermacher-Auswahl* (München and Hamburg: Siebenstern Taschenbuch Verlag, 1968), p. 293.

6. To my knowledge, the most impressive effort is an article by Wilfried Härle in the *Zeitschrift für Theologie und Kirche* 72, no. 2 (1975), 207–224.

like a father to Barth. Although he did not sign the declaration of the German intellectuals, he did support the German war effort, though with more circumspection than most (which lost a good many subscriptions to *The Christian World*). Barth's disapproval of Rade was further complicated by the fact that Barth's brother, Peter, was engaged to Rade's daughter.

On September 8, shortly after receiving the first wartime issues of *The Christian World,* Barth wrote Rade, taking sharp issue with the position he had taken on the war.[7] Barth said he did not want to make a political judgment about which country had right on its side in the war. The matter, he thought, was too complex. Historians will have to decide. Precisely for that reason, he expressed astonishment that everything Rade had written was based implicitly or explicitly on the premise that the German cause was just. That assumption led Barth to the major problem he had with Rade's position: Rade had asserted that the premise of right was the necessary precondition for "pious readiness for war."

> For me that is the saddest of all things in this sad time, to see how today all over Germany love for the fatherland, enthusiasm for war, and Christian faith are all hopelessly mixed up together and how now on principle *The Christian World* acts just like the whole of Germany acts. . . . In this decisive moment, *The Christian World* ceases to be Christian and lines up simply with *this* world.

Certainly, he continued, Germany has to carry on the war, whether its cause is just or not. But why not leave God out of "this whole secular, sinful necessity"? To proclaim God's blessing is to invite the Germans to kill and destroy with a good conscience, but

---

7. *Karl Barth—Martin Rade: Ein Briefwechsel,* ed. with an Introduction by Christoph Schwöbel (Gütersloh: Gütersloher Verlagshaus Gerd Mohn, 1981), pp. 95–98. At Rade's suggestion, Barth's letter and a response from Rade were printed in *Neue Wege,* a journal of the Religious Socialists, edited by Leonhard Ragaz and published in Switzerland. Barth stated his preference for their publication in *Die christliche Welt* or in the *Zeitschrift für Theologie und Kirche,* both of which Rade edited. Barth noted that the border between Germany and Switzerland had been sealed and that Germans would not be able to read the exchange if it were available only in a Swiss journal.

the only possible frame of mind with which Christians can go to war is with a bad conscience.

> We say: *Hominum confusione et Dei providentia mundus regitur* ["The world is ruled by human confusion and the providence of God"]; protect us from confusion as long as it continues, and fill us with bitter shame when it is over. And then believe that God's providence, in spite of us, accomplishes what God wills.

As we saw, Barth remembered this as the time when the bottom fell out for him, leaving him, we might assume, without theological grounding. In his letter to Rade, however, we can see theological themes at work, and these themes would develop quickly as he began to wrestle anew with the apostle Paul in his letter to the Romans. Those themes are (1) the utter difference between God and human beings, (2) the sinfulness of all human endeavors, (3) the impossibility of identifying the providence of God with anything human beings do, and thus (4) the necessity of keeping a theological distance from all political judgments.

If these were budding themes that, together with their corollaries, would be worked out in his work on Romans, then sources for their development outside the arena of both Liberal and Positive theology began to suggest themselves to Barth in connection with his trip to Marburg in 1915 for the wedding of his brother, Peter, to Rade's daughter. He did not, of course, find these sources in Marburg. Marburg, indeed, no longer existed for him theologically. Rather, he found them on a stop he and his close friend, Eduard Thurneysen, also a minister in the Aargau, made on their way home from the wedding.

Barth suggested they stop at Bad Boll in southwest Germany to visit Christoph Blumhardt. Thurneysen had been urging Barth to make this pilgrimage for some time. Blumhardt carried on the community and retreat center founded by his father, who had been widely known for his healings and his Bible-centered proclamation of the kingdom of God. The son was an impressive personage, and he affected Barth profoundly. After their Sunday visit with Christoph Blumhardt at Bad Boll, Barth read works by both son and father. He said that he found illumination in the message of the two Blumhardts. He was impressed by its thorough rooting in the Christian hope.[8] In this way, Barth came under the influence of Schwabian pietism and was led to read Bengel (died 1752), whose biblicism led him to establish text criticism in Germany as a means of recovering the original form of the biblical text; Oetinger (died 1782), who soared beyond pietistic biblicism to mystic and esoteric speculations; and Beck (died 1878), who, when biblical criticism was reaching a zenith, tried to recall theology to the sufficient and final authority of the Bible, if not to a doctrine of verbal inspiration. Under these influences, Barth says he began to move beyond the insurmountable difficulties of Liberal theology and religious socialism.

> The thought of the kingdom of God in the biblical and real otherworldly sense of the concept began to press itself upon me more and more. At the same time, the textual basis for my preaching, the Bible, which I had considered self-evident for much too long, became more and more problematic to me.[9]

This crisis raised for him the problem of the sermon in the sharpest way. Preachers are supposed to speak of God, but as human beings they cannot speak of God. God is beyond everything human. God is the "Wholly Other." Human beings cannot break out of this impasse. But, Barth became convinced, God can and God has. The issue, then, is not how human beings can find God; the reality is that God has found us. God has spoken God's word in Jesus Christ, the crucified and risen. This word is God's "yes" to the world, and to us who are totally alien to God. But we cannot hear that "yes" without also hearing God's resounding "no" to all human pretentiousness. The word of God is Jesus Christ; that revelation is found in the Bible; and it is uttered again today through the preacher who attends to the message of the Bible. This message turns everything upside down, and there is no other way by which God can be heard.

Barth turned to the Bible anew, prepared to read it with eyes

---

8. See Barth's 1927 autobiographical sketch in *Karl Barth—Rudolf Bultmann Briefwechsel: 1922–1926,* ed. Bernd Jaspert (Zürich: Theologischer Verlag, 1971), p. 307.
9. Ibid.

unassisted by lenses ground by his theological training. He set himself first the task of understanding Paul. He chose the letter to the Romans, and he set out to read it as the truth and as the truth here and now, the word of God revealed once for all to humankind, unencumbered by historical considerations. Thus in 1916, under the crisis of the war and the collapse of the Second German Empire and the theology that had prevailed within it, Barth began work on *The Epistle to the Romans*.

In an autobiographical statement prepared for the Protestant theological faculty at Münster in 1927, Barth recalled that at first he intended this work only for his own edification and for circulation among a small circle of friends.[10] In his Foreword to the reprint of the first edition in 1963, he recalled that when he finished it in 1918 he decided to seek a publisher. He reported that three well-known Swiss houses refused it before his well-to-do friend from Zurich, Rudolf Pestalozzi, paid for an obscure press in Bern to print one thousand copies.[11] However, letters from the time to his friend Thurneysen reflect a quite different series of events.[12] In these letters, we learn that as early as 1917, Pestalozzi had put a fund at the disposal of Barth and Thurneysen for the publication of their works. This fund was used for the first volume of sermons by Barth and Thurneysen and for the publication of *Romans,* which Barth was already planning with the Bäschlin press in 1917, fifteen months before he finished the manuscript. There is no mention of sending it to three other publishers.

In any case, it was published by Bäschlin; but by the time three hundred copies had been sold, Georg Merz, a pastor in Munich and later a colleague of Barth in the journal *Between the Times,* convinced the prominent publishing firm, Christian Kaiser in Munich, to take it over. The other seven hundred copies quickly sold in Germany. A new theology was born. In time it would be designated as "Dialectical Theology" (for its oscillation between God's "no" and "yes" and its assertion of opposites) or "theology

---

10. Ibid.
11. Karl Barth, *Der Römerbrief (Erster Fassung) 1919,* ed. Hermann Schmidt (Zürich: Theologischer Verlag, 1985), p. 6.
12. *Karl Barth—Eduard Thurneysen Briefwechsel,* vol. 1: *1913–1921,* ed. Eduard Thurneysen (Zürich: Theologischer Verlag, 1975), pp. 227–228 (letter of Sept. 6, 1917) and p. 260 (letter of Jan. 23, 1918).

of crisis" (for its focus on what Barth believed to be the absolute crisis of everything human in the presence of God).

Kaiser urged a reprinting, but Barth had moved beyond the first edition. By that time, he later reflected, he thought it was too much under the influence of thoughts from Bengel, Oetinger, and Beck "in a roundabout way from Kutter and Schelling," which he had come to consider unproductive.[13] He therefore declined a reprint. Instead, he set to work on a thorough rewriting. A second, even more forthright and strident, edition appeared in 1922, and essentially in this form it was reprinted repeatedly in Germany until the Nazis came to power.

Barth stated his premises in his prefaces. In the Preface to the first edition, he states:

> My whole energy of interpreting has been expended in an endeavour to see through and beyond history into the spirit of the Bible, which is the eternal Spirit. What was once of grave importance, is so still. What is today of grave importance— and not merely crotchety and incidental—stands in direct connexion with that ancient gravity. If we rightly understand ourselves, our problems are the problems of Paul; and if we be enlightened by the brightness of his answers, those answers must be ours. (1)[14]

This statement, we may rightly say, reveals Barth as a "biblicist," but the label can easily mislead us. We would be tempted to use the label to explain him and thus transfer to him connotations of the label that we have picked up from others whom we have learned to call "biblicists." Barth's approach to the Bible was, however, distinctive. To be sure, he wrote in order to explain why,

---

13. See Barth's autobiographical sketch for the Protestant theological faculty in Münster, *Karl Barth—Rudolf Bultmann Briefwechsel,* p. 307.

14. Karl Barth, *The Epistle to the Romans,* trans. Edwyn C. Hoskyns (London: Oxford University Press, 1933). Quotations from Barth's commentary on Romans will be from this translation and will be noted by the page number in parentheses at the end of each quotation.

Hoskyns's translation is sometimes quaint. For example, he uses "thee" and "thou" as a means of retaining the familiar second person usage in German. This English translation and others I am using are perhaps more sex exclusive than their German authors intended.

if he had to choose between the historical-critical approach to the Bible and the doctrine of inspiration, he would choose the doctrine of inspiration. But we must note that he put this choice in a hypothetical framework. He thought that a choice between the old alternatives is not necessary. Certainly, his approach to Romans was different from the historical-critical method of Liberal theology. Those who stood in that ring characteristically approached the Bible with the assumption that those who wrote it were human beings like themselves, subject to currents of thought, modes of life, and views of the world in their time. Thus, in order to understand such texts from the past, one must view them critically in their historical contexts and try to distill their creative contributions from their time-bound and often unconscious assumptions. Barth boldly set that method aside and proceeded to read Paul as if he were speaking about a subject that concerned Barth and his contemporaries as much as it did Paul, and he read Paul as if what Paul said is the truth of God.

Thus, if he had to choose, he said he would choose the doctrine of inspiration. But Barth did not read Paul like the Positive theologians with whom he was entirely familiar and most certainly not like those who are generally designated "fundamentalists" in the present day. For Positive theologians, to take the Bible as truth meant that one finds in it accurate information about God, Jesus Christ, human being, salvation, and so forth. That is, there could be a sense of distance between the reader and the text as there is a distance between the Latin student and Caesar's *Gallic Wars*. In his exposition of Romans, Barth showed remarkably little interest in information, and he tried to collapse the distance between himself and Paul. Thus the word is to be heard with "fear and trembling," and although it presents a "clear and objective perception," that perception "demands participation, comprehension, co-operation . . . faith in the living God, and . . . creates that which it presumes" (28). Barth's treatment of Paul was as strange to Positive theologians as it was to Liberals.

In the Preface to the second edition, Barth states:

> If I have a system, it is limited to a recognition of what Kierkegaard called the "infinite qualitative distinction" between time and eternity, and to my regarding this as possess-

ing negative as well as positive significance: "God is in heaven, and thou art on earth." The relation between such a God and such a man, and the relation between such a man and such a God, is for me the theme of the Bible and the essence of philosophy. Philosophers name this KRISIS of human perception—the Prime Cause: the Bible beholds at the same cross-roads—the figure of Jesus Christ. When I am faced by such a document as the Epistle of Paul to the Romans, I embark on its interpretation on the assumption that he is confronted with the same unmistakable and unmeasurable significance of that relation as I myself am confronted with, and that it is this situation which moulds his thought and its expression. (10)

Another way of stating this assumption, if less clear at first glance, is much more succinct: "God is God" (11). This sentence may appear to be a meaningless tautology (where the predicate is identical with the subject) that is, simple repetition. One thinks of Gertrude Stein's "A rose is a rose is a rose" or, more sophisticatedly, of the philosopher's proposition "A is equal to A." But the illustrations do not illustrate.

The reason is that this kind of tautology in fact does have implications. If "a rose is a rose is a rose," then a rose is not a pansy. If "A is equal to A," then A is not equal to B, C, D, and so forth. But these inferences do not help us understand Barth's foundational proposition because roses, pansies, and all other kinds of flowers are alike in being products of the earth, and A, like B, C, D, and so forth, is a letter of the alphabet. God, however, is the ultimate reality beyond this world. Therefore, to say that God is God is also to say that nothing in this world is God, and especially not human beings—*especially* not human beings, because human beings always want to elevate themselves or something they designate in the world to the place of God and thereby to negate the truth of the only seemingly meaningless proposition—God is God. That proposition, then, is only a shorthand way of putting the First Commandment, "You shall have no other gods before me." God is the "Wholly Other," and there is an "infinite qualitative distinction" between God and everything in this world, including human being.

To acknowledge the truth of this statement is to recognize that the primal human sin is the constant human impulse to deny its truth. In his exposition of Paul's letter to the Romans, Barth wanted to explore the implications of the statement in a relentlessly radical way—in a way, he was confident, for which the theological generations before him had no sense and which, he feared with near certainty, the generation of his teachers would not be able to comprehend. In this respect, his book is an unmistakable polemic against all existing theologies. But the polemic is only the reverse side of a fresh and utterly radical understanding of God that Barth unfolds with unremitting consistency and astonishing forcefulness, both in spite of and by means of his penchant for bold opposites and frustrating paradoxes.

God is God. That means that human beings are not God, even though invariably they try to be. God is *God*. That means that God is the Wholly Other, the mystery above and beyond this world and the entire cosmos whose reality not only accounts for the world but also judges it by an immeasurable standard and thereby negates everything that is in it, above all, human beings. Thus human beings are placed in annihilation, reduced to nothingness before God. The human situation, therefore, is one of total hopelessness.

That is, it would be if it were not for the gospel of God, "Jesus Christ our Lord," as Paul put it often, the meeting and parting of two worlds, the intersection of two planes, "the one known and the other unknown" (29). The gospel is "something quite new and unprecedented, joyful and good,—the truth of God" (28), but human beings want always to domesticate and pervert this joyful and good news. Thus the gospel itself is judgment as well as grace.

> The Gospel is not a religious message to inform mankind of their divinity or to tell them how they may become divine. The Gospel proclaims a God utterly distinct from men. Salvation comes to them from Him, because they are, as men, incapable of knowing Him, and because they have no right to claim anything from Him. The Gospel is not one thing in the midst of other things, to be directly apprehended and comprehended. The Gospel is the Word of the Primal Origin

37

of all things, the Word which, since it is ever new, must ever be received with renewed fear and trembling. The Gospel is therefore not an event, nor an experience, nor an emotion—however delicate! Rather, it is the clear and objective perception of what eye hath not seen nor ear heard. Moreover, what it demands of men is more than notice, or understanding, or sympathy. It demands participation, comprehension, co-operation; for it is a communication which presumes faith in the living God, and which creates that which it presumes. (28)

The truth and the power of the gospel were missed by Liberal theology because, in Barth's judgment, it tried "to inform mankind of their divinity or to tell them how they may become divine." For the Liberals, the gospel could be an experience, an event, or an emotion, but Barth finds no trace of that sort of thing in Paul, whose premise, Barth is convinced, is that *God is God*. Therefore, the gospel can be received only "with renewed fear and trembling," what no one has ever seen or heard. It demands "participation, comprehension, co-operation." It demands faith in the living God, which no human being can accomplish by her or his own intention and effort. Thus far, this is nothing but bad news. The good news is that the gospel "creates that which it presumes." That is, faith in the God who saves human beings from their situation of total hopelessness cannot be a human work. It is the decisive act of God in human life. Therefore, Christians rightly sing, "Praise God from whom all blessings flow."

In all this, Barth is trying to press the doctrine of justification by grace through faith apart from works of the law to its limit and thus to come closer to Paul's understanding of it. This classic teaching in Christian faith means that no human being can by disciplined goodness earn for herself or himself the favor of God. Persons may have a sense for what is right and good, but they cannot do it thoroughly so that, so to speak, they can "stand in the presence of God." To come into salvific relation with God can happen to a person only as a gift of God. That gift is called grace, and it is to be received through faith. It seemed self-evident to Barth that if one thinks this teaching through to its furthest implication, it means that all human effort is seriously tainted before God: "Since power belongs only to God, it is the tragic story of every man of God that he had to contend for the right of God by placing himself in the wrong. This must be so if the men of God are not to usurp the place of God" (57). Further, it means that even faith, the condition for the reception of God's grace in Jesus Christ, must be given by God. The gospel "creates that which it presumes." If faith were a human possibility, then being set right with God would be dependent on the achievement of a human possibility. That is, it would be a human work. But reliance on one's own work is a negation of God's gift.

> Grace, then, means neither that men can or ought to do something, nor that they can or ought to do nothing. Grace means that God does something. Nor does grace mean that God does "everything." Grace means that God does some quite definite thing, not a thing here and a thing there, but something quite definite in men. Grace means that God forgives men their sins. (215)

God is God, not human beings. If a person comes really to acknowledge this reality, then that person can only give thanks to God for having created the acknowledgment in himself or herself. By this gift of God's grace, the person becomes weak, last in line, withered away, small, and therefore strong, first, growing, great.

> Therefore we are righteous before God and in our weakness we are strong. We are first, because we are last; we grow, because we wither away; we are great, because we are little. God justifies Himself in our presence, and thereby we are justified in His presence. By making us His prisoners, He sets us free; by rejecting us as we are, He affirms us to be what we are not; He takes our side and uses us for His purpose, and thereby His side becomes our side, His right our right, and His good work is begun in us. He acknowledges us, and is with us. He promises us salvation in His Kingdom. (150)

Barth speaks of this event as the "impossible possibility." Any human being who considers it an actual possibility will be driven to utter despair—or that person has by an act of mind reduced God, an act of self-assertion against God.

39

Barth's conviction that God stands as judge over against every human possibility extends to what Barth argues is the highest human possibility—the human effort to reach God by piety or religion. Religion is the highest form of ethics. It is a mode of human activity in the world, and it is directed toward God or toward what one supposes to be God. Thus religion in all its forms is negated just as morality and social ethics are negated. *Humanum non capax infiniti* ("What is human is not capable of infinity"). This fact shows itself most poignantly in religion.

> As men living in the world, and being what we are, we cannot hope to escape the possibility of religion. . . . Knowing ourselves to be thus circumscribed, we are able to see that the last and the most inevitable human possibility—the possibility of religion—even in its most courageous, most powerful, most clearly defined, most impossible "variety," is after all no more than a human possibility, and as such a limited possibility: and, because limited, peculiarly dangerous, since it bears witness to, and is embraced by, the promise of a new and higher order by which it is itself severely limited. (230)

"Religion compels us to the perception that God is not to be found in religion" (242). It is "the working capital of sin" (248). It is "an abyss . . . terror" (253).

This total negation of religion, the highest human possibility, follows from the doctrine of justification by grace through faith apart from works of the law. God is God, the Wholly Other. Human beings are not God. "No other possibility is open to me except the possibility of being a man of the earth" (269). God, however, has other possibilities; and in Jesus Christ, the one who is both God and human being, God has bridged the gap that we cannot bridge and has given the gift that makes ours the impossible possibility.

> Jesus Christ is the new man, standing beyond all piety, beyond all human possibility. He is the dissolution of the man of this world in his totality. He is the man who has passed from death to life. He is—what I am not—my existential I—I—the I which in God, in the freedom of God—I am! Thanks be to God. (269)

For the person who is troubled by the question of ethics (What shall I do?), this radical exploration of the premise "God is God" and of the doctrine of justification by grace through faith apart from works of the law has to be unsettling, if not mystifying. If all human works are brought to nothing in the presence of God, then can it make any difference at all what one does?

Barth's exposition of Romans leads him inevitably, repeatedly, and, in the last main section, concentratedly to the question of ethics. He gives us a clue in his treatment of religion. We should expect it, because religion, in his judgment, is the highest human possibility, that is, the highest level of human activity, which is the sphere of the ethical. "We do not escape from sin by removing ourselves from religion and taking up with some other and superior thing—if indeed that were possible" (240). We cannot avoid religion (or any of the lower human possibilities) so long as we are creatures of this earth. This recognition, of course, intensifies the enigma of ethics because it makes us aware that all human activity, all working at human possibilities, even the highest human possibility, is marked by sin. "Grace means the recognition that a bad conscience must be assumed in the daily routine of an evil world" (428). But as creatures of the earth, we have no alternative, worst of all the alternative of trying to abstract ourselves from the earth and doing nothing. "Grace means divine impatience, discontent, dissatisfaction: it means that the whole is required" (430). Because we live, then, we are impelled, and we dare to work at our human possibilities. What is important is that our activities remind us of our distance from God's realm.

> The veritable KRISIS under which religion stands consists first in the impossibility of escape from it as *long* as a man *liveth;* and then in the stupidity of any attempt to be rid of it, since it is precisely in religion that men perceive themselves to be bounded as men of the world by that which is divine. Religion compels us to the perception that God is not to be found in religion. (242)

Once again, we have come full circle and see the most basic premise guiding everything Barth wants to say. It is also the presupposition of ethics.

> God is God: this is the pre-supposition of ethics. Ethical
> propositions are therefore ethical only as expositions of this
> pre-supposition which may never be regarded as a thing
> already known, or treated as a basis of further routine
> operations, or as something from which it is possible to hurry
> on to a new position. (439)

One can see how this premise guides ethics in certain ways. If God
is God, then human beings are limited to this life here and now in
the world. It would be the most serious violation of the premise if
one were to try to escape this life here and now by turning one's
back on it or by trying to transcend it in some way. But this life
here and now is characterized by communities of people with their
various forms of order and mutual responsibilities. Also, if one
acknowledges the difference between God and human beings,
then one comes immediately to know that nothing one does in the
context of the forms of order and mutual responsibilities pertaining to communities of people will span the chasm that separates
God and the world of humanity. Thus no matter how satisfied one
might be with a particular action or set of actions, one does them
with a bad conscience. That is, one recognizes that they are
ambiguous in quality and do not come close to the perfection of
God's realm. Barth's ethics, therefore, evokes rigorous self-
criticism. Because of that, it gives a basis for the criticism of all
human actions and institutions. Barth's ethics is a good buffer
against sentimentality, preoccupation with the trivial, and being
duped by the demonic. It trains the eye to see disfigurement and
sham.

The premise only indirectly gives guidance for the mode of life
for people of faith. As we have noted, it causes people to see
themselves as inescapably a part of the world and thus to accept
their responsibilities for and in the world. In order to describe
more positively the mode of life of faithful people, Barth gives a
rather strained exposition of Romans 12:4–5: "For as in one body
we have many members, and all the members do not have the
same function, so we, though many, are one body in Christ, and
individually members one of another." He denies that this
comparison is an organic metaphor that sets forth individuals as
" 'partial' things comprehended in a larger whole" (441). Also, he

denies that it supports "that romantic, conservative attitude towards individual human personality which underlies the Catholic doctrine of the Church and other similar doctrines which are derived from it" (441). ("God does not delegate His claim upon men to any directly observable human formation, however spiritual" [441].) The conception of individuals as parts of an organic whole cannot refer to the kingdom of God, as Barth believes the comparison does, and he cannot see why thinking this way would "impose so severe a limitation upon men as to remind them of God" (441). No, human beings encounter God "in their own particular, individual, tribulation and hope, and not through some notion of the 'whole' " (441).

The likeness does, however, "remind the individual of the fact of the community . . . of the existence of other individuals. And, indeed, the ethical problem—*what shall we do?*—appears at the point where the existence of these 'others' itself emerges as a problem" (442). The other is the neighbor; the neighbor is every other person; and it is the neighbor who is the parable of Christ, the one in and through whom God is revealed.

The life of faith in this world, then, is a life of service in behalf of the neighbor. "Service means so to bind up our temporal wounds that our eternal wounds, which no human operation can heal, are left gaping. Service means so to care for the body that the souls of men are not destroyed thereby" (447). Further, it is a service motivated by a love that wars against self-interest (thus *agape* in struggle with *eros*).

> AGAPE is the question which is addressed to the others—
> What is good? What is evil? AGAPE is the KRISIS in which
> the others stand. AGAPE can never be the simple, direct,
> unmistakable thing which sentimentalists yearn after—
> because it is indissolubly linked with the AGAPE which is
> directed toward God. Love is therefore both sweet and bitter.
> It can yield; but it can also be harsh. It can preserve peace;
> but it can also engage in conflict. (454)

In none of this does the reader find specific instructions about what to do. That absence of instructions is not an oversight. "Be thyself the neighbour; and there is no need for any further question" (495). The context within which people of faith venture to decide what to do, however, is clear: the intention to serve the others, the impulse of love that is not self-serving, and the recognition that whatever one does is not and cannot be equal to God's realm (thus the constancy of self-criticism that goes with the criticism of all human acts and institutions).

In 1919, before his commentary on Romans was known in Germany, Barth was invited to give one of the three lectures at a conference on religion and social issues in Tambach, Germany. The two German pastors who organized the conference recognized that there were others like themselves who were in restless ferment after the German collapse in 1918 and who feared that the church would become "a piece of the past in a changed world."[15] The two pastors leaned politically toward the radical Socialist party (USPD) as did most of the hundred pastors and professors who attended.[16] They thought it would be good to invite a representative of the religious-socialist movement in Switzerland, which was older and stronger than the comparable movement in Germany. They invited both Leonhard Ragaz and Hermann Kutter, the leading spokespersons for the Swiss movement, but both declined. A Swiss acquaintance suggested they invite Barth. He was asked to speak on the third and final topic of the three-day meeting, "The Christian's Place in Society."[17]

Günther Dehn reports that what people expected (because

---

15. Quoted in Karl Kupisch, *Karl Barth in Selbstzeugnissen und Bilddokumenten* (Reinbeck bei Hamburg: Rowohlt Taschenbuch Verlag, 1971), p. 43.

16. Günther Dehn, whom we will encounter later in connection with the famous "Dehn Case" that brought Barth and Hirsch into open conflict, attended the conference and later recalled remarking about the conference to another person: "If one should confess [here] to being a supporter of the SPD [the moderate Socialist party], one would be suspected of being a reactionary." Dehn, *Die alte Zeit, die vorigen Jahre: Lebenserinnerungen* (München: Christian Kaiser Verlag, 1964), p. 217.

17. Translated by Douglas Horton under the title "The Christian's Place in Society" and included in Karl Barth, *The Word of God and the Word of Man* (New York: Harper & Brothers Publishers, 1928). The references to this lecture that follow are from Horton's translation and will be noted by page numbers in parentheses after each quotation.

Barth was thought to be a part of the Ragaz school of thought) and wanted was a sharp rejection of the still dominant capitalistic ordering of economic and social life, and a resounding call to work together for the new socialist order. That is not the message they heard, but, except for a few, they were overwhelmed by Barth's lecture and found in what he said the "new" grounding for which they were groping.[18]

Barth began, "The thought of the Christian's place in society fills one with a curious blend of hope and questioning" (272). He asked why we should be concerned with the *Christian's* place. Then he explained that society—that is, marriage, family, civilization, the economic order, art, science, the state, the party, international relations—has its own laws and inner workings that keep it going. Today, in the catastrophe in which we live, we are able clearly to see that the familiar course of society is wrong. We would like to turn our backs on the whole scene, but we cannot escape life. The *Christian*, however,

> is a new element in the midst of the old, a truth in the midst of error and lies, a righteousness in the midst of a sea of unrighteousness, a spirituality within all our crass materialistic tendencies, a formative life-energy within all our weak, tottering movements of thought, a unity in a time which is out of joint. (273)

By "the Christian," however, Barth did not mean "the Christians," those who are members of the church. He was under no illusions about the accomplishments of Christians. He meant, rather, the Christ, "that within us which is not ourself but Christ in us" (273), but he warned against a narrow view of the "chosen" that separates Christians from non-Christians, Jews from Gentiles. It is the power of Christ in human beings that offers promise that "society, in spite of its being on the wrong course, is not forsaken of God" (275).

---

18. Wilhelm Wibbeling, an attending pastor, reflecting on the event forty-five years later (1964), wrote, "The impact was colossal." *Evangelische Theologie* 24, no. 10 (October 1964), 556. The electrifying impact has been confirmed by others who were present.

The hope, then, is in the power of God at work in the world. Our need arises from the recognition of the difference between ourselves and God, "an unhappy separation, a thoroughgoing opposition between two dissimilar magnitudes." We have no solution to this problem. The only solution is in God. The best we can do is to engage in "a candid, absolutely thorough and . . . *priestly agitation*" (282). Barth saw it as his task to indicate the points of departure for this agitation.

The first and most fundamental point of departure is to attend to the movement of God in history or, better, in the human consciousness, "the movement whose power and import are revealed in the resurrection of Jesus Christ from the dead" (283). He insisted he was not talking about some kind of human "experience," and he was adamant that he was not talking about "religion." On the contrary, he meant "the world of God breaking through from its self-contained holiness and appearing in secular life, . . . the bodily resurrection of Jesus Christ from the dead" (287). Those who participate in the meaning and power of Christ's resurrection discover a new motivation, influencing "our life on earth in every part" (289). It evokes unyielding criticism: Barth said we must side with the youth in their rejection of the dead world of their elders and "issue a categorical challenge" to all the authorities in life (economic, national, political, and so forth). It also leads to thoroughgoing participation: "To understand means to take the whole situation upon us in the fear of God, and in the fear of God to enter into the movement of the era" (294). And it gives hope: "God in history is *a priori* victory in history" (297).

Second, "Insight into the true transcendence of the divine origin of all things" allows, even commands, us to see that the orders of this world are caused by God. We are led, first, not to the denial but to the affirmation of "the world as it is" (299). God "desires to be known even in the profligate, degenerate, and confused ways of men" (300). The reign of nature is therefore also the reign of God. In this confidence, we accept the orders of creation in the social world (e.g., family, State) just as we accept the orders of creation in the natural world. "For life as it *is* means something" (306). God "remains the Creator even of our fallen world." So it is not ours "to be onlookers," but to accept our "solid responsibility" (308). Barth might have been invited to membership in the Solid Citizens Club except for his repeated acerbic remarks about the values and achievements that middle-class moralists cherish.

Third, the resounding No after the Yes: "Tears are closer to *us* than laughter. *We* live more deeply in the No than in the Yes, more deeply in criticism and protest than in naïvete, more deeply in longing for the future than in participation in the present" (311–312). "The same moving force that bids us take life as it comes presently prohibits us from doing so" (313). "The Kingdom of God advances to its *attack* upon society" (314).

> Why, with a *sacrificium* ["sacrifice"] of our intellects and more than our intellects, do we bow before the message of the *Sermon on the Mount*, which acclaims men blessed who do not exist; which opposes what was said to them of old time and what we must continue to say to each other, with a "But I say unto you" that can be applied neither to modern nor to any conceivable society; which preaches a morality that presupposes that morality is no longer necessary? . . . No relegating of our hopes to a Beyond can give us rest, for it is the Beyond itself standing outside and knocking on the closed doors of the here-and-now that is the chief cause of our unrest. (315, 317)

Consequently:

> [W]e must enter fully into the subversion and conversion of this present and of every conceivable world, into the judgment and the grace which the presence of God entails, unless, remaining behind, we wish to fall away from Christ's truth, which is the power of the resurrection. . . . The Kingdom of God is *at hand*. (318, 319)

Finally, we must understand that the synthesis of the Yes and the No is in God alone and not in anything we can do. "While it is God who gives us that rest and this greater unrest, it is clear that neither our rest nor our unrest in the world, necessary though both of them be, can be final" (320). "The synthesis we seek is in *God* alone, and in God alone can we find it" (322). "The *resurrection* of Jesus Christ from the dead is the power which moves both the world and us, *because* it is the appearance in our corporeality of a *totaliter aliter* ["wholly other"] constituted corporeality" (323).

Barth ended his address with a question: "What can the Christian in society do but follow attentively what is done by *God*?" (327). The attentive listener, however much he may have been stirred by Barth's address, and the serious reader, of whatever year after it was published, might well be mystified about how she or he should actually act in this world outside of the qualified Yes and the resounding No, and the proclamation of the final, eschatological reality, which only God through Christ, the resurrected Lord, can bring. But there could be no mistake about the qualified Yes and the resounding No.

Barth tried to make clear both the Yes and the No, as well as the final resolution in the power of the resurrection of Jesus Christ and God's bringing his kingdom to the world, in a statement near the end of his exposition of *Romans:*

> Who then is justified? Who dares to say, "I have faith"? Who dares to take upon himself responsibility for others, or even for himself? Who dares to harp upon the theme of his own autonomy? There is but one thread in all this grim uncertainty. Hold thee to God! But who can maintain his hold, if he be not himself held? (522)

We began this exposition of Barth's commentary on Romans with a reference to two premises. The one was his statement that if presented with the alternative of choosing between the Liberal approach to scripture, as a collection of human documents, and the doctrine of inspiration, he would choose the doctrine of inspiration. The other was the pregnant proposition that God is God. Now we are in a position to see that the second of these, as Barth explained it, determines the first. If God is God, the Wholly Other, whose realm has no point of contact with this realm except as God establishes it, then there is no possibility of receiving the Word of God except as God speaks it or accounts for its being written down. Given what Barth says about God and Jesus Christ, there is no alternative to a high view of the Bible; and it is not surprising, therefore, that he defined faith as the acceptance of the "incredible testimonies" in the Bible.[19] "Only God can say to us in a way that we will hear it, what *we* can*not* hear."[20] As powerful as this premise may be, it has an Achilles heel, as we will see.

Whether that is the case or not, Barth's theology, with its fresh and radical understanding of God and with the exceptionally vigorous style in which he wrote and spoke, found an enthusiastic response in a large segment of the rising generation of theologians and ministers in Germany. The Tambach lecture opened the doors to Germany for this pastor from the obscure Swiss village of Safenwil, and his *Epistle to the Romans* became one of the most widely read theological books in Germany through the years of the Weimar Republic. Over the fourteen years from 1921 to 1935, he would become one of the most potent theological teachers in Germany, first at Göttingen, then at Münster and at Bonn. In 1935, the Nazi government dismissed him, stripped him of the German citizenship he had been awarded with his appointment at Münster, and deported him to Switzerland.

---

19. From the 1932 debate between Adolf von Harnack and Barth, which appeared in *Die christliche Welt,* translated by Keith R. Crim and edited by James M. Robinson in *The Beginnings of Dialectical Theology* (Richmond: John Knox Press, 1968), p. 181.

An engaging anecdote pertaining to Barth's position on the Bible comes from the noted church historian Walther von Loewenich. In 1924–25, Loewenich studied under Barth at Göttingen, belonged to his circle of devotees, and once, along with a few other Bavarian students, was described by Barth as "my joy and my crown" (*Karl Barth—Eduard Thurneysen Briefwechsel,* vol. 2: *1921–1930,* ed. Eduard Thurneysen [Zürich: Evangelischer Verlag, 1974], p. 329; cf. Loewenich, *Erlebte Theologie* [München: Claudius Verlag, 1979], p. 47). In the years after his study with Barth, Loewenich distanced himself from Barth theologically and presented as one of his theses for *Habilitation* exams in Erlangen the following: "In exegesis the concept of the canonical may not be introduced as the point of departure but only as a point at the end" (ibid., p. 231). Loewenich reports that when Barth saw this thesis he said, *"Ganz übel, ganz übel"* ("Very bad, totally wrong") (ibid., p. 89).

20. *The Beginnings of Dialectical Theology,* trans. Crim, ed. Robinson, p. 181.

EMANUEL HIRSCH

2

EMANUEL HIRSCH AND
GERMANY'S DESTINY

Emanuel Hirsch was one of the most brilliant persons in the field of theology of his or any other generation. During the twenty-seven years between the end of the Second World War and his death, blind and in poor health, he published a massive, five-volume history of modern Protestant theology, translations of Kierkegaard from the Danish with historical commentary, eleven novels and collections of stories, and eight theological books.[1] In addition to his brilliance, he was a rigorously moral person, and the question of social ethics was a cardinal feature of his theological work. Even so, he not only hailed the assumption of power by the Nazis in 1933, he also continued to believe in Hitler's mission for Germany throughout the years of the Third Reich and afterwards—so far as we know, as long as he lived.

Like Barth, Hirsch was the son of a minister who belonged to the Positive party. Unlike Barth, the conservatism of his father does not seem to have had a particularly strong and certainly not an enduring influence on Hirsch. He was precocious and worked himself free of any confining horizons of his religious upbringing with no sense of conflict or upheaval. In his brief autobiographical reminiscences, written in 1951, he noted that his home was strict

---

1. For a description of this astonishing set of accomplishments, see Wolfgang Trillhaas, "Emanuel Hirsch in Göttingen," *Zeitschrift für Theologie und Kirche* 81, no. 2 (April 1984), 236ff.

and pious and that his parents were faithful members of the Positive movement in the church, but he added that precisely because of this early environment he decided that he should listen to critical theology.[2] Even before he began his theological study at the University of Berlin, he had appropriated critical presuppositions without sharp transition. He set aside the doctrine of inspiration and began to view the Bible as "a human book that related to me the mysterious history of the human heart with God."[3] Consequently, when he began to study with the Liberal professors in Berlin, he experienced no tension. He thought he was able to retain values from his upbringing while appropriating fully the critical method in theology. Both of these, he said, lived within himself, while he determined to find a way for himself alone that would stand beyond both Liberalism and orthodoxy.

When Hirsch wrote his reminiscences in 1951, the German church and theological world was embroiled in a divisive conflict over Rudolf Bultmann's so-called program of "demythologizing the New Testament." To Hirsch, it seemed to be nothing more than a somewhat noisier reenactment of the old Liberal-Positive conflict over the Bible. Hirsch said he viewed the altercation with a smile, like the smile older people have when they see children discovering how large the earth is and how high the mountains are. Early in his life, he moved fully into the sphere of liberal, critical theology, and "the inescapable earthquake" that normally accompanied that movement left him unshaken.[4]

Be that as it may, critical theology, with its premise that the Bible must be read like any other book and with its strong moral impulse to carry out the implications of the premise with rigorous intellectual honesty, was like a gift of God to Hirsch. "I belong to those theologians who through theology, more precisely through a critical theology that backs away from no question, were saved for Christian faith."[5] Later we will have to recall this statement by Hirsch. At one most decisive point, he made a fatal exception to the principle of criticism.

---

2. In *Freies Christentum,* ed. Friedrich Manz: 3, no. 10 (October 1951), 2–4; 3, no. 11 (November 1951), 3–4; 3, no. 12 (December 1951), 3–6.

3. *Freies Christentum* 3, no. 10 (October 1951), 3.

4. Ibid.

5. Ibid., p. 2.

Unlike Barth, who studied at four universities (typical of most German students), Hirsch did all of his study at the University of Berlin. The professor there who had the greatest impact upon him was not the famous and venerable Adolf von Harnack but Harnack's younger colleague, Karl Holl.[6] Hirsch studied with Holl for several years until he completed his first theological examinations in 1911.

Holl became the foremost Luther scholar of the twentieth century. In 1917, on the four hundredth anniversary of the beginning of the Reformation, he presented a lecture on "Luther's Understanding of Religion." This lecture, especially when it appeared in expanded form in a volume of essays on Luther in 1921, had an effect comparable to Barth's *Epistle to the Romans*. It inaugurated a renaissance of Luther studies that continues to this day.

Hirsch studied with Holl in the years when his work on Luther was beginning to show its yield. They were heady years. Hirsch said that Holl led him most thoroughly into historical criticism and opened for him most profoundly the power of the doctrine of justification by faith.[7] "As a historical and dogmatic critic, as an inexorably sharp analyst of the history of dogma and theology, at least in his younger years when I studied under him, Karl Holl . . . was far more radical than his colleague Harnack."[8]

Holl's grasp of Luther was utterly fresh, enduring in most of its insightful analysis, and earthshaking in its impact. Moreover, like Barth's work on Romans, Holl's interpretation of Luther transcended the existing debate between Positive and Liberal theology. He saw that the crisis of faith Luther encountered was engendered by Luther's recapturing a radical and authentic understanding of God as God. God is the awesome reality above and beyond this world. No human being can win the favor of God by her or his own effort. With this understanding, one becomes frightfully aware of the wrath of God. But in Christ, this same God seeks out the human being and draws that person into genuine

---

6. Holl was twenty-two years older than Hirsch and fifteen years younger than Harnack. He died prematurely in 1926 at the age of 60. He had been appointed full professor of church history at Berlin in 1906 at the age of 40. Hirsch knew him as a "young" professor.

7. *Freies Christentum* 3, no. 10 (October 1951), 3.

8. Ibid.

relationship through love. The resolution of this struggle does not come easily because the self always wants to be its own God.

The resolution of the struggle can be received only as God's free and undeserved gift through Jesus Christ. The gift of faith in Jesus Christ creates a new being, a person who has died and risen, so to speak, with Christ. The new being in Christ does not obliterate the old being. The two live together in one and the same person, but the grace of God in Christ, which constitutes the new being, has a redemptive effect in the life of faith. It liberates the "I" from itself and makes one free to live one's life in the world. One wants above all to love God and the neighbor.

One now receives one's life in the world as the gift of God, and one joyfully pursues one's vocation in the context of God-given orders (such as State, people, economy, family), recognizing that these orders themselves are revelatory of God. Moreover, one is emboldened to act, to decide in murky situations, confident of the ever-renewed grace of God that forgives and transforms. (As Luther once said to Melanchthon, "Sin boldly, but all the more boldly believe.")

The locus for decision and the direction of activity in the world is the human conscience. "Luther's religion is conscience religion in the most pronounced sense of the term."[9] The conscience in turn is governed by God's Word (the gospel, grace) and by love of the neighbor.[10]

---

9. Karl Holl, *Gesammelte Aufsätze zur Kirchengeschichte,* vol. 1: *Luther* (Tübingen: J. C. B. Mohr [Paul Siebeck], 1948), p. 35.

10. Perhaps he did not make it clear enough. Some have said that all of Holl's students, appealing to Luther's faith as "conscience religion," became supporters of the Nazi regime. The judgment is patently false. There were Holl students who never were enticed by Adolf Hitler. But it is the case that a number of Holl's students did hail the advent of Hitler on the basis of a decision of conscience. Here is a statement one of them wrote twenty years after the end of the Second World War. It is fraught with background: "Perhaps Holl himself knew better than we, his students, that historical knowledge is limited in its applicability. It can give only 'indirect communication' to the present, and only in this way can it be an essential and meaningful communication. Perhaps we were guilty of misunderstanding when we took the Reformation point of view as a direct answer to our questions of the moment" (Hanns Rückert on Karl Holl in *Tendenzen der Theologie im 20. Jahrhundert,* ed. Hans Jürgen Schultz [Stuttgart and Berlin: Kreuz Verlag; and Freiburg im Breisgau: Walter-Verlag, 1966], p. 107).

Holl ended his famous essay with a question that was poignant in 1917. "Is this conception of religion peculiarly German?" He answered first with a "yes":

> Certainly, it is German in its emphasis on the courage to bear personal responsibility, the determination to think things through to the end, the power to hold opposites together in their tension, the proportionate sense for the heroic, and the tender warmth of heart that beams through everything, but also the inclination to melancholy, the brooding inclination that moves toward action only under the strongest pressure of the conscience, the angular character of the construction of ideas, and the impetuosity of discourse.

Then he qualified and broadened the "yes":

> Even so, it would be overweaning presumption on our part and a restriction of Luther's greatness if we claimed him for ourselves alone. Precisely in him it becomes transparent how what was born out of the deepest spirit of a particular people conceals and bears with it what is universally human. . . . He belongs to humanity. And therefore we bear the confident trust that his work will remain for the whole human race.[11]

The understanding of Christian faith and the rigorous standards for scholarly work that Holl communicated to Hirsch were most likely the strongest influences that gave Hirsch the stamina to endure the devastation of the First World War, and Hirsch's distinctive appropriation of Holl's influence helped him establish a new and hopeful course when the collapse of Germany in 1918 brought his world to an end.

When the war broke out in 1914, Hirsch was the director of the house for theological students in Göttingen. This was a good position for an aspiring scholar. It provided a modest living and permitted him time to work on a doctorate, which he completed in 1914 with a dissertation on the early nineteenth-century German Idealist philosopher Fichte, who remained important to him in his later work. Like the overwhelming majority of people in the

---

11. Holl, *Gesammelte Aufsätze zur Kirchengeschichte,* vol. 1, p. 110.

western countries that entered the war, he was a strong patriot and nationalist. He had a deep sense of identity with his people (*Volk*) and would have liked to enlist, but it was out of the question. He was small of stature and physically weak, weighing only a little over a hundred pounds. More decisive was his poor eyesight. One eye had been damaged by a detached retina, the other by the slip of a barber's razor.

In order to work on his second dissertation, the final step in qualifying for an academic career, he accepted the position of director of the house for theological students in Bonn, which he took up in November of 1914. In early 1915, both church historians on the theological faculty at Bonn were called into service. Hirsch was asked to take the place of both of them and was made an assistant professor. For a year and a half, this beginning teacher taught a double load. Wolfgang Trillhaas says that "in tenacity and efficiency" his discipline was "without comparison."[12] He worked day and night to prepare his lectures and seminars. By dogged discipline, he mastered the literature of his field. His students consisted mainly of those who had been so severely wounded that they could not be reassigned to military service. Hirsch gave himself to them utterly and without reserve. He viewed the long days and nights of study and the care with which he attended to his students his "war service."[13]

Hirsch experienced the disintegration and collapse of Imperial Germany as an unmitigated tragedy for his German *Volk*. He had witnessed and shared the sacrifices of the home front, and he believed in the German cause to the end. When Germany surrendered, Hirsch was devastated, certainly because of the bitter pill of defeat but especially because of what happened afterward—the institution of the Weimar Republic and the dominance of the Allied Powers, particularly England.

The Weimar Republic was a parliamentary democracy, and Hirsch thought that this form of government, with its parties and principle of majority rule, would intensify the disunity of the people (*Volk*) by emphasizing factionalism. He did not see how it could evoke a common mind, and he was certain it would feed the

---

12. Trillhaas, "Emanuel Hirsch in Göttingen," p. 222.
13. *Freies Christentum* 3, no. 11 (November 1951), 4.

self-destructive tendency of individuals and groups toward narrow self-interest. On the other hand, the victorious powers, he thought, were motivated by self-righteousness and acrimonious rancor. With respect to the values he treasured most, he viewed the situation of Germany as all but hopeless. The nature of his faith in God, however, would not allow him the despair of utter hopelessness.

His theological convictions struggled with the realities until he found a new basis for hope. He set forth his position in ten public lectures that he gave at the University of Bonn in the summer term of 1920. Five of the lectures developed a distinctive theology of history; the other five applied this theology of history to the German situation. Later in 1920, he published the lectures under the title *Germany's Destiny: State, Volk and Humanity in the Light of an Ethical Point of View*. The book had a strong impact on many of his people, especially younger Germans.

> In Germany today there is much reflection, by both the learned and the unlearned, about the riddles of human history, about the great questions of conscience that have to do with the common life of people. No *Volk* more than ours struggles so earnestly to comprehend what is right and true in this sphere. To be sure, none has more occasion to do so than we who, as a consequence of the war, sacrificed life and freedom to a world of deceptive illusions. (1)[14]

These sentences stand at the beginning of the Foreword to his book, and they introduce us to three major themes. First, he refers to "the riddles of human history." What Hirsch wanted to find was not a balm to ease the symptoms of Germany's trauma. Rather, within the context of a desperate crisis that drives one to final questions, he wanted to comprehend the mystery of human history and out of that comprehensive view to locate the ray of hope for Germany. The position he developed was theological to the core. That is, he was convinced that the incomprehensible power of God hovered over human history. It was impossible for

---

14. Emanuel Hirsch, *Deutschlands Schicksal* (Göttingen: Vandenhoeck & Ruprecht, 1920). Citations from this work will be noted by page numbers in parentheses at the end of the quotations.

him to believe that God is unconcerned about the course of human affairs. It would be misleading to say that he believed God "acts" in history, if we mean that God intervenes, directs, moves to change things in this or that case without respect to human agency. Hirsch's position is a relative of the philosophical view of German Idealism that saw the reality of God moving and active throughout human history and inducing it ineluctably and necessarily to self-fulfillment. As we will see, he distinguished what he called his "theistic" view from the Idealist position, but like Idealists, he wanted to comprehend the relationship of God to the whole of human history.

Second, we see that he was concerned with "the great questions of conscience." Noting this concern will help us understand (1) how he distinguished himself from the Idealist metaphysics of history and (2) the inseparability of theology and ethics for him. The power of God, according to Hirsch, does indeed permeate or hover over human history, but in no way does it negate human freedom and responsibility. Human beings must struggle to recognize what God wants to make of the world. In this struggle, they have no objective certainty, and therefore they must decide with fear and trembling what to venture. (Hirsch was influenced as deeply as the Barth of *Romans* by the nineteenth-century Danish philosopher-theologian Kierkegaard, though in different ways.) He was under no illusion that historical conditions could be so transparent that a decision coordinate with the reality of God would be straightforwardly self-evident, but he was sure that the locus in human beings for a decision related to God is the conscience. Thus God and human beings are related through the conscience, and it is by decisions of the conscience that human activity in the world (ethics) is directed.

Third, Hirsch was concerned for "the common life of people." This theme is more difficult for readers in the United States to grasp sympathetically. Society in the United States becomes more pluralistic rather than less, and the historic value of "rugged individualism" seems to have metamorphosed into an even stronger but "pure and simple" individualism. There are numerous instances of identity, even primary identity, with a group, large or small, but there has been an evident erosion of a sense of primary identity with "the American people." But when Hirsch wrote of "the common life of people," he thought above all of entities as encompassing as a people, and he saw a foundational value in individuals finding their primary identity in such an entity, just as he saw such entities as "the German people," "the French people," "the American people" as the key to the highest cultural developments and the enhancement of spiritual life in the broadest and most amorphous sense of the term.

Although Hirsch wanted to comprehend theologically the whole of human history, he directed his book specifically to the German people, as his title indicates. His Introduction goes straight to the point:

> The collapse of our Fatherland and the socialist revolution have caused a great confusion in our souls. The most difficult questions of corporate human life have been awakened in us. But we lack the power and clarity, the unity of mind, for their solution. The only thing we have in common is a feeling, the pain of Germany's fate, which for the more honorable among us is the deepest pain of their lives. Beyond that feeling everything is contested. We do not know how we should judge the past. We do not know which way we should go now in order to have a future. We have different ideas of good and evil, of justice and life, of *Volk* (people) and community, of destiny and history, of humankind and God.
>
> There is only one way out of this confusion, and providence is at hand to lead us to it. It is the way of common, tough destiny. Only because all, without distinction of opinion or conviction, stand under the same heavy pressure from outside, will a divided mass of human beings become a *Volk*. The more cruelly and shamefully our oppressors of the present act toward us Germans, the more we ought to hope for that moment when the German understands what is German. . . . In that moment of decision, Germany will require upright persons who are prepared to comprehend her command. (5)

Hirsch looked forward passionately for that moment, and he tried to prepare his people for it by calling them to draw on the most potent resource they—at least most of them—held in common: faith in God, revealed in Jesus Christ, understood, he believed, with singular insight and power by Luther and permeating the German soul.

Hirsch developed a position that he distinguished from sceptical relativism (Nietzsche, Spengler), which views human action as meaningless, determined by the conditions of time and space, and from the absolutism of German Idealism, which eliminates the boundary between God and world by viewing the human drama as a part of the dialectical process of divine self-realization. His position acknowledged that we are, indeed, in many ways determined by factors over which we have no control (time, place, family, inborn gifts or lack of them, *Volk*), but he affirmed human responsibility and creativity as well. He thought scepticism could not account for the fact that from time to time something entirely new happens, the effects of vibrant, creative human spirits. He argued that one cannot account for these creations by supposing that they result simply from hard work. One must believe that an invisible power activates them. The fact of genius poses for us "the whole metaphysical problem" (16).

In the distinction between good and evil, in the yearning for what is true and good, in the establishment of moral norms, people come to sense in the depths a certainty, an eternal, holy will that stands behind the good and true and our yearning for it. "This certainty is the living power that breaks forth from our hearts in the risk of making moral decisions" (17). "To have the power of truth means to stand in inner relation to the final, eternal necessity in and behind every reality" (18).

The creations of the human spirit and our decisions are our own. Thus we bear a final responsibility for them. Also, because they are ours, they are conditioned by our time and place, and they are flawed by the fact that we are not God. There can be no identity with the divine power, only a relationship with it; and, so to speak, we "take our lives in our hands" when we venture decisions of conscience in the hope of confirming that relationship. Hirsch thought he appropriated what is right in both relativism and absolutism while at the same time accounting appropriately for human creativity and the sense of responsibility. He called his position "theistic."

Having placed his theistic metaphysics of history between

scepticism and idealism, Hirsch argued in a similar way that history is governed exclusively neither by the universal ideas of reason nor by the particulars of individual life, but in part by both. Human life, he said, is characterized by a remarkable gift, the earliest expression of which is speech. The higher development of speech is reflection, the power of thinking about something. Without reflection, memory is not possible. To remember means to recall moments of life that by reflection have transformed themselves into images. In this respect, we become like observers of the past. That distance gives us a freedom toward the past. That is, we can appropriate what we judge to be great and honorable, and we can try to improve on what we deem needs improvement. "It is clear that culture is not possible without a clear relationship to the past that is formed as remembrance and criticism" (26). Happily, not every generation has to start at the beginning.

Reflection about the past leads inevitably to the impulse to try to make sense out of history. This effort involves us in the process of reasoning that leads to the construction of ideas that have universal range. In this way, people think that what has come to us from the past needs to be re-formed according to the universal laws that reason discovers. One wants everything to conform to the ideals of rational understanding. For example, this tendency, he said, is what stands behind the present-day craze to "organize" everything.

"A dark feeling" in us objects to this tendency. The rationalist treatment of history breaks down in the face of the distinctiveness of the individual. "Every historical appearance is an interlacing of the most varied elements, a knotting of conditions that happen to converge only in this particular time and place and nowhere else" (29). Rational reflection about the past is critically important, but it goes awry if it overlooks what is unique or ignores differences. "In its essence, history is not the realization of the dominance of the idea but the revelation and unfolding of the variety of individual life that has ordered itself by critical relation to the idea in the unity of the human" (31). All higher cultures depend on the unresolvable interpenetration of rational ideas with the uniqueness of individuality in particular times and places.

If this is the case, if in our search to discover the task that is right and true for us we cannot simply derive our judgments from the generally applicable dictates of reason, then every historical judgment and activity involves risk. Decisions have to be made in the dimness of a present that remains in no insignificant measure a riddle to us.

We must, however, remember that human history is not purely the result of human judgment, decision, and activity. It is also in large measure something that is given to us and by which we are determined. The result is that history is an oscillation, an intertwining of what is given and of what human beings decide. Both of these factors undergird the theistic premise: what is given comes from beyond us and is the mystery that shapes and forms us, and the possibility and necessity of decision, our power to reshape the present and the future, points us in our conscience to the good and the true, which we ourselves have not created. Hirsch believed that this historical view could give the German people hope in their dark hour.

He was very much aware that some of his people were finding what hope they could in the nineteenth-century doctrine of progress coupled with the Enlightenment ideal of universal humanity. Those who did so had to believe that, in ways they could not at present understand, Germany's destiny contributed to the progress of that ideal in history. He acknowledged development in history, but he thought no realistic person could believe in progress. Development means that historical life is held together by a firm and necessary web of happenings in which the parts are conditioned by the individual whole mysteriously expressing itself in them. Development is not simply a straightforward matter of cause and effect. Any new stage, any new epoch, is more than a simple re-forming of what has gone before. It is a new creation. Development reveals an inner direction. It is a process with a purpose, and because no stage of development can be simply derived from the past, each stage is a mystery. It is not, however, necessarily progress.

To Hirsch, both the remarkable accomplishments of the past, even the distant past, and the horrors of the present rendered impossible a belief in evolutionary progress. Of more importance, he thought the exponents of that doctrine never were able to encompass "the authentic soul of historical life" (40). He believed with Leopold von Ranke, the father of modern historical study, that "every epoch is immediate to God." Therefore, it is not possible to reduce the higher life of humanity into a single, somehow rising line of development that has a definite goal.

Those who espouse an evolutionary view posit such a goal of history, but they prove themselves to be provincial. Either they take as the guiding principle the tendency of their own epoch, or they base the principle on their religious tradition. Hirsch recognized that the world is much larger.

Moreover, he thought the doctrine of evolutionary progress ignored the living will of humankind as "a real power in its own right" (45). If we give proper consideration to the role of the human will in history, belief in the doctrine of evolutionary progress is not possible. Human beings commit free acts. Therefore, all necessary connection between epochs and stages reaches only to a possibility for existence. The human will is decisive. Thus history is always a task that is resolved for better or worse in human freedom. It is not simply an always progressive development.

Hirsch thought his view should not discourage those who found what hope they could in the evolutionary progressive position. He emphasized that a total sacrifice, in order to be worth making, does not require a world change or a major step upward in human development. What is important is that it is considered necessary and demands the whole person.

One can sense the movement in history of the divine power only in one's own specific historical situation. For Hirsch, that last phrase was synonymous with the situation of one's *Volk*. However, he continued to emphasize that everything human beings try to do is limited by the unmovable boundary separating what is human from what is divine.

Hirsch's theistic metaphysics of history, with its twofold focus on the divine power penetrating human history and on the free and responsible individual, and with the difference between the two set as a border or limit, issues in the summons to a "community of conscience," the point of contact with God. His conception of history, therefore, if we attend to his own intention, would more appropriately be named "theistic-ethical."

Both themes in this twofold focus lead him to emphasize the importance of the *Volk* and of the nation-state that preserves and enhances the life of the *Volk*. The traditions, mores, modes of thought, distinctiveness of culture, special forms of creativity that shape the life of the individual are given to people by birth. The most encompassing context within which these shaping forces are given is the people, or *Volk*. What is given results, to be sure, from what those before us have done, but not exclusively. The mystery of the Eternal also moves in and through the life of the *Volk*. The divine reality, God, is also revealed in and through the life of the *Volk*.

Just as the most encompassing sphere that shapes us is the *Volk*, so the most basic and encompassing sphere within which we live, decide, and act is also the *Volk*, more particularly, the State, the institution for the preservation and enhancement of the life of the *Volk*. "All individual morality exists solely by virtue of the fact that one, together with one's mind and life, is absorbed in the richly faceted life of the State and finds the substantive foundation and aim of one's existence in it" (53). Then one can understand the proper and close relation between patriotism and morality.

> Insofar as one understands by patriotism that frame of mind that experiences the duties of civil life as privileges and therefore views life in the State as that through which above all one's own life is spiritually quickened and truly becomes reasonable and free—to that extent are patriotism and morality one and the same. (54)

The importance of the *Volk* and the nation-state that supports and preserves it as the basic community becomes even more clear, Hirsch thought, when we consider the foundational importance of faith in God to this theistic-ethical metaphysics of history. If human beings are to be bound to one another at the deepest level, one must think of a community that is rooted in the spiritual life, a community of consciences, of souls. Hirsch described such a community from three sides. First, it is a true community rather than simply an abstract agreement between individuals. Second, it is a community in God and toward God: in God, in the sense that God is the one who effects the mysterious bonding of one conscience to the other; toward God, in the sense that although the knowledge and faith of the individuals are quite different according to degree and clarity, they are similar in that they are related to the one God, that within one and the same arena God is the object of their thinking and living. "The inner unity of this community depends on this identity" (60). Third, it is a community that extends through all peoples (*Völker*) and across all times, one single church of God for the whole of humanity. Hirsch was convinced that behind all the historical differences in the varied peoples of humankind there is hidden a "single, living heart" (61). "From each of its [humanity's] moments there is an entrance into the community of conscience in God" (61).

As convinced as Hirsch was of that universality in diversity, he was equally certain that the specific communities of conscience of which individuals can be a part are related to external, earthly organizations. One can know the universality only in and through the specific and distinctive context. "All knowledge of God and God's will comes to us through the mediation of the life history we experience" (62). The broadest arena in which it is possible for human beings to experience such a "life history" is in and through the life of their *Volk,* the organizational form of which is the nation-state. The relationship, then, between the invisible community of conscience, on the one side, and State and society, on the other, vivifies a *Volk* and gives it substance.

Hirsch concluded the theoretical part of his book with what he considered the only key to the meaning of history available to finite human beings: "One understands history only when one sees it as a concrete interplay between earthly-natural life and ethical-religious life. Both sides belong to history in the authentic, true sense" (62).

Hirsch was convinced that his theistic-ethical metaphysics of history realistically accounted for finite human life, with its possibilities for glory and shame, for well-being and suffering, for life and death. He was also convinced that it yielded practical understandings and guiding principles that could lift the German people out of the morass that threatened to engulf them. He drew out these practical implications by addressing the issues of law, the State, *Volk,* humanity, war, and society. There are no surprises in his application, but what he said is less alarming from the point of view of 1920 than from that of the present. We will have more to learn if we try to assume, insofar as possible, the point of view of 1920.

Law is necessary for the establishment and preservation of order in the life of a State (the organized and ordered life of a *Volk*). Just as the steady and safe flow of traffic is not possible without traffic lights and stop signs and rules for driving, so no people can live, much less flourish, in a society that is not ordered by law. There are decent and good folk who could manage to give their neighbors a sense of regular expectations free of fear, but decency and goodness do not prevail in all members of any people. Without law, decisively and strongly administered by those designated for that difficult responsibility, individuals would have to be so concerned for their own safety and well-being that neither higher culture nor higher morality could develop. The persons who are designated to institute and enforce law need to be strong leaders, and they must have the power to act with firmness. They have the responsibility to institute laws that coordinate and express the particular spirit of the people.

The purpose of law is to establish equitable and just conditions within which a *Volk* can live, but it has to do only with external matters. It cannot touch the heart. The order of law is not the order of the kingdom of God. External and internal matters are not, however, unrelated. The ordering of social life by law frees people from the necessity of having to defend their lives and property by their own power. Without such freedom, the inner persuasions of morality and ethics cannot develop. Moreover, in submission to law, whose foundation is the good of the whole, we begin to experience the claim of morality and ethics that goes beyond law. It is an elementary teacher that helps us learn the value of having a primary identity in the whole in contrast to self-centered and short-sighted individualism.

Law can foster a sense of belonging to one's people, but it cannot establish this sense in the most authentic way. It should give institutional expression to the special traits of a *Volk,* but it cannot cause members of a *Volk* to internalize these or other common traits so deeply that the genuine and special life of the *Volk* flourishes in culture, creativity, and mutuality. This deeper level of communal life occurs most notably through a common faith in God. Hirsch thought faith in the God revealed in Jesus Christ was uniquely potent in this regard. Where this faith takes root, people are turned out of themselves, oriented to the good of the neighbor, and ready to sacrifice themselves for the whole body.

Hirsch was certain that the government established by the Weimar constitution was ultimately destructive of the basic value of common life among the German people. Its democratic premise called for the rule of the majority over against the minority, and its party system necessarily led to factionalism among the people and to single-issue orientations. Monarchy was much better able to recognize, express, and evoke the special character of the German *Volk* and to develop strong leadership, but he realized that there was no possibility for reinstating the monarchy. He made no proposal for a different form of government, but he did state his conviction that the existing State could be strengthened by concentrating more power in the offices of the President and the Minister of Economics (not the office of Chancellor, the leader of the party that by virtue of a majority or plurality in the parliament held the reins of government). Again, the overarching value Hirsch assigned to corporate life in submission to which individuals are to find and realize their freedom is evident. (What Hirsch called for is what tends to happen even in democracies in times of great crisis that call for sacrifice and the subordination of the individual to the whole. Note, for example, the central roles assumed by Roosevelt in the United States and Churchill in Great Britain during the Second World War.) Hirsch believed that Germany in 1920 was in its most severe crisis. He found no hope in the Weimar Republic and especially not in its leading party, the Social Democrats.

Ostensibly, hope would have to come from a strong leader who would recall the German people to their authentic character as a *Volk*, evoke from them a willingness once again to endure sacrifices for the good of the whole, and strike the chord that would create anew a community of consciences determined by the gospel, in which the God-given character and order of the *Volk*, their free ethical decisions, and their response to the mystery beyond all life and history would ring harmoniously. We may say that his hope was for a Germany that would be both National and Social, though Hirsch did not use these terms in 1920. Nonetheless, the terms make sense in the context of Hirsch's thought.

1. "National" reminds us of Hirsch's sense for the limits under

which human life takes place. He respected the ideal of universal humanity, but he was severely critical of those who expounded it without respect for the limiting diversity of humankind. When we take account of the diversity of peoples, we realize that a world government is utterly inconceivable and could take place only by virtue of one people ruling all others. Far better it is to recognize the God-given restraints of history and envision the display of universal humanity in the particular peoples of the world, that is, in nations.

It is, then, the mission of a people so to order itself in a nation-state that its own special characteristics will show forth and thereby reflect universal humanity. There is no alternative to this diversity, and, as regrettable as it may be, there is no escape from tensions and conflicts between peoples. Some wax, and others wane. Some become great; others do not. Some grow such that they require more space for living. War is a part of the mystery of history. It is "a necessary piece of the divine order of creation" (95). It is not, however, a happy reality of life. "All talk about an invigorating or joyous war is foolish" (95). One might wish for a world that was always at peace, but we did not create the conditions of our common life in the world. "Behind them stands another will, a totally other wisdom" (95). Hirsch tried to show that all arguments to determine when a war is just or who is the aggressor fail in the face of a range of ambiguous factors, such as national borders, responsibility for firing "the first shot," and so forth. Also, in an effort to be consistently realistic, he concluded that it is illusion to suppose that right is always victorious in war. All one can say is that the stronger will and the stronger force wins. A great war, he thought, is a hot and passionate question to God in which a people strives for its national being. At best it can be undertaken with a good conscience and the conviction that God is greater than the State. "If war is really a question to God, yes, a struggle with the God who hammers testingly on the foundation stones of the national being, then it is an irresolvable mystery" (109).

2. We can readily see that the term "Social" applies to Hirsch's position in connection with the primary value he placed upon *Volk,* community, and society. It was most certainly not "Social" in the sense in which that term was used by the Socialist and

68

Communist parties. These parties, he thought, fostered a factional spirit among the workers, and the radical Socialist and Communist parties were Marxist and therefore erred in being utopian and idealistic on the one side and international on the other. His distaste for the left-wing parties, however, should not be taken as a signal that he had no sense for the oppression of the poor and powerless in society. To be sure, he thought that underprivileged conditions could be helpful in building character, but that value by no means justified social oppression. Hirsch was aware that under the conditions of unrestrained capitalism the poor get poorer and the rich richer. As a matter of fact, he was as critical of capitalism as he was of moderate socialism. Capitalism not only fosters factionalism, it is both fiercely individualistic and international, and those who possess the concentrated wealth have too much power. He supported the right to private property, but he believed that right had to be limited in any number of ways to ensure the economic well-being of all the people. He was not, however, an egalitarian. The variety of gifts and accomplishments justifies a measure of stratification in society. But if the *Volk* is to approach the goal of being a community of consciences in which the individual subordinates himself or herself to the higher good of the *Volk,* and if the State through its law is not only to express the special character of the *Volk* but also to protect and enhance the life of the whole people, then the State must ensure and enhance the economic well-being of all its people. Hirsch's position was not socialist, but it was social.

Hirsch intended his position to be religious at its roots. His theistic-ethical metaphysics of history recognized contingency at every point and therefore placed the greatest weight on the free decision of people and the corporate will. The nation-state can help with these two claims, but because it is an "external" institution it cannot by itself call forth authentically free decisions. It cannot constitute a corporate will or create a community of consciences. Only faith in God could transform the inner life of a people and establish those values.

Hirsch was convinced that this faith had molded the German soul and could permeate it again in this darkest hour. In this faith, he saw the key to the possibility of hope that the German people would overcome their current disaster and transform their destiny into the fulfillment of their glorious mission in the world.

> We Germans must become a pious *Volk* in whom the gospel has power over the conscience. Otherwise, we will not master our destiny.
>
> Faith in God gives us two things that are crucial for our *Volk*. The one is . . . a clear sense of humanity and history, of *Volk* and State, which sharpens right and duty in our conscience so that we can do and suffer everything for our own *Volk* and our own State, transcending our own person. . . . The other is rather personal. Faith in God awakens those traits of character and soul that we Germans so desperately need. (153–154)

With this faith, he was confident, the German people would no longer be like stone smashed to dust by the hammer blows of God but like a mighty metal forged by God for the fulfillment of its authentic destiny and mission in world history.

$$* \quad * \quad * \quad * \quad *$$

> The old faith has become a superstition. I do not say: Let the new faith come. One does not wish into being or expedite things of this sort; they spring forth from creative distress. Our task can be only to provide clarity and purity. Then the ground is prepared for things that are ready to come.[15]

Barth's *Epistle to the Romans* and Hirsch's *Germany's Destiny* were utterly different books, but they had some things in common. Both spoke to the crisis of the German people after the collapse in 1918, though for Barth the crisis began in 1914. Both presented new theological positions that moved outside the old arena in which the Positives and Liberals had struggled with each other for more than a century. Both books were widely read and hailed by people their age and younger, though not by the same people.

Although Barth and Hirsch did not know it, the lines of a future battle were drawn. In the ensuing years of the Weimar Republic, those lines would shift and alliances would change, sometimes to

---

15. Döblin, "Jenseits von Gott!" p. 395.

the astonishment of Barth and Hirsch, who first, unwittingly, drew the lines.

It is ironic that another thing the books had in common was that they won for their authors appointment to the respected professorial ranks at the same German university. In 1923, Karl Barth, because of the impact of his *Epistle to the Romans,* was invited to be Honorary Professor of Reformed (Calvinistic) Theology at the University of Göttingen. The position did not carry with it full professorial rights, and it was funded primarily by Presbyterian churches in the United States, but it was Barth's entrée to the German university system as a professor in spite of his not having gone the regular route of writing two dissertations under professorial guidance. Also in 1923, because of his book, Emanuel Hirsch was invited to be Professor (*Ordinarius*) of Church History at the University of Göttingen.[16] Even more ironically, Hirsch and Barth became close discussion partners in the four years that they were on that faculty together. Although their discussions were mutually stimulating, they knew before they began that the possibility for agreement was remote.

---

16. It is doubly ironic that Hirsch's appointment was made by democratic-inclined officials in the Ministry of Culture (the government). Only two of the seven professors on the faculty at Göttingen (Conservatives!) listed him first. The other five placed him third on the list. The government ministry had the right to choose among the three. "Under the strong influence of his recently published *Germany's Destiny* the philosopher of law, Rudolf Stammler went to the Ministry of Culture and categorically declared that the author of that book must receive a professorship." That declaration apparently swayed the ministry to select Hirsch, the candidate least appealing to it politically. (Trillhaas, "Emanuel Hirsch in Göttingen," p. 222.)

PART II

BETWEEN THE TIMES:
1920–1932

CONTROVERSIES OVER THEOLOGICAL
FOUNDATIONS FOR ETHICS

> The death watch ticked for the German Republic, which had just
> begun to awaken from the agony of the emergency. The terrible
> flood of time was already rising; one day soon it would be up to our
> necks. It was all the more urgent what one did now to bring about
> something good and to establish a firm position before the ground
> under our feet was washed away. What counted now was to make
> use of the time and to squander nothing.—CARL ZUCKMAYER[1]

Among the pastors who heard Karl Barth present his lecture on
"The Christian's Place in Society" at Tambach, Germany, in 1919
were two who would become close colleagues of Barth in the
development of the new "Dialectical Theology." We have already
noted the presence there of Georg Merz from Munich, who in his
enthusiasm for this new theological voice persuaded the Christian
Kaiser publishing house in Munich to buy the rights to Barth's
Epistle to the Romans so that it could have its effect in Germany.
The other was Friedrich Gogarten, pastor in a small Thuringian
village. Unlike Barth, he had come to theology from the outside
(his father was not a pastor), but like Barth, his theological
education had been primarily in the Liberal tradition. Also, unlike
Barth, but like most Germans, he had been a patriot in 1914, but
like Barth, his theological world had collapsed, and he was seeking
something new. Barth's Tambach lecture struck a tone that
resonated with the voice that was already beginning to sound in
him.

Before the crucial second edition of *Romans* was published,

---

1. Zuckmayer, *Als wär's ein Stuck von mir*, p. 357.

73

Gogarten crashed on the scene with a forceful declaration of severance from the Liberal theological heritage. He titled his essay "Between the Times," and he published it in the leading Liberal religious weekly, *The Christian World*.

"It is," he began, "the destiny of our generation to stand between the times."[2] Speaking for his generation of theological students, he addressed his Liberal professors:

> The tormenting question never left us, the question of whether we, who were supposed to give everything with the word, could have anything at all to give. Indeed, we received nothing [from you]. We received much that was scholarly, much that was interesting, but nothing that would have been worthy of this word. . . . Did you not teach us to see the work of man in each and every thing? . . . Now we draw the conclusion: Everything that is somehow a human work not only has a beginning, but passes away again. . . . This distrust [of everything human], which questions everything, is only possible because there must be in us a germ of the knowledge of the opposite, of that which is not human. We cannot, however, conceive of God. But we can know more and more distinctly what . . . [God] is not, what . . . [God] cannot be.
>
> But now if we fully comprehend this plight we can ask about God. Then the question does not get entangled in the human and find false answers in it—false because the answers are human and not divine. . . . We stand not before our own wisdom, but before God. *We* have no time now. *We* stand between the times.[3]

The phrase vividly captured the sense many people had about the postwar years. Karl Barth had used it a few times in his Romans commentary. Whether Gogarten borrowed it or spontaneously created it anew, Barth was ecstatic about him. Barth, whose tradition was Calvinistic, had found a theological soulmate who was Lutheran. Shortly, he wrote his close friend, Eduard Thurneysen: "Have you read Gogarten's 'Between the Times' in *The Christian World?* I sent him a greeting at once and called upon

---

2. *The Beginnings of Dialectical Theology,* trans. Crim, ed. Robinson, p. 277.

3. Ibid., pp. 277, 279, 281–282.

him to cry aloud. This is good."[4] A few months later, after Gogarten had spent several days with him, the conversation going on day and night, Barth wrote again: "Here is a dreadnought on our side and against our opponents. Who knows, perhaps one day yet he will teach us something!"[5]

Barth and Thurneysen in Switzerland joined with Merz and Gogarten in Germany to found a new journal. The journal quickly became the most controversial and important theological journal of the time. It was the vehicle for the development of Dialectical Theology, the most discussed theological movement of the Weimar years. Karl Barth and Friedrich Gogarten were its major moving forces and contributors. The journal took its name from Gogarten's essay.

It contains a good bit of the most vigorous theological writing of the twentieth century, but it lasted only eleven years. It was brought to an abrupt ending by Barth in October 1933 after his coeditor Gogarten sided with the German Christians, the church movement that sought to bring the church in line with Adolf Hitler and the Third Reich.

Even before the first issue of the new journal appeared, Gogarten gave Barth cause to furrow his brow, a gesture we should not take seriously as a foreseeing of what Gogarten would do in 1933. Barth furrowed his brow easily, especially when considering his theological peers, and sooner rather than later he distanced himself from almost every one of them. His motto, as he explained to his close friend Thurneysen, was "in necessary issues not to give an inch, in uncertain issues not to pay attention, at all times not to let my pipe go out."[6] Barth usually managed to keep his pipe lit, but he was so intense a theologian that it was not easy for him to find uncertain issues. Almost every issue, so far as he could see, impinged in one way or another on the most necessary issue of all—the sole priority of God and the Word of God in Jesus Christ as revealed in the Bible and proclaimed by the church in

---

4. *Revolutionary Theology in the Making: Barth–Thurneysen Correspondence,* trans. James D. Smart (Richmond: John Knox Press, 1964), p. 52. Cf. *Karl Barth—Eduard Thurneysen Briefwechsel,* vol. 1: *1913–1921,* p. 399.

5. Ibid., p. 53 (German ed., p. 435).

6. *Karl Barth—Eduard Thurneysen Briefwechsel,* vol. 2: *1921–1930,* p. 30.

obedience to scripture. One by one he came to believe that most of his theological peers distorted that one most fundamental issue.

A few weeks before the first issue of the new journal appeared in early 1923, Barth mentioned Gogarten again to Thurneysen. At first, he commented, "I am more than ever convinced that both of us are biting on the same bone," but a few lines later he referred to an indistinct "element of distrust that somewhere at the bottom of things I have in regard to him."[7] In the early years, however, that element of distrust did not diminish Barth's expectations from Gogarten or dampen his enthusiasm for working with him. Together they became the acknowledged leaders of Dialectical Theology.

Both Barth and Gogarten were aggressively polemical, and this trait led them inevitably into controversies. Dialectical Theology developed in large measure by attack on other positions and by counterattack against those who criticized it. All of these controversies were through and through theological. The conviction from which Barth, and Gogarten with him, started and to which he always returned was God as the Wholly Other. Even so, the controversies revolved, directly or indirectly, around the issue that seemed to be most opaque in the paradoxical yes and no dialectic—the problem of ethics. What should I do?

---

7. Ibid., p. 126. The translation is from *Revolutionary Theology in the Making,* trans. Smart, p. 122.

FRIEDRICH GOGARTEN

3

ETHICS OF CONSCIENCE
OR ETHICS OF GRACE?

GOGARTEN AND BARTH
VERSUS HIRSCH

The first issue of the new quarterly journal *Between the Times* came out in early 1923. It consisted of basic, programmatic articles by Barth, Gogarten, and Thurneysen, and a review of events of interest to theologians by the general editor, Georg Merz.

Barth's essay was a lecture he had presented to a pastors conference the summer before at which he had been asked to explain his theology. He did so by emphasizing the transcendent reality of God, the incapacity of human beings from their own resources to speak of God, the initiative of God in revelation, and the necessity of proclaiming a theology of the cross in which all glory is given to God and everything human is called into question.

Gogarten's essay "The Decision" echoed Barth's. The fundamental question, he claimed, is the question of God. This is not a theoretical question, not a question about whether God exists. Rather, it is a question regarding whether God is hidden or revealed, invisible or visible, infinite or finite. The question places human beings in the crisis of decision. It cannot be answered by our own powers of thought or feeling. It is answered by God in revelation, and human beings are called upon to obey, that is, to have faith in the Word of God.

Some readers doubtless were mystified by the assertiveness of the essays and wondered how one could know, but many others surely were moved by the power of the message and resonated with the focus once again on a God who is above and beyond all things. In both cases, the issue was a good and forceful introduction to the new movement.

In the second issue, the editors were ready to get on with more specific business. The first project was to take on Emanuel Hirsch, who in the second edition of *Germany's Destiny* wrote an afterword in which he claimed that Barth and Gogarten dissolve questions of conscience into dialectical assertions that lead nowhere. Gogarten accepted the assignment and wrote an extended critique of Hirsch's book. He titled his essay "Ethics of Conscience or Ethics of Grace." Barth supported Gogarten by printing a lecture, "The Problem of Ethics Today," which he had given to another conference of ministers in the fall of 1922.

For Gogarten, the basic issue, of course, is the priority of God and the centrality of the teaching that God relates to human beings by the gift of grace received in faith with no respect whatsoever to human activity. He began with Luther, to whom Hirsch had appealed, and argued that for Luther, Christ is not the condition without which there can be no righteousness in human life. Even the Turks, Luther thought, though they do not know Christ, can be upright and honorable, and they have established an enviably solid order of state and society. The point, for Gogarten, was that Luther did not think God is an ethical principle. Hirsch is wrong, Gogarten asserted, in his contention that the Protestant reformers thought the eternity of God enters our human life and judges it in the moral sphere. Gogarten claimed that they held that God reveals God's self solely in the forgiveness of sin, and forgiveness is not an ethical principle. Rather, it is a break with the ethical and stands on the far side of good and evil. To say that the conscience is immediately related to God as the source of ethical activity would be, he thought, a form of blasphemy to Luther, robbing God of God's deity. God's forgiveness is free and is not conditioned by a person's moral worth or lack of it. Faith is not a human work. It is a passive response to God's gift.

Gogarten boldly formulated what he believed to be the difference he and Barth had with Hirsch: Hirsch determines the relation of human beings to God by the category of the ethical, whereas we, he said, hold that ethics is determined by grace, by God's relation to us. But Hirsch is not simplistic in his representation of that position. He is not idealistic or utopian. He knows the difference between God and humankind. He recognizes that human life is limited by the Eternal and thus that there can be no absolutizing of state, society, or anything human. Given these insights, Gogarten was puzzled that Hirsch did not found his view of law and social order on them. He concluded that they were not substantially important to Hirsch, and he thought the reason was that these insights do not break through into the moral sphere. Where they govern one's thinking, one sees that the conscience perceives nothing but the judgment of God. Hirsch, however, wanted to understand conscience as the locus, "better the organ," of revelation.[1] Hirsch accused Gogarten and Barth of dissolving ethical truths into general dialectical statements. Gogarten objected. In order to hold grace and judgment together, he insisted, one must speak dialectically. He complained that Hirsch did not engage them at the root of their dialectical method. The voice of conscience, to be sure, is loud, but it is the roar of judgment. Conscience is the locus of autonomy in human beings; by the gift of grace, autonomy is destroyed and the believer places himself or herself under God's revelation. The problem with Hirsch, Gogarten thought, is that he puts creation and redemption on the same plane, and therefore his understanding of the difference between God and humankind becomes simply one idea alongside others, rather than the dominant insight that affects everything else.

The distinction between God and humankind has the sharp dynamics of exclusivity—either God or the human being. However one decides, the underlying opposition remains. If one decides for the human being, one is all the more troubled by God; if one decides for God, then one is overwhelmed by the sense of sin. This understanding, Gogarten explained, is the basis for the criticism of culture he and Barth made. In contrast, Hirsch believes the moral act is the highest human act and, in its certainty, gives one a sense of relatedness to the Eternal. Hirsch roots this view in his doctrine of creation, but because he does not

---

1. *Zwischen den Zeiten* 2 (1923). Reprinted in Friedrich Gogarten, *Illusionen* (Jena: Eugen Diedrichs Verlag, 1926), p. 30.

subordinate creation to redemption, he does not see "the danger of making earthly powers into idols."[2]

Drawing on the traditional theological terms, law and gospel, Gogarten said that Hirsch can view law apart from gospel, with the result that he succumbs to the fatal flaw of the law: he wants to see in it the possibility of an immediate relation to God. There is, he insisted, no relation to God except under the gospel alone, as God's free gift. Then the gospel becomes the foundation for ethics, and one knows that this ethics will have its special character in the fact that its acting is without any immediate relation to God. A soul does not "unite itself to the Eternal by the affirmation of a specific duty," as Hirsch claims.[3] Moreover, even moral acts done in faith have no effect on the relation between God and the person. Ethical activity is an effect of faith, but it does not affect faith. The first and most pressing concern of an ethics that is grounded in faith is to give God the glory.

Finally, Gogarten considered Hirsch's work as a construction and exposition of the meaning of human history and the ordering of society with its laws and necessities. Hirsch and others try to give a positive, religious meaning to human history; and Hirsch, especially, wants to see a positive relation between God's ordering of the world in creation, God's power at work in the world, and the possibility of human decisions of conscience that draw on the power of God to bring about what is right and good. Hirsch realizes, as not all others do, that humans can make a mess of things. Gogarten picked up on this proviso and pressed it to make his own point. He was certain that if one takes this proviso seriously and contemplates the decisions that human beings make, especially if one has a sense of the majesty and righteousness of God, then one is overwhelmed by the destructive and bewildering powers that are unleashed in history. If one views human history from the standpoint of faith, one is struck with a sense of sin and will necessarily view the course of history in dialectical relation with the kingdom of God (No and Yes). He believed that if one ponders Hirsch's proviso, one cannot possibly see a relation to

---

2. Ibid., p. 35.
3. Ibid., p. 38.

God in decisions of conscience. One will see nothing but God's judging No to the world and thereby sense the desperate need for forgiveness. The cross of Jesus Christ becomes the symbol of human history. It is both God's No and God's Yes. The cross does not bring an immediate relation to God, but a mediate one. It is mediated through the stark conviction of sin and God's free gift of grace, which in turn intensifies the sense of sin.

To be sure, in the cross of Christ all creation is sanctified. That means we have earthly duties to perform, and they can be fulfilled only in an earthly way. We know, however, that in and of themselves they have nothing at all to do with our relation to God, which is given to us by God in grace.

Gogarten thought this position was consonant with Luther's response to the ethical question. He cited Luther's 1518 Heidelberg disputation:

> "If you ask, What then should we do? Shall we do nothing since we can do nothing but sin? Answer: No, but when you hear that, you should fall on your knees, call on God for grace and put your hope in Christ, in whom is our salvation, life and resurrection."[4]

Barth's lecture "The Problem of Ethics Today" followed Gogarten's essay in the second issue of *Between the Times*.[5] Although he did not deal explicitly with Hirsch, he did in almost all respects sound the same themes Gogarten developed. If one is permeated by the mystery of God's grandeur and absolute righteousness, then faced by the question, What shall I do?, one is utterly abashed. Within oneself one hears nothing but judgment. The question will not go away, but the answer to it is itself a question from God. Near the end, Barth told his hearers that he

---

4. Ibid., p. 47. The statement is quoted from Luther's clarification of the Heidelberg disputation in 1518.

5. This lecture was included in a collection of Barth's addresses under the title *Das Wort Gottes und die Theologie*. An English translation of the essay is in *The Word of God and the Word of Man*, pp. 136–182. Quotations from the address will be from the English translation with occasional modifications. In the footnotes, I will indicate the location in *Zwischen den Zeiten* and will note in parentheses the page reference to the translation, preceded by E. T.

did not want to leave them with a riddle, but what he said in answer to the riddle was no more specifically helpful in guiding human activity than Gogarten had been: "If I have led you to an impasse, at least I know what I have done."[6]

However, Barth did go beyond Gogarten's brief points near the end of his essay. Gogarten had affirmed the sanctification of creation by the cross of Christ and the necessity of performing our earthly duties in an earthly way. Barth confessed that he belonged with those contemporaries who saw the ethical objective in the form of the socialist ideal, though for him this ideal was a hope for the last things, the millennium, the eschaton. Even so, he saw it as the goal of earthly history. Like Hirsch (whom he did not mention), he could not conceive the ethical question yielding an answer in individualistic hopes and goals; but sharply unlike Hirsch, he thought the goal had to be in terms of "the universally valid humaneness."[7] To think the ethical question is to think oneself in identity with all other human beings.

Barth's socialist orientation is well known. For a time during his pastorate in Safenwil, he held membership in the Swiss Social Democratic Party, and, as we will see, he joined the German Social Democratic Party after Hitler gained control of Germany and membership in the party was possibly dangerous. However, Barth's theology led him to have no illusions about final solutions to the social problems, and he believed that the judgment of God fell as severely on revolutions from the left as on revolutions from the right. He held that God judges all existing forms of government. Every answer to the ethical question, he believed, was finally also a question. Human beings live under the power of the fall, and they cannot extricate themselves.

> All the human being can desire is things. Things are not spirit. All the human being can do is to unfold the self. Such a display, however, is not love. All the human being can achieve in history is the colorful image of a pluralistic, layered community with all the crying injustices that go with

---

6. *Zwischen den Zeiten* 2 (1923), 55 (E. T., p. 179).
7. Ibid., pp. 42–43 (E. T., p. 157).

this kind of ordering or a coercion, the boredom and stupidity of the barracks, where the highest right is transformed into the greatest injustice. In no case, however, can a human being achieve freedom in love and love in freedom.[8]

Barth believed that the only kind of love of which humans are capable is eros, the desire of the self in contrast to selfless love. Consequently, human possibility is limited to a modicum of civil justice. (Note the connection with Gogarten's emphasis on "earthly duties.") We can make things a little better, but we remain always at an infinite distance from the final goal. We can ask the ethical question, but we cannot find an answer.

The pressure of the question, however, never eases, neither in its urgency nor in the judgment it imposes on us. "It is because God says Yes to us that we must remain so radically, so inescapably in the No."[9] This is what it means to say that the law is still in force. (Note again the resonance with Gogarten and the contrast with Hirsch, who, though he, too, acknowledged judgment under the law, thought the law could be perceived in creation and guide the conscience.)

The positive side of the recognition that the law is still in force is that it will not let us rest in the face of the ethical question. However, for Barth, that did not mean taking recourse in the doctrine of older and more recent Lutheranism, that is, the orders of creation. (Contrast Hirsch.) Barth thought that doctrine was an evasion of the ethical question. The ethical question places us before the ultimate reality, and he insisted that the orders are not ultimate. Only God is ultimate. This truth

> *not only* assures the continuance and proper continuance, in
> all its relative dignity and authority, of that system of human
> ends which is wholly profane, wholly set up from below by
> fallen man, *but also* authorizes and necessitates a struggle for
> relatively higher ends—with, or if possible, without revolu-
> tion—in the political, social, and other spheres.[10]

---

8. Ibid., p. 47 (E. T., pp. 165–166).
9. Ibid., p. 49 (E. T., p. 169).
10. Ibid., p. 51 (E. T., p. 172).

There is, Barth believed,

> the possibility—and this possibility is the necessity—of saying
> an unrestricted Yes not only to the ethical question but to the
> answers as well, without pessimism and scepticism, in spite,
> no, because of its very questionableness, in spite of, no,
> because we have not been able to resolve the decisive ethical
> questions.[11]

Barth had no ultimate confidence in human possibilities for
accomplishing something really good in history, but without
diluting his belief in the judgment of God on everything human
beings try to accomplish, he affirmed the impulse to make things a
little bit better.

It will not surprise us that he ended his lecture with a reference
to the last things, to eschatology. In good dialectical fashion, it was
an unsettling word of comfort.

> And now let me close with a word from the story of Lazarus.
> "Whosoever liveth and believeth in me shall never die." I beg
> you not to take religious rest in this, for the question asked of
> each one of us is, "Believest thou this?"[12]

Emanuel Hirsch, slight as he was and visually impaired, was not
one to walk away from a fight, especially with Dialectical
Theology, which he recognized as his most potent opponent. He
wrote a rebuttal to Gogarten's essay and sent it to the editors of
Between the Times. It was published in the next issue together with
a final response from Gogarten.[13]

It is characteristic of the vigorous and aggressive style of
Hirsch's polemics that in an extended footnote to the first
paragraph he analyzed Gogarten's citations from Luther for the
purpose of showing that his opponent had misconstrued the
Reformer, quoting him out of context, and that he had misused
Karl Holl (Hirsch's teacher). It is not important for us to try to

---

11. Ibid., p. 52 (E. T., p. 173).
12. Ibid., p. 57 (E. T., p. 182).
13. "Zum Problem der Ethik: Emanuel Hirsch an Friedrich Gogarten,"
Zwischen den Zeiten 3 (1923), 52–57.

adjudicate these historical and interpretive points, but it is interesting to note Hirsch's concluding statement to these charges: "On the basis of these two examples the reader will surely have from the outset a bit of scepticism about Gogarten's treatment of me."[14]

In the main text of his response, Hirsch claimed that Gogarten had misrepresented him on so many points that he could not possibly deal with every instance of his wrongheadedness. Instead, he said he would restrict himself to the main points. I will paraphrase these main points.

1. Gogarten used my book, *Germany's Destiny,* to make a sweeping judgment on my appropriation of the gospel. He could not resist the temptation to note how rarely in that book I referred to Jesus Christ. What he failed to take into consideration was that my book was not a systematic theological treatise but an effort to construct a philosophy of history and of the State. The moral-religious view of life grounded in the gospel is important to me in every respect, and it is necessary in order to understand the ground, the mode, and the goal of life in history and the State. But, because of the subject matter of my book, I dealt with it only at those points where it impacted the subject matter.

If Gogarten had taken the trouble to consider my other works, he would have seen, for example, that I am as critical as he of the optimistic view of humankind, that Luther's view of the justification of the impious in distinction from the pietistic view of the justification of the pious is the cornerstone of my conception of the gospel, that I affirm religious determinism and predestination. This position, however, as others acknowledge, does not necessarily exclude a freedom of the human spirit toward nature; it has to do only with the relationship between God and human beings. Thus Gogarten's volleys passed over my head.

The essential difference between him and me lies within the truth about God's providence, which we hold in common. It has to do with one's attitude toward the State and history. But Gogarten chose not to address this point, which is the subject of my book. Perhaps he avoided it because on these issues, in sharp distinction from his friends, he does not think so differently from the way I

---

14. Ibid., p. 52.

think. [This comment is an omen when we look ahead and realize that Gogarten joined forces with Hirsch in several publications after Hitler came to power. In his reference to Gogarten's "friends," Hirsch is referring above all to Karl Barth with his socialist ideal.]

2. Over and over again, Gogarten took issue with my statement "Out of the certainty of their relatedness to something eternal individual souls unite themselves with this Eternal by saying Yes to a specific duty."[15] In my book, this statement occurs in the context of a theoretical struggle with sceptical positivism. I was making the point that a human being is not an animal. A person is distinguished from animals by being related to the truth, which includes within it a relation to God. I acknowledge that the specific content of my statement seems questionable, but I explained that the statement does not for me posit an apparent divinity in the human being but rather a relatedness to God. To be a person means to stand before the question of God. At this boundary, where God and human beings meet, all the vitality we have is kindled. My statement does not, as Gogarten thinks, refer to the moral act but rather to moral judgment. Moreover, it does not understand moral judgment as the perfection of community with God, but as the acknowledgment that there is a God above me whom I should obey. Gogarten's objection that my statement amounts to works righteousness misses the mark. I know what a soul experiences in justification by grace through faith, but this was not my point. In order properly to reject my statement, Gogarten would have to say that human beings are animals with no sense at all for God until they encounter Jesus of Nazareth. He does well to leave that consequence alone.

3. Gogarten complains that I stop short with the religious criticism of human beings and their enterprises. He says I exempt the conscience from criticism. I do not recall saying that the conscience is the "organ of revelation," and if Gogarten knew my thought as a whole, he would know that for me all human knowledge of God is a gift and breaks into our lives from the outside. In my judgment, we are human beings only insofar as we are addressed by God. Thus for me, the conscience is activated most purely and completely in the act of prayer. Therefore I have

---

15. Ibid., pp. 53–54. Hirsch quoted from his book *Germany's Destiny*.

no objection to the statement that the conscience is a liar until God's revelation sets in and frees the conscience.

I do refer to conscience as the "locus"—better, the arena—of revelation. What I mean is that the question of God does not arise in a person's yearning for happiness or for a better life, or in striving for knowledge, or in the sense of beauty. Rather, it arises in a personal relation to the good. God wants to be understood by us in God's holy goodness in that God makes us responsible to God for ourselves. God speaks to us in the conscience.

Gogarten objects and contrasts my view with that of the Protestant Reformers who, he contends, held that God's revelation takes place in forgiveness. Well and good, but forgiveness presupposes judgment, and that points us to morality. That is what I mean by the locus. For me that locus is the starting point, not the completion of community. Where does Gogarten think it happens? He says that the locus is not the conscience, but Jesus of Nazareth. I fully concur with him in affirming that Jesus is the coming of the suprahistorical into our mundane history, but the danger is that one might see in Jesus nothing but a piece of reality. In the cross, Jesus addresses me about my guilt and God's wrath. But where do I hear what he says? I hear it in the place where I, through God's Yes, first know myself truly as myself, in the conscience. That is where I perceive God's truth and my lie. That is where I perceive the reality of the suprahistorical. At this point, Gogarten, on the contrary, can take recourse only in arbitrary authority. His position is like that of Tertullian in the early church: I believe because it is absurd.

4. I do not want to end this response on a negative and personal note. Maybe I am wrong. If so, it is not at the points where Gogarten attacks me. The issue has to do with the law. Luther understood the law as the revelation of God. He knew that it reveals both God and our guilt. The law demands love from the whole person. We cannot understand the revelation of the gospel except in connection with the revelation of the law. Gogarten often gives the impression that the gospel has done away entirely with the law, that Luther was an antinomian. He is wrong. What the gospel does is to show us the perverted use of the law. That is, it makes us see the lie in thinking that we can claim for ourselves a relationship with God on the basis of our good works. Luther

understood the "terrors of the conscience," and he realized that these terrors are an act of prevenient grace.

The one who understands that God justifies the sinner by grace through faith senses at least that law and gospel do not contradict each other but interpenetrate at the deepest level.

Gogarten thought nothing Hirsch wrote in his rebuttal dealt with the points he had made in his essay. He was confident that he had already answered every objection Hirsch had made. He decided to respond only because the issue was so crucial. It had to do, he thought, not just with a difference between himself and Hirsch but with the fundamental theological issue of the distinction between law and gospel, the righteousness of the law and the righteousness of faith, which Hirsch, he insisted, had eliminated. I will paraphrase Gogarten's comments as I did Hirsch's rebuttal.[16]

I would have had no occasion to criticize Hirsch if he had done nothing more than his title promised, that is, to construct an ethical view of history. He tried to do more, but he has no idea how far it is from an "ethical-theistic view of history" to a view of history that is based on the gospel. Hirsch said he wanted "to understand rightly the foundation, mode, and goal of the life of the State and history" on the basis of the gospel. His relation to the gospel should, therefore, have been at the center of his work. Doubtless, Hirsch knows everything there is to know about justification and the bondage of the will. That is not at issue. What is at issue is whether he has appropriated what he knows when he speaks personally about the gospel of justification. If so, that should show itself when he speaks about "the foundation, mode, and goal of life in the State and history." I can only conclude that he knows everything as a historian and as a philologian but not in reality. Otherwise, he could not criticize me for having focused on the wrong points.

My contention is that Hirsch has actually written nothing more than an ethical-theistic view of history, but he holds that his work, because of its ethical grounding, is the view of history most

16. "Erwiderung an E. Hirsch von Friedrich Gogarten," *Zwischen den Zeiten* 3 (1923), 57–62.

appropriate to the gospel. I argue with him because of this transference, which is the universal malaise of theology today of which Hirsch is only an example.

In fact, there are two utterly different views of history. One has nothing to do with the gospel; the other is determined by the gospel. The fundamental distinction between the two is faith. There are secondary distinctions, but they are here at issue only in that they (including all moral qualities) may not in any way be decisive. It is not possible to know who is a Christian by that person's moral qualities. One can know only by the person's faith, and no one can see that except in faith.

Thus the sharpest point of this debate is the opposition of law and faith. Hirsch sees this opposition, but I want to put it more sharply. Hirsch distinguishes between a perverted and a right use of the law. Is that really a distinction? He sees a difference between the conscience thinking that it ought to fulfill the law and the conscience saying Yes to the norm and claim of the law. But does not the conscience say Yes when it thinks it should fulfill the law by its own powers? Can the conscience, when it says Yes, intend anything other than that it ought itself to fulfill the law? Then does it not necessarily happen that the "right" use of the law willy-nilly becomes a perverted use of the law?

Whatever one may know in one's head about justification does not protect one here from falling back into the notion that one can be related to God on the basis of what one does (works righteousness). It is not the conscience that says Yes to forgiveness, but faith, and it does so against the conscience, which can only condemn. Therefore faith, not conscience, is the locus of that conversation in which Jesus Christ speaks to the believer about God's wrath and favor. Jesus Christ, not conscience, is the locus of revelation, and there is no special mode or attribute of Jesus that can be a proof that he is the revelation of God. "If he is the revelation, then he is it absolutely because he is it."[17] Any other grounding does nothing but negate the revelation. When one finds revelation exclusively in Jesus Christ rather than in experience, this affirmation no longer seems absurd. Then also the primacy of morality is broken through, and the optimistic doctrine of human being is destroyed.

---

17. Ibid., p. 61.

4

ETHICS OF WRATH, GRACE
OR GOODNESS?

GEORG WÜNSCH VERSUS GOGARTEN

The debate on the issue of ethics involving the Dialectical Theology of Barth and Gogarten did not end with the exchange between Gogarten and Hirsch. In order to follow its most illuminating extension, however, we have to look at a critique by a theologian outside the set of six on whom we are focusing.

In 1923, Georg Wünsch was at the beginning of his academic career, an assistant professor (*Privatdozent*) of Systematic Theology at Marburg. In 1931, he would be given Marburg's first professorial chair in Ethics, Social Ethics, and Apologetics. It was his life goal to write what no German had yet written, a constructive and comprehensive treatment of social ethics that would be both theoretically sound and practical. The question of ethics (What should I do?) was his passion. He was strongly influenced by the Liberal theologian and philosopher Ernst Troeltsch, who with his massive work *The Social Teaching of the Christian Churches* had in effect created the discipline of social ethics; but other influences were also important, especially Martin Luther.

Wünsch was convinced that the gospel yields positive guidance to Christian people for the conduct of their lives, not only personally but socially and politically as well. He had a deep concern for the socially and economically oppressed. Even before he won his beginning appointment to the theological faculty in Marburg, he was a respected voice among Religious Socialists in

Germany, and he became the leader of a branch of that movement in Germany and the editor of its journal. (His role in the movement brought him into contact with Paul Tillich.)

When he read the articles by Gogarten and Barth in the second issue of *Between the Times,* he could not keep silent. He did not write to defend Hirsch. In 1923, they stood at opposite ends of the political spectrum. He wrote because he felt impelled to call attention to what he thought was the major weakness of Dialectical Theology—its failure to venture a helpful answer to the question, What should I do? His essay "The Ethics of Wrath and the Ethics of Grace" was published in the *Journal for Theology and Church.*[1]

Wünsch was convinced that the new Dialectical Theology yielded nothing but negativity with respect to what Christians—for that matter, all people—might try to accomplish in this world. Dialectical Theology, he said, asserts that no human activity in the world has value. Only the forgiveness of sin changes the human situation, but forgiveness as Barth and Gogarten understand it only makes one more aware of the wrath of God. For them, he thought, there is no assurance of grace and salvation. There is nothing but "fear, shaking, weaving back and forth in doubt, for no one can be certain whether he or she stands under damnation or in grace."[2] He acknowledged that they had performed a service by pressing the distinction between God and humankind to its last consequence, thereby shattering (or trying to shatter!) the crystal shell of comfort in the church. But even this service is negative. Dialectical Theology, he thought, walks a narrow ridge between two abysses: the total lostness of the world, on the one side, and the inescapable wrath of God, on the other.

In reading Barth and Gogarten, Wünsch found no help in answering the basic question, What should I do? Gogarten, in his essay against Hirsch, argued that morality does not determine faith; faith determines morality. However, after playing with paradoxes and proclaiming the judgment of God on everything that human beings undertake, all Gogarten could suggest was

---

1. "Ethik des Zorns und Ethik der Gnade," *Zeitschrift für Theologie und Kirche,* Neue Folge 4, no. 5 (1923–1924), 327–352.

2. Ibid., p. 327.

that we have faith in Jesus Christ and get on with our earthly duties in an earthly way. Barth's ethical yield, he thought, was even more scanty. He holds so tightly to the doctrine of original sin and the fall that he can say no more than that we are able to affirm ethical demands only in dying. He talks about Christian ethics, but it remains hypothetical for him because he repeatedly tells us that no one can be sure of the grace of God, which is the foundation of Christian ethics. No wonder we find no reference in their writings to the Sermon on the Mount or to being disciples of Jesus.

The view of the Dialectical Theologians is so one-sided in its preoccupation with the hiddenness of God and God's wrath that Wünsch wondered if it could be called Christian. What they miss, he thought, was the revelation of the goodness of God. To be sure, it is right to avoid all talk of God's goodness if by that goodness one understands the transference to God of nothing more than the ordinary rational attitudes and acts we call good in human beings. There is, however, another way to understand the goodness of God, a way that exceeds human rationality but is comprehensible in Christian experience. This goodness is God's acceptance of the sinner out of sheer grace, with no petty conditions whatsoever. Barth and Gogarten, to be sure, do not overlook grace, but they do overlook its significance.

The goodness of God in grace is mightier than God's wrath, and when it takes hold of a person, that person is made new and given a new understanding of God and a new orientation to life in the world. The transformed person experiences the presence of the kingdom of God, is permeated by the naïve joy of the children of God, and has a new conscience. Grace does more than forgive sins; it brings to birth the new creation by the pouring out of the Spirit. It is the work of Christian ethics to describe the kind of life in the world that characterizes the new creation. Using an image from the Sermon on the Mount, Wünsch compared faith and ethics to a good tree bearing good fruit. His point is that Christian ethics has positive content. God's goodness evokes love (a word Wünsch rarely found in the writings of Barth and Gogarten), and, he insisted, we not only can but must try to explain concretely what it means to love in the social world in which we live.

In developing a Christian ethics with positive content, we are helped further by the goodness of God. This goodness causes us to see the world in a new light as the creation of God. We come to see God's hand and guidance in the structures and orders of creation. We believe that God pursues God's aims in the world, and we want to trace these aims and try to bring our actions into conformity with them.

God's goodness, then, impels us toward Christian ethics, and the positive content is elaborated on the basis of the two pillars: love and the world as God's creation. Wünsch was aware that Christian people are not preserved from error, but by the grace of God they must have the courage to err. "The experience of the goodness of God presses us into action."[3]

Gogarten responded to Wünsch's essay typically with an "or" in his title instead of Wünsch's "and": "Ethics of Goodness or Ethics of Grace?" It came out in the next issue of the *Journal for Theology and Church*.[4] Clearly, he did not care for Wünsch's overwrought rhetoric, such as his claim that the religious crisis of which Dialectical Theology spoke is "a terminal illness in its last stages."[5] Gogarten thought the entire essay was supercilious and utterly wrongheaded. Throughout his rebuttal, Gogarten repeated the phrase "In this entire essay I do not find one sentence that speaks to . . ."

Wünsch thought the fundamental issue revolved around the relation of law and grace, of wrath and goodness, but Gogarten could find no place where Wünsch dealt seriously with the relation of law and gospel. He said frequently that the two belong together, but he said nothing about their relationship. Neither was Gogarten able to find any place in the essay that argued that what he and Barth say about the judgment of God is false.

Moreover, Gogarten found relatively little in the essay about grace. What he found was a facile move from God's grace to God's

---

3. Ibid., p. 352.
4. "Ethik der Güte oder Ethik der Gnade?" *Zeitschrift für Theologie und Kirche* 4, no. 6 (1923–1924), 427–443.
5. Ibid., p. 427. Cf. Wünsch, "Ethik des Zorns und Ethik der Gnade," p. 344.

goodness. That, he thought, was the key to Wünsch's position. Only by this transference was Wünsch able to talk about "childlike naïveté," "health," "self-evident joy," and so forth. To speak of grace, Gogarten reminded the readers, is to remember one's sin and thereby to be reminded of judgment. This hard reality that we know through grace eliminates the possibility of any naïveté in this world.

Gogarten thought it was evident that when Wünsch referred to goodness he was not speaking about grace and therefore was not serious about wrath and law. He claimed that the goodness of which he spoke was not the rational goodness of human beings transferred to God, that he was speaking of the sheer grace of God that accepts persons with no conditions, which is beyond the reach of reason. But unfortunately he goes no place with this understanding. It is for him something comprehensible and thus remains in the rational sphere. Had he worked with this understanding, he would have been pressed ineluctably into dialectical statements. He would have been led to acknowledge that grace is also judgment. He would have seen that the goodness of God is not something that takes hold of our lives from this day forth and forever. On the contrary, the grace of God in Jesus Christ puts us in a constant struggle. It is something that has always to be received again and again. It is something that we have and do not have. The human situation is always dialectical. It is no wonder, Gogarten insisted, that Wünsch stays clear of dialectics: he has no understanding of grace.

Wünsch held that the two pillars of Christian ethics are the acts of redemption and creation. Gogarten agreed, but he did not agree that these pillars are "positive." It was apparent to Gogarten that Wünsch meant by that term that there was a straight line for thought from redemption and creation to positive, substantive statements about how to live in the world. But for Gogarten, neither the reality of God nor the reality of the world can yield undialectical straight lines to any place. The reality of God does not come to us simply as goodness; it comes as grace and thus also as wrath. Moreover, the world, as beautiful as it is, is also ugly; as wonderfully supportive of life as it is, it is also harsh, mean, and destructive. Wünsch, he thought, may be right in saying that Christians must have the courage to err, but is his erring pious deed . . . really any better than nothing? And the "struggle" for content in the answer to the question, What shall we do? is certainly not worse but also no better "than to clothe oneself in the prophetic mantel of inactive sublimity over the always useless work in the world."[6]

Gogarten insisted that he had given a material content to Christian ethics when, with Luther, he had said that we should place our hope in Jesus Christ. Wünsch, he noted, thought that was little help for Christian ethics. Gogarten agreed with him if he could put it his own way. It is, indeed, little in relation to all the high-minded ethical undertakings of the present that know the positive goals of this world and work to achieve them. He added that there can be none of that nonsense when one knows one can do nothing but sin. This understanding, he thought, is what Wünsch gave up with his emphasis on the positive, the outpouring of the Spirit.

Gogarten did not entirely disagree with Wünsch's talk about the new life in Christ, but he insisted that this new life is not a firm possession but is based on faith and hope. But, again, to say that means that one has to deal with God's wrath as well as God's goodness. He was also willing to grant Wünsch's point that Christian ethics tries to act only out of the renewal in the Spirit, but life in the Spirit, Gogarten insisted, is not naïve. Faith destroys all naïveté. One can be positive; but like the negative, the positive is given only in faith—not in experience, as Wünsch thought.

Everything the Christian has, Gogarten believed, is given in faith alone; and because faith is never a firm possession, what it helps us see in creation is the need for redemption, and what it helps us see in the new being is the dialectical, continuing life of the old being. This understanding, Gogarten thought, was the contribution of Christian faith to ethics. Theology, therefore, does not guide ethics in the secular realm. For Gogarten, that guidance should be left to those disciplines that are specifically oriented to that realm. The business of theology, he was convinced, is to make clear the actual reality of this world, and he was certain that

---

6. "Ethik der Güte oder Ethik der Gnade?" pp. 436–437.

theology could accomplish this goal only by proclaiming what has been entrusted to it—the gospel of forgiveness.

The editors of the *Journal for Theology and Church* gave Wünsch the opportunity to respond to Gogarten's rebuttal.[7] In his response, he charged that Gogarten's essay was surly and contributed nothing to the discussion. The only thing he knew to do, therefore, was to repeat what he had said to gain greater clarity. He restricted himself to three points.

The first was the relationship between goodness and grace. Grace, he repeated, not only brings forgiveness but gives birth to a new creature and thereby enables a new judgment of the total divine work in the world and humankind. Gogarten put an "or" in his title (Ethics of Goodness or Ethics of Grace?). Wünsch insisted that the "or" would be appropriate only if Gogarten had meant by goodness what he specifically said he did not mean. The grace of God is the way God expresses God's goodness by means of the forgiveness of sin.

Wünsch's second point had to do with the contrast of the old and new being. He repeated his conviction that in Gogarten's thought one could never be certain of God's grace and therefore one could know nothing about the new creation. Wünsch agreed that no one can "know" that God is gracious to her or him. One can only "believe" it. The certainty that goes with that belief is the presupposition for the possibility of Christian activity with respect both to the impulse to do the best one can in this world and to the discovery of what is best to do. Certainly, he admitted, the Christian lives after faith as before "in the flesh," and the new creation also sins, but the Christian knows that his or her sin has been sublimated by the underlying and ongoing sense of trust. Certainly, he agreed, grace is not a once-for-all act that ends all struggle in this worldly life, but this struggle takes place specifically in the ethical sphere. The Christian, in distinction from others, is determined by courage to act—to act with circumspection, joy, and, indeed, naïveté because the Christian is a new creation. If one does not believe that a good tree is possible, one cannot believe there can be good fruit.

---

7. "Nochmals: Ethik des Zorns und Ethik der Gnade," *Zeitschrift für Theologie und Kirche* 4, no. 6 (1923–1924), 444–448.

Gogarten, he thought, was right if we must judge all human actions in relation to God, but human actions are in relation to other human beings, and in that sphere some actions are better than others. Christian ethics should and can try to distinguish what is better and what is worse.

Wünsch's third point had to do with Gogarten's reservation about his two pillars of Christian ethics: redemption and creation. Gogarten complained, he noted, that he had not made clear that both the act of redemption and the act of creation reveal both sin and grace. Wünsch expressed mystification: how could they be otherwise conceived in the new creation of God? But his reservation was that he did not see why one always had to speak about both sides. There is a point at which one needs to explain what Christians ought to do.

Wünsch's last comment directed itself to the concluding reference in Barth's lecture on "The Problem of Ethics Today." Wünsch wrote: "In the gospel one reads not only the story of the resurrection of Lazarus but also the story of the good Samaritan. How we today in our industrial-military age can be good Samaritans is my problem."[8]

One would hope that puzzling about how to be a good Samaritan was a preoccupation for others besides Wünsch, with or without reference to the Dialectical Theology of Barth and Gogarten. And one can see why Wünsch put the problem specifically before Barth (to whom he referred more than I have noted) and Gogarten.

Gogarten offered all but no help with that problem. At this stage in his development, he gave the impression of being disdainful of all efforts on the basis of Christian faith to make the world a bit less painful to those who hurt or to make it structurally a bit better for the whole. The way he worked out the implications of the infinite majesty of God has both depth and power, and no doubt the Protestant church of that time and place needed to be shaken to its roots and branches by his relentless pressing of the doctrine of justification by grace through faith. It is by no means clear that he would have had to violate his understanding of grace

---

8. Ibid., p. 448.

in order to struggle with Wünsch's problem of how to be a good Samaritan there and then, but he did not.

Before long, he would decide that it is, after all, important as a theologian how human beings hear the gospel, what effects that hearing has upon them, and in connection with that, what those effects mean for the attitudes and activities of people in the world. Unfortunately, it was that development in his thought that, for a complex set of reasons, led him in 1933 to join the "German Christians" and to give qualified support to Hitler.

If what was to happen to Gogarten is poignant and perplexing, then so also was what happened to Wünsch. He never gave up his passion to struggle for concrete answers to the ethical question, What shall I (we) do? But in the years after 1923, he began to develop the tenuous connection he made near the end of his essay against Gogarten between redemption and creation, and he did so to the point of giving creation all but an independent status as revelation. He coupled this theme with a growing interest in history as the arena in which God's will can be known and with a new conviction that it is necessary to recognize historical conditions and limitations. Thus he came to believe that one must concentrate on what is possible in *Volk* and State. He was not the only one in the early thirties to move from socialism to National Socialism, from Marxism to fascism. After the war, he was suspended from his professorship at Marburg for five years. His case was contested, but the evidence in his massive work *A Protestant Ethics of Politics* (1936), as well as in other places, was overwhelming.

One would think Gogarten's sense for the absolute difference between God and human being, between the kingdom of God and all human social constructions, would have led him to sharp criticism of a regime whose advent was hyped by religious fervor and whose claim was total. One would also think Wünsch's struggle for what it means to be a good Samaritan in this world, especially because he knew that question had to be posed in its societal dimension, would have caused him to be repelled at the least by the hatred in the Nazi rhetoric. That these expectations did not materialize is an unsettling reminder that in darkening times human thought does not always follow straight lines. In the case of Gogarten, we will have to trace the turns in his thinking.

PAUL TILLICH

5

THE WAY TO ETHICS: CRITICAL
AND POSITIVE PARADOX

TILLICH VERSUS BARTH
AND GOGARTEN

After the publication of the exchange between Gogarten and Hirsch and about the time Wünsch entered the debate, Karl Ludwig Schmidt, the editor of the widely read fortnightly magazine *Theological Leaves,* asked Paul Tillich to write a piece on the new Dialectical Theology. It was a brilliant move on the part of the gifted editor. Tillich had points of identity and difference with all who had becomed involved in the melee. Like Barth and Gogarten, Tillich was dialectical, but unlike them he was deeply engaged in a philosophical-theological analysis of culture. Like Wünsch, Tillich was a Religious Socialist, but they worked in different groups. Most striking of all was the affinity and difference between Tillich and Hirsch.

Tillich and Hirsch first met in 1908 at a meeting of the Wingolf fraternity in Berlin. Tillich was twenty-two and Hirsch, twenty. From the beginning, they recognized in each other common interests, inclinations, and goals. Both were students of theology; both thought theology should have a solid base in philosophy; both were oriented to the German philosophical tradition of Idealism, though Hirsch was drawn more to Fichte and Tillich to Schelling; both had absorbed and made their own the critical method in theology; both sensed massive changes in the offing and wanted to contribute to new ways of thinking about God and human life. Each recognized in the other the intellectual power and self-discipline to fulfill his vocation.

Their friendship was instant, intimate, and enduring. They took long walks together during which they tirelessly discussed problems in philosophy, theology, and culture. They wrote essay-length letters to one another. Each was a strop to the other on which his own thinking was honed, and the affinities in their developing thought led friends to say they could not tell them apart. However, beginning with their first publications after the war, their thinking, in spite of structural similarities, went in opposite directions politically. In 1933, when Hirsch gave his "joyous Yes" to Hitler, Tillich's "No" was so clear and definite that he was on the first list of professors to be suspended.

Like most Germans, Tillich had been a strong nationalist and patriot in 1914. He enlisted in the army at first opportunity and was made a field chaplain assigned to an artillery battalion. He experienced all the horrors of the western front. He lived with the troops in the trenches, and under heavy fire he carried the wounded to safety. For his bravery, he was awarded the Iron Cross and the Iron Cross, First Class. Twice he had to be treated for battle fatigue. Like so many others on the front, his spirit was broken, and he came to see the war as the end of a world. He began to believe that the new world would have to be international in character and address the deprivations of the laboring class, the workers whose comrade he had become as their chaplain. He moved toward socialism, and he believed it was incumbent on theologians to be concerned about what happens and can happen in this world.

His first major public lecture, in Berlin on April 16, 1919, was "On the Idea of a Theology of Culture."[1] In that lecture, Tillich set forth in embryonic form the structure within which his thought would develop and many of the concepts and themes that would preoccupy him throughout his career.

---

1. Paul Tillich, "Über die Idee einer Theologie der Kultur," in *Religionsphilosophie der Kultur* (Berlin: Reuther und Reinhard, 1920) Philosophische Vorträge, Kantgesellschaft Nr. 24; also in Tillich, *Gesammelte Werke*, vol. 9: *Die religiöse Substanz der Kultur* (Stuttgart: Evangelisches Verlagswerk, 1967), pp. 13–31. William Baillie Green translated the lecture into English in Tillich, *What Is Religion?* ed. James Luther Adams (New York: Harper & Row, 1969), pp. 155–181.

His approach to history and human agency in history was, like Hirsch's, primarily speculative in the philosophical sense. He took it to be his vocation to try to develop conceptual schemes that would show the coherence of culture in its manifold expressions and at the same time give beneficial direction. Like Hirsch, he wanted, insofar as possible, to be universal, though, also like Hirsch, he realized that universality is not attainable in human constructs. The reality behind, beneath, and above everything that is and that happens he called "the Unconditioned" (compare Hirsch's "the Eternal"). The Unconditioned impinges on human life in all its cultural forms, and where its transcendent power is perceived, one senses overwhelmingly its No to every human effort to give it content through form and, at the same time, its Yes to the human spirit and the impulse to express its content anew through new form. However, every form and thus every expression of content is human, of the world, conditioned. Because of this inescapable fact and because human constructs are susceptible to demonic distortions of what is seeking to be expressed, the Yes carries with it, once again, the No.

The free confluence of the reality of the Unconditioned with an expression of its content in new form is an instance of theonomy. Theonomy (literally, the law or standard of God) stands in stark contrast to heteronomy (literally, the law or standard of the other). Heteronomy is control from the outside, the imposition of authority, whether that be the rules of harmony that have lost their creative power for a composer, oppression by a State, the exercise of authoritative power by a church, or whatever. Autonomy (literally, the law or standard of the self) is the natural reaction against heteronomy, and it finds its fulfillment in theonomy.

In its rejection of heteronomy, autonomy has the possibility of moving toward a new theonomy. Tillich called such a time of creative potential a *Kairos* (literally, "a right or pregnant time"), especially if a set of cultural forms (e.g., artistic, intellectual, social) seems simultaneously poised for that kind of movement. He came to believe that the postwar years were moving toward a *Kairos* and that the societal form best suited to bring it to expression was Religious Socialism. Although he realized that the negative force of demonic powers could wreak havoc and loss, he was philosophically optimistic.

Tillich's philosophical constructs and his descriptions and analyses of culture cannot, however, be separated from his specifically theological work. His commitment to and understanding of Christian faith suffused almost everything he thought and did. In this connection, it is most important for us to comprehend what he meant by "the Protestant principle." Tillich used the term "principle" to refer to "the power of a historical reality" as that historical reality is "grasped in concepts."[2] The principle or conceptualized power of a given historical reality is derived from an understanding of the reality, but it is never fully active in it. Thus the principle of a reality is not only the means for understanding that reality and its development in the world but also the basis for criticizing it in its own name. For example, in the 1950s it was in the name of democracy (its "principle") that many in the United States criticized the systematic exclusion of African-American citizens from the ballot box and from other rights of citizens.

For Tillich, the Protestant principle is found in the doctrine of justification by grace through faith. The "No" side of this doctrine was the proclamation that no matter how good one tries to be or is, one can never merit the grace and acceptance of God. Its "Yes" side was the conviction that whatever one's moral or ethical state, God makes right the relationship to God and accepts one unconditionally. Tillich saw that this doctrine rightly extends to thinking as well as to acting. As he put it, "Not only he who is in sin but also he who is in doubt is justified through faith." He thought this meant that "you cannot reach God by the work of right thinking or by a sacrifice of the intellect or by a submission to strange authorities, such as the doctrines of the church and the Bible."[3] Works of piety, morality, and intellect do not establish relationship with God, but they do follow from a relationship with God, and one constantly tries to see and understand what kind of ethics and what kind of thinking properly issue from this accepted

---

2. Paul Tillich, *The Socialist Decision,* trans. Franklin Sherman (New York: Harper & Row, 1977), p. 10. The original edition in German appeared in early 1933.

3. Paul Tillich, *The Protestant Era,* trans. James Luther Adams (Chicago: University of Chicago Press, 1948), pp. xiv, xv.

life in the consciousness of the presence of God. That, again, is its positive side.

Its negative side implies that all human constructions—intellectual, ethical, social, cultural—stand under the judgment of God. God is God; human beings are human beings. Thus the Protestant principle is also the critical principle, freeing human beings to look at every historical phenomenon and product with utter honesty and the most searching questions—and that includes the way we look at church, dogmas, and Bible. The Protestant principle produces what Tillich called "believing realism," and he identified it with the spirit of the prophets in ancient Israel.

These concepts and their corollaries were already formed in the mind of Tillich in the first years after the war. He had hope in their power to help form a better society, though he knew that any improvement in society would in time show its own failings and have to be reformed. His view also revealed both affinity with and distance from the new Dialectical Theology of Karl Barth and Friedrich Gogarten.

Tillich wrote about the new theology under the title "Critical and Positive Paradox: A Discussion with Karl Barth and Friedrich Gogarten."[4] He began by stating that he was reluctant to write the essay because he did not want to do anything to ease the discomfort Barth and Gogarten were causing with their sound and unyielding criticism. By pointing to occasional weaknesses in their position, he did not want to give comfort to the consciences of those who would like to evade the crisis and paradox Barth and Gogarten were proclaiming. What he decided to do, then, was "to venture the attempt at a discussion which, while acknowledging critical negation, seeks to demonstrate the position [that is, the positive foundation] on the basis of which negation first becomes possible"(133). He used the term "paradox" to refer to the dialectic, because when the Yes and the No are sounded side by side, the result is statements that appear paradoxical.

---

4. English translation in *The Beginnings of Dialectical Theology,* trans. Crim, ed. Robinson, pp. 132–141. The original essay in German appeared in *Theologische Blätter* 2 (1923), 263–269. Citations will be from the English translation, and page numbers will be given in parentheses at the end of the quotations.

Any talk about the Unconditioned in relation to the conditioned (humankind, the world) requires the dialectics of Yes and No, and that dialectics cannot be transcended. It keeps going on and on as long as we are in this world. But what Barth and Gogarten have not acknowledged is that their dialectical method, sound as it is, is grounded in a presupposition they themselves have assumed, and that presupposition is not itself dialectical. In short, they have a position, and it is a "positive paradox" in the sense that it is a "position" that they themselves, human beings, have taken with reference to God. Such a positive paradox is inescapable for human beings who want to talk about the Unconditioned, but realizing this necessity makes one more circumspect than Barth and Gogarten have been.

> The dialectician must perceive that as a dialectician he has one position among others which does not cease through any dialectic self-transcendence to be a position, and he must, as he is prepared to do—despite his conviction of the truth of his position—submit to the No, and concede to the other positions—despite the No which he pronounces on them— the same. (135)

Tillich accused Barth and Gogarten of provincialism (a term to which I will return in Part IV) in the sense that they made a claim for what they said (their province) the likes of which they would not grant to others. If they could acknowledge this point, they would have to grant a Yes, without surrendering their No, to other positions. Tillich did not see this opening as an introduction of relativism. The truth is at issue, but it has to be decided, as best we can, on the basis of arguments to which all sides have equal access.

By "position," Tillich also meant a positive, undialectical foundation underlying the dialectical Yes and No of Dialectical Theology. He believed he could demonstrate such a positive, undialectical foundation, and he tested his view of the matter with respect to God and nature, God and the human spirit, and God and history. Each test followed the same pattern.

1. God and Nature. Nature has its No: in it we see judgment, irrationality, and death. But we could not know these horrors if we were not aware, at the same time and before, of "the world as unity of form, nature as unity of configuration, life as reality. . . . For the negative can reveal itself only in terms of the positive, not of the negative" (136). To find grace without judgment in nature, to feel the unparadoxical unity of the Unconditioned and conditioned in nature is "idolatrous idealism." On the contrary, to think of destruction in nature outside of a paradoxical unity with grace is "demonic realism" (136). In the Christian doctrine of the Trinity, he observed, the three persons interpenetrate in their respective activities and the Son is regarded as the agent of creation in the New Testament. Thus, theologically, "the order of creation and the order of redemption belong together," a judgment that can be "comprehended only in faith" (136).

2. *God and the Human Spirit.* This topic led Tillich to comment directly on the debate between Gogarten and Hirsch. He noted that Gogarten thought Hirsch had absolutized conscience as the locus of revelation and that he took this as an act of autonomous rebellion against God. Tillich thought Gogarten was right to criticize Hirsch for failing to be dialectical. In Hirsch, the connection of ethical, personalistic piety with the Eternal is too direct and free from criticism. But Gogarten did not acknowledge that his appeal to revelation is finally *his* appeal. It posits an act of the human spirit that implies a connection of that spirit with God. According to Tillich, there is no escape for the responsible person from autonomy. One must only take care to see, insofar as possible, that this autonomy does not become demonically distorted. In order to avoid that distortion, one must acknowledge one's position as one's own judgment, place it on equal footing with others in the public forum, and realize that it, too, is subject to the dialectical unity of judgment and grace, to God's No as well as Yes. Tillich thought Barth's work was subject to the same criticism. Barth's brilliant criticism of all religion in *Romans* is flawed in that Barth should have acknowledged that his own understanding of faith is itself also religion.

Tillich's argument here has decisive significance for the question of ethics. If one acknowledges that every theological work is an act of autonomy but that one must nevertheless venture to speak theologically, to express the Unconditional in a way one knows is conditioned, then one will similarly venture to deal in a theological way with the specific question, What shall we do?

3. God and History. Tillich praised the Dialectical Theologians for their unyielding criticism of everything historical and human. In this way, they have rendered impossible any identity of salvation history with secular history, on the one side, or miraculous history, on the other. There is, however, a quite specific claim (a position) that undergirds their criticism and that is not itself subject to historical ambiguity, but calls for straightforward, arbitrary acceptance. Tillich meant their Christology, the claim that what happened in Christ happened beyond human history but in the historical person, Jesus. Gogarten had claimed that this once-for-all event is a "purely objective fact," that "only here is the No not valid for that in which it appears," and he had exclaimed "O contradiction of all human knowledge of God" (140).

For Tillich, the arbitrariness of this claim meant that the criticism Gogarten and Barth employed is founded on "a theology of the positive absurd" (140). He was convinced that this founding of their theology on the sheer acceptance of a historical fact constituted an abandonment of their own premise, and he believed it opened a Pandora's box out of which would fly the ills of heteronomy, law, and absolutistic religion. It opened the door to heteronomy, because in order to accept the "fact," one is forced to reject as irrelevant all critical historical work on Jesus because historical criticism is autonomous. For Tillich, autonomy, including the autonomy of biblical criticism, is "in service of the truth" (140). Insisting on the arbitrary acceptance of something, Tillich thought, amounted to the reintroduction of law, because it was a work of intellectual self-denial no less than the mystic's practical discipline of self-denial. Moreover, he thought absolutistic religion would surely follow, because those who commit this act of intellectual asceticism would believe they hold the truth and all others are in error.

He argued that these ills could be avoided only if it is acknowledged that the revelation of God in Jesus as the Christ is permeated by ambiguity for human beings. "Faith is not a work of the affirmation of the absurd, but it has grown up on the ground of the imperceptible history of revelation, which passes in hidden manner through history and has found in Christ its complete expression" (140).

Christian faith does not rest on positing something human as divine but in perceiving Jesus as pointing to the Unconditioned as its symbol. Seeing faith in this way retains fully and on a coordinate foundation the all-pervasive dialectic, but it also opens the possibility of seeing something of the Unconditioned, dialectically to be sure, in nature and spirit, and in culture and religion. Faith perceives the imperceptible when it finds redemption in the Christ as complete symbolic power. Thereby it perceives the imperceptible redemptive power of God in its struggle with demonic powers throughout human history. For Tillich, this positive paradox undergirds the critical paradox.

Karl Barth responded to Tillich under the title "The Paradoxical Nature of the 'Positive Paradox': Answers and Questions to Paul Tillich."[5] He, too, found no pleasure in taking issue with Tillich, who in some respects, he acknowledged, was not distant from Gogarten and himself. He said he was also reluctant because the philosophical thought world of Tillich was so distant to him, and he claimed no competence in it.

He expressed astonishment that Tillich apparently thought he had told them something they did not know when he insisted that their dialectics rested on something positive. Barth readily admitted it but immediately emphasized that the most crucial issue is to determine rightly what that positive base is. He was baffled by Tillich's raising the issue: "Is it possible that he sees at the conscious, positive point something so entirely other from what I see, that he, by an optical illusion, believes he perceives in me at the same point an empty spot?" (143). There is an empty spot, he continued, if what we are doing is conceived "as a part—perhaps even the most impressive part—of a philosophy of culture." Having made such a mistake, Tillich thinks we are in error "as soon as we fail to stick to the matter at hand and let theology be theology" (143). (We should note that Barth abhorred any attempt to connect the subject matter of theology with one or another human enterprise, as represented,

---

5. *Theologische Blätter* 2 (1923), 287–296. The English translation is in *The Beginnings of Dialectical Theology*, trans. Crim, ed. Robinson, pp. 142–154. Citations will be from the English translation, and page numbers will be given in parentheses at the end of the quotations.

for example, in the phrase "theology and culture.") As theology, however, Barth was confident that their "dialectical transcendence" is a warning against overlooking the crisis to which all attitudes are subject—not just Tillich's, with his theology of culture, but their dialectic attitude as well.

Tillich thinks this "dialectical transcendence" constitutes a "position" that he and Gogarten had taken. Barth asked why it could not rather be an allusion to the "real transcendence," the Wholly Other. (Barth either ignored or missed the point of Tillich's claim that he and Gogarten were in the same arena with the rest of them and had, therefore, to argue it out on equal footing with the others.) Consistent with that indirect claim, Tillich's effort to construct "on the basis of the unconditioned" an understanding of nature, mind, history, science, and even a doctrine of the Trinity impressed Barth as "so rebellious" (148). He objected to Tillich's method, which he thought tried to establish a first principle for which church and Holy Spirit, scripture, and Christ "are basically superfluous" (148).

> It is this *method* above all which is always strange and incomprehensible to me even at the first step in Tillich's temples of thought, and its point of departure makes his conclusions, however often I rejoice in the agreement with him in the subject matter, as a whole so improbable as theology. (148)

Barth was willing to grant that what Tillich was up to was a possibility, alongside any number of other possibilities, but he was unwilling to grant Tillich's assumption—and the assumption of those who pursued the myriad other possibilities—that it was theology. At best, what Tillich did was bad theology. When we grasp the reason for this judgment by Barth, we see the nub of the issue between these two. Both of them, though in utterly different ways, pointed to the same place. And not only was there no basic agreement between them, there was a genuine impasse. That is, they differed radically on the foundation of theology, and there was no way to adjudicate the difference in a public arena, though it had been one of Tillich's major points that Barth and Gogarten—for that matter, everyone who talks about the Unconditioned—cannot avoid the public arena, where every idea is appraised on the basis of common ground rules, the positive side of autonomy for Tillich.

It was precisely that form of autonomy that Barth found "so rebellious" and so utterly out of place in theology, whose subject matter is the Wholly Other. Barth and Gogarten were not only willing to admit but insisted that their dialectical warnings stood under the judgment of God just as much as any other talk of God, but they were unambiguously certain that only God, the Wholly Other, can give not only the revelation but the acknowledgment of it as well. From the human side, this may look like arbitrary acceptance. In his controversy with his former teacher, Adolf von Harnack, Barth said it clearly: "The *acceptance* of these incredible testimonies of the Scripture I call *faith*," and that acceptance is itself the act of the Holy Spirit.[6] He was more elaborate in expressing the same point to Tillich:

> One does not talk this way [Tillich's way] of the "positive paradox" if he knows that as a theologian he is dealing with the *divine* paradox, that is, not with this "imperceptible," but with what is real *and* knowable really only on the basis of God's own free will, only by laying aside his majesty, or what is the same thing, only out of love and in love in the world and for man, with the revelation which is by no means a relationship to be designated with a general "there is" or "there are," or to be discovered merely by man; not some secret given but something very special, made known only by God, and only, in that we are known by him, an *occurrence* to be known, an *event* from person to person, a *communication*, a *gift* in the strictest sense of the word, and therefore both the subject matter *and* knowledge of it. (150)

For Tillich and a good many others, this assertion by Barth was reminiscent of the notorious confession of the late second- and early third-century Christian, Tertullian: *Credo quia absurdum est*

---

6. "An Answer to Professor von Harnack's Open Letter," *The Beginnings of Dialectical Theology*, trans. Crim, ed. Robinson, p. 175. The exchange between Harnack and Barth was published in *Die christliche Welt* in 1923.

("I believe because it is absurd"). Barth's comment about this connection was typically aggressive:

> What is "absurd" from the Christian or *theological* point of view is not at all what Tillich so designates the "once and once for all" which is rather simply our theological duty to affirm. What is "absurd" is all unreflecting, unclassical, disrespectful deviation from the formula of the Council of Chalcedon [the ecumenical council of the early fifth century that defined Christ as having two natures—of the "same being" with God and with humankind], for to hold quietly to this confession would still indicate, *mutatis mutandis* ["with appropriate adaptations"], good insight even today. (152)

In conclusion, Barth, consistent to the end, denied that the clash with Tillich was over "Gogarten's dogma of revelation" or the "theology of crisis." He insisted it had to do with "our reference to the indissoluble correlation of the theological concept of truth with the concepts 'church,' 'canon,' 'Holy Spirit' " (154). He ended with a quotation from Augustine (late fourth and early fifth century): "In the church it is not significant that I say this, you say this, he says this, but rather that the Lord says thus" (154).

Tillich responded briefly to Barth.[7] He focused on the necessity of dealing with human access to truth in contrast to Barth's arbitrariness. He held that it is "not possible to say and do just anything at any given time, but that each time has its task of creating anew the eternal meaning of all time out of its life and in its words" (155). He meant by this that one has to resist every form of authoritarianism that claims truth for itself without explanation in terms people can understand as they understand other things. Thus he thought it was necessary for theologians to pay attention to the intellectual situation of their day and to try to speak in ways that are clear and persuasive to contemporaries. He was unwilling to accept as alternatives either the loss of salvation or the sacrifice of the intellect.

---

7. "Antwort," *Theologische Blätter* 2 (1923), 296–299. The English translation is in *The Beginnings of Dialectical Theology,* trans. Crim, ed. Robinson, pp. 155–158. Citations will be from the English translation, and page numbers will be given in parentheses at the end of the quotations.

He alluded to what had been critically important to him in his own development as a theologian, that justification by grace apart from human works had to do with works of the intellect as well. That is, even doubt is embraced by the grace of God in justification. Thinking rightly does not make a relationship with God, but thinking well (that is, according to the best standards humans can develop) is incumbent upon human beings in this finite life—for the theologian no less, if not more so, than for others.

The theologian, therefore, must be attuned to the intellectual situation of his or her day. For Tillich, that meant the necessity of finding new language for words that had lost their immediacy and power. Thus he chose to speak first of the "Unconditioned" rather than of God, not as a way of substitution but as a way of recovering the richness and power of the word "God." He thought "Jesus Christ" had also been trivialized. Thus he looked for the power and reality of the Christ as it comes in some measure to expression in the variety of cultural forms—again, not as a way of substituting for Jesus who is the Christ, once and for all, but as a way of recapturing the singular richness and power of the redemptive act in Jesus.

> Theology must, for the sake of the spirit of truth and of love, . . . explain that the Holy Spirit cannot breathe on us wherever it will [arbitrariness], and that the Spirit of Christ, the Spirit of the concrete paradox, *can* blow on us from the splendor and the wilting of the flowers of the field, from the creative power and the despair of a work of art, from the profundity and the self-transcendence of logic, more strongly . . . even than words, tales, and pictures, which always still bear the seal of the Grand Inquisitor for our consciousness. (157)

Tillich was concerned with the problem of giving human beings access to the truth. Barth, on the contrary, believed that God creates God's own access to human beings.

It was that tenet of Dialectical Theology that most troubled Tillich. He saw it leading to an undialectical supernaturalism and a simple No to the world, "the fate of which is always to remain unattainable in practice, and at some point unexpectedly to be transformed into a Yes that is all the more positive and undialectic" (158). In this comment, Tillich expressed: (1) the root cause of his difference with Barth and Gogarten, (2) his intellectual affinity with Hirsch in the search for a theistic view of history that points the way toward helping to form destiny, and (3) his fear that what he saw as an uncritical acceptance behind Barth's No could "unexpectedly" be transformed into an uncritical acceptance of a Yes. One can only wonder if he had a premonition of his friend Hirsch's "joyous Yes" to Hitler in 1933.

The exchange ended with a brief statement from Gogarten.[8] He said he could concur without reservation to what Barth had written in the exchange, but because the public debate concerned him as well, he thought he had no right to keep silence. He picked up on Tillich's emphasis on engagement with the intellectual situation of the time. He chose to focus on that issue because he thought that was the place where he and Tillich had the most in common—not in their theological work, but in their backgrounds. Gogarten, we should note, did not come to theology by inheritance. His father was not a pastor, and his first studies concentrated on art history, German philology, and psychology. He knew, almost as well as Tillich, the intellectual and cultural situation of twentieth-century Germany, and he had felt its lure.

However, once having discovered what he believed to be the authentic and sole subject matter of theology—the revelation of God in Jesus Christ—the possibility of working with the broader cultural context was over for him. Thus he disagreed absolutely with Tillich's contention that theologians *as* theologians in the present day needed to become philosopher-theologians of culture. "The most dangerous deficiency, it seems to me, is the lack of a thorough and honest theology concerned with its object and *only* with its own object" (160). The problem with a so-called theology of culture, no matter how much one talks about the "Uncondi-

---

8. "Zur Geisteslage des Theologen," *Theologische Blätter* 2 (1923), 608. The English translation, "The Intellectual Situation of the Theologian," is in *The Beginnings of Dialectical Theology,* trans. Crim, ed. Robinson, pp. 159–162. Citations will be from the English translation, and page numbers will be given in parentheses at the end of the quotations.

tioned," is that its subject matter is human being rather than the revelation of the Wholly Other God in Jesus Christ, the exclusive subject matter of theology. Certainly, one can take human being, nature, or history as one's subject matter, but in so doing one ceases to be a theologian and should not pretend to be one. Every attempt so to concern oneself *as* a theologian is bound to fail.

> The reason is that for us there is no reality outside that of the God who was revealed in the man Jesus Christ. I say this explicitly, say it as a theologian, and see no possibility of saying differently what should be said here. It is precisely by means of *this* direct and unmediated statement that I know I am guarded from *that* directness and unmediatedness which Tillich rightly rejects. For by means of this statement, provided I know what I am saying, and I think the same holds for the attentive hearer, I am referred directly and unmediatedly to the reality of my life, to what is "existential" for me. (161)

Gogarten was painfully aware that when the theologian is honest about the subject matter of theology, he or she will inevitably alienate what Tillich called "the community with those who in all areas of culture struggle for the revelation of paradox, for a glimpse of the Spirit of Christ" (161). Gogarten felt the poignancy of that alienation because he recognized that community as his "homeland." "I gladly confess to Tillich that my *homeland* is *over there,* and that I left home and went abroad when after long hesitation I entered a theological lecture hall for the first time, and that his talk strikes my ears like a call from home" (161). But the vocation of theology "calls upon us to carry through the painful renunciation of this community, in order to perform the service which we have to render them as theologians" (161).

Gogarten concluded by saying that he—and he thought he could speak here for Barth as well—was "seeking in terms of Jesus Christ, yes, more precisely, in Jesus Christ, the reality of the world and of life and the knowledge of it, while Tillich seeks for the knowledge of Jesus Christ, or, as he so characteristically says, of the Spirit of Christ, in the knowledge of the world and of life" (162).

Gogarten's statement shows more than meets the eye at first glance. Already he sensed, without having worked it out and awed by the sense for the reality of God as the reality utterly beyond this world, that the gospel of God has to do fundamentally with the way people understand their lives in this world, their "existence," and thus their activities. Before long, he would recognize clearly what he dimly sensed in 1923. But this recognition, combined as it would be with his special appropriation of the base of Dialectical Theology as the "Lordship" of Jesus Christ and with other factors in his development, would issue in conclusions that led to qualified support for Hitler in 1933 and then, disillusioned, reduce him to silence from 1937 until the postwar years.

PAUL ALTHAUS

6

BASIC PROBLEMS OF SOCIAL
ETHICS . . . AND OF
DIALECTICAL THEOLOGY

ALTHAUS VERSUS BARTH
AND GOGARTEN

Academically speaking, the most precocious—or the luckiest—of our six professors was Paul Althaus. He was appointed to a regular professorship at an earlier age than any of the others. When he was 32, in 1921, he was invited to be Professor of Systematic Theology and New Testament Exegesis at the University of Rostock. It was not his final destination. In 1925, he moved to the university in Erlangen in Bavaria. Erlangen was the major center that supported ecclesiastical-conservative Lutheranism and allowed for its rejuvenation at the same time. Paul Althaus is the most shining example in the twentieth century of a challenging and up-to-date restatement of conservative (Positive) Lutheranism in Germany; and, especially after the Second World War, his influence extended to the United States by the translation into English of several of his works, particularly those dealing with the theology and ethics of Martin Luther.

Althaus came by his conservatism naturally. His father had been formed by the Erlangen conservatism and was Professor of Systematic Theology and Practical Theology in Göttingen from 1897 (when Paul was nine years old) to 1912, when he became Professor of Systematic Theology and New Testament at Leipzig, where he remained until his death.

The son studied theology at Tübingen, where he was influenced most by Adolf Schlatter, a distinguished conservative New

Testament scholar, and at Göttingen, where Carl Stange, his father's successor, taught him Martin Luther. He never studied with Karl Holl, but he felt more grateful to Holl than to anyone else. Years later he would succeed Holl as president of the Luther Society.

During the First World War, he was a field preacher stationed in a German community in Poland. He was deeply moved by what he perceived to be the difficulties experienced by this community of fellow Germans in an alien land and the oppressions under which they suffered. This experience greatly enhanced the sense of *Volk* he imbibed from his family and context. The German defeat in 1918 affected him deeply.

He was passionate about theology and confident in the positions he took, but he was by nature conciliatory. He did not, however, back away from differences; and when he thought he saw theological error, he contested it with thoroughness and vigor, though always, to use a term of yesterday, as a "gentleman" in debate. His course was clear to him, and he pursued it with competence. This course in its application unfortunately led him to hail the advent of Hitler, though after four years of the Third Reich, he fell silent about it. After his "de-Nazification" at the end of the war and his reinstatement as a professor, he resumed his course with chastened application and achieved a broad influence, especially in world Lutheran circles.

In 1921, the year of the second edition of Barth's *Romans,* he wrote a typically irenic but also critical short book on Religious Socialism.[1] His own political position was well to the right of socialism, but he was able to affirm some of the socialist ideals and criticisms of capitalist society. In his work, he included Karl Barth among the Religious Socialists, though he considered Barth a "moderate."

Barth responded with a review essay in 1922, which he titled "Basic Problems of Christian Social Ethics: A Discussion with

---

1. Paul Althaus, *Religiöser Sozialismus: Grundfragen der christlichen Sozialethik* [Religious Socialism: Basic Questions of Christian Social Ethics] (Gütersloh: Bertelsmann, 1921), 99 pp.

Paul Althaus."[2] Since his work on Paul's letter to the Romans, Barth had stood at a considerable distance from the Religious Socialist movement in Switzerland, not to speak of its counterparts in Germany, but his political convictions were socialist. In any case, in this essay he chose not to mention his criticisms of Religious Socialism. His target was Althaus.

The following are a couple of characteristic statements from Althaus's book that show how far removed from Barth he was:

> The Christian fulfills Jesus' command to love by dutiful participation in the orders of the world, yes, precisely through them.[3]

> For one simply dare not permit the new Christian radicalism, by appeal to Jesus and the Sermon on the Mount, to confuse the conscience with respect to law, Fatherland, the State, and military service.[4]

Barth was less strident in his review because he recognized that Althaus himself was more irenic about his position than other political conservatives. He was, however, no less definite and pointed. For example, in a comment on the second citation from Althaus above, he wrote, "It is to be hoped that Althaus sees *who* it is who 'confuses' the consciences here, if he wants to express it that way!" (46). And a few lines later: "Perhaps Althaus should discuss with those who are basically closer to his position, such as Emanuel Hirsch . . . , why it is that his book did not turn out to be less ambiguous, more devastating" (47).

Barth acknowledged that Althaus saw that the gospel has to do with conditions of society and that the church is not free of criticism for having ignored that connection. (Althaus had stated that the church missed an opportunity when it had not taken Adolf

---

2. In *Das neue Werk* 4 (1922), 461–472. The English translation is in *The Beginnings of Dialectical Theology*, trans. Crim, ed. Robinson, pp. 46–57. Citations will be from the English translation, and page numbers will be given in parentheses at the end of the quotations.

3. Althaus, *Religiöser Sozialismus*, p. 76.

4. Ibid., p. 32.

Stöcker seriously. Stöcker was a late nineteenth-century conservative with a program for the alleviation of the plight of workers. In 1878, he had founded the "Christian-Social Workers" movement. He was anti-Socialist and anti-Liberal.[5]) What Barth missed in Althaus was a sense for how far the gospel presses one to criticize. In this respect, he thought Althaus had no understanding of eschatology, Barth's basis for his unremitting criticism of all human constructs, and he was disappointed that Althaus apparently could not see that the Social Democrats were so far ahead of the church (and Stöcker!) that the church could only "feel ashamed of itself" (47).

Barth further acknowledged that Althaus agreed with "us who are chastised with the name of 'religious socialists' " (46) that a more socialist ordering of society is relatively right and that, in any case, what the Christian does in society cannot avoid inconsistency. He regretted, however, that Althaus did not go further with both points.

In noting these points of agreement (which consequently called for understated criticisms), Barth admitted to straining Althaus's text in a way with which Althaus would probably not agree. He did so because he was convinced that the main issue between them was not "religious-social" but theological. "We are not . . . unequivocally united in what we call 'God' " (51). Then the familiar Barthian theme: "The chasm which divides men from God is absolute; the chasms which divide men from one another are relative, even when it must be so for the sake of God" (51). Barth objected to two points where Althaus seemed to him to presume to know God and God's will.

1. Althaus touched Barth's theological nerve when he wrote about the "very elementary necessity of law and the State" and observed that everyone knows that "governance by natural law and law in personal relationships are the two basic presuppositions of all personal as well as of all social life" (52). He pressed that tender spot harder by asking the rhetorical question whether one could possibly think of love as the only structure of the world. To

---

5. Cf. Adolf Stöcker, *Christlich-Sozial: Reden und Aufsätze,* 2nd ed. (Berlin: Verlag der Buchhandlung der Berliner Stadtmission, 1890).

that question Barth answered unequivocally with a Yes. Love as it is presented in the Sermon on the Mount was to Barth either an illusion or the basic "structure of the world," to use Althaus's term. Therefore it is the crisis of everything human beings call their love for God and other human beings. We live, to be sure, under the law of a world order that is anything but love, and that reality should be a reminder to us of the crisis. "The gospel . . . speaks of God and of faith and not of what 'everyone knows,' of ultimate things and not of penultimate" (53).

Althaus touched the raw nerve when he argued further that one can find in the "living movement" of history and its "organic laws" at least an approximation of the will of God. In this way he concluded that (as Barth summarized his position) "the vocation of a nation should be a 'question of transcendental depth' . . . , because here the 'irrational' and the 'creative deed' are at home . . . , and politics is now suddenly 'in its depths a religious matter' " (53). It is on the basis of this utterly wrongheaded position, Barth claimed, that Althaus could move further to speak of war not as murder but as a " 'mighty self-measuring of the nations for leadership and for the future' " and urge people to " 'live through the competition and die' " (53–54).

Barth's response shows the critical power of his apparent tautology, God is God.

> Why is it not vital to faith in God and in the living Christ to forget the ineradicable limit of all moral ordering of the world: life as nature, destiny, and struggle; indeed to forget it as such an ineradicable limit, that is to say, to contrast it as the perishable to the imperishable, as what is totally dissimilar to it, incomparably less than it in significance and dignity? How should it be more pious "to bow before the God who has placed us in this world under such laws of life" . . . ? Who is this God then? Is he really God? (54)

For Barth, the norm for politics is the righteousness of the one true God, and no human political righteousness whatever, to any degree, can be identical with it.

2. Barth thought Althaus was particularly enthusiastic about " 'Christendom,' the 'congregation,' the Kingdom of God as the

'lordship of the gospel in the heart' " (54). He noted that Althaus had high expectations of Christianity, also of politics, and believed that one could appropriate Christian faith in one's heart and life. He cited Althaus's statement that the Christian could fulfill the love commandment of Jesus by being dutiful to the orders of the world, and his claim that "the Christian can, even in undertakings of raw, hard work in the life of law, the State, and war, live completely according to the spirit of the Sermon on the Mount" (55).

Barth had moderately praised Althaus's sobriety about what human beings can accomplish in the world, but he was aghast at Althaus's claim for what Christians could accomplish psychologically. Barth informed his readers (and Althaus!) that the same standard of judgment (based on the contrast between the eternal and the temporal, the eschatological end time and the here and now) applies to the inner life as well as to the outer life. Althaus's problem, Barth said, is that he has missed the critical power of eschatology.

> At the basis of the removal of eschatology from ethics there lies the intention of making the former harmless and of removing the latter from the threatening shadow of the former *ad majorem gloriam hominis* ["to the greater glory of human being"]. . . . Whoever can bring the will of God into such dangerous proximity to the little bit of experience of heart and conscience of so-called Christians and the little bit of "common life of the congregation" will also of necessity bring it into the quite fatal proximity to history, nature, and fate. (56)

As a way of responding, at least in part, to Barth, Althaus wrote a long essay against Dialectical Theology. He titled it "Theology and History: In Opposition to Dialectical Theology," and he published it in a new journal that he edited along with Emanuel Hirsch and two others.[6] He posed the issue between himself, on the one side, and Gogarten and Barth (especially Barth), on the

---

6. "Theologie und Geschichte: Zur Auseinandersetzung mit der dialektischen Theologie," *Zeitschrift für systematische Theologie* 1, no. 2 (1923–1924), 741–786.

other, as a radical difference in the understanding of God. He thought the Dialectical Theologians' concept of God was one-sided and inadequate to Christian faith. Their representation of God, he asserted, is in such total contrast to the world that it is without content. Consequently, they can give no helpful guidance on the pressing problems of ethics and the meaning of our common history.

1. Althaus rightly saw that the Dialectical Theologians root everything in the tautology that God is God and in the premise that God is the Wholly Other. This foundation, he thought, leads them to draw a sharp contrast between "the other side" and "this side," between eternity and time. The utter incompatibility between these poles means that on this side—that is, in time and history—nothing can be known about God except the contrast. There is no revelation of what God is or wills in history. Rather, everything in time stands under the crisis of judgment, even religion. Althaus saw a healthy warning in this scepticism and negativity, but he thought that warning had been sounded by many others in the Christian tradition. If one does nothing more than sound the warning, he argued, one has oversimplified the faith.

Alongside the warning, Althaus added a sense for the presence of God in history. He thought that, from the Christian perspective at least, one cannot think of history without thinking of the reality of God showing itself in the moral law. Ethics is the key to the understanding of history. In the many responsibilities that claim us, we are grasped by one responsibility above all others, our responsibility to God; in the varied, thoroughly conditioned tasks that weigh upon us, we encounter the unconditioned Lord; in history we meet the eternal. In Christian faith, by the Holy Spirit, the God by whom we are so grasped is characterized by love. Love, he believed, is the positive content of theology. To be sure, as love God is veiled, not unambiguously clear, but God as love is also revealed. Moreover, God's love unites in itself law and gospel. It is both God's commandment and God's gift.

2. In Dialectical Theology, not only is the concept of God entirely negative and without content (God is the "Unknown"), but also it cannot account for the fact that in Christian faith we speak to God. In our speaking, we address God in the familiar

form as "you." In Christian faith, God is known as a person characterized by love. Dialectical Theology misses this positive content in the doctrine of God. It consistently pursues its contentless concept of God as the Wholly Other and therefore sets up the contrast between time and eternity on the basis of which everything in time is subject to nothing but judgment. This judgment, however, has nothing to do with morality. Temporality is the human condition for which human beings are not responsible. Thus guilt loses all meaning. It follows from this, he added, that Dialectical Theology can have no comprehension of the transforming power of God's love. It cannot speak of new life in this world in the love of God that is experienced in the conscience as both judgment and grace.

3. Althaus believed it was consistent with the fundamental concept of God in Dialectical Theology that Barth had no interest in the salvific pertinence of Jesus as a historical person. He thought Barth saw no positive content in what Jesus said and did but only the same contrast between eternity and time. It seemed to him that Barth saw nothing in the resurrection of Jesus but the appearance of the "Other" over against history. Althaus believed that Christian faith originates in Jesus—his life, death, and resurrection—who to faith is both a veiling and an unveiling of God. Jesus veils God because it is incomprehensible and a "scandal" to suppose that the reality beyond all things appears in a human being, but he unveils God because it is precisely in Jesus that the reality of God meets us decisively. Althaus wanted to keep these two themes in tension with each other. Jesus becomes the ground of faith that permits us to overcome the "scandal." He grounds faith both in his call for obedience to God and in his forgiving of sinners.

4. Finally, Althaus criticized Dialectical Theology for interpreting redemption unhistorically. Barth, he thought, could find new life only on the other side. He viewed this exclusive orientation to eschatology (last things) as simply an extension of the tautology with which Barth started. Thus Barth not only devalues history and creation but has no sense for the new being in faith.

In contrast, Althaus was convinced that in faith people begin something new. A living power changes them such that they are drawn toward selflessness in love for the neighbor, which is a form of love for God. For him, justification by grace through faith was not a contentless abrogation of sin promising salvation only in the hereafter but an acceptance by God that changes one's life in the world. He did not mean that the transformation here and now is complete and perfect. He insisted, rather, that the life of justification is always a back and forth, a having and a not-having. As a not-having, it leads to criticism and mistrust of self and everything human and to the constant sense of "ought." As a having, it is liberating and gives an authentic sense of the new being in God. Thus it is always both freedom and demand. Justification has ethical content by holding these two together.

Althaus's essay is an impressive criticism of Dialectical Theology. The points he argued are similar to points Hirsch, Wünsch, and Tillich made. All four of these critics struggled with the concrete problem of ethics, convinced that Christian faith makes and should make a difference in the way people live in the world. They thought theology has a responsibility to help people of faith understand more specifically the kinds of activities that are appropriate to faith and required by it. All of them thought Dialectical Theology, with its unfailing sense of the infinite distance between God and human beings and its consequent sense of the judgment of God over everything human without exception, was unable, if not unconcerned, to venture the movement from theology to ethics.

More clearly than the others, Althaus pointed to the root of the issue in the concept of God and drew all of his criticisms from that understanding. He rightly saw that everything in Dialectical Theology flowed from its concept of God. Karl Barth surely would have agreed with him. Althaus can be faulted for not having seen that for Barth Christian faith carries with it an irrepressible ethical impulse; but he can, at least in some measure, be excused, because Barth tended to avoid specific ethical guidance. In Barth's defense, we should note that he seems to have thought that the direction of life in the world for Christians was self-evident, especially with respect to social ethics. Moreover, he had asserted that some activities are better than others, even though all come under judgment, and all accomplishments, if we may use that word, become in turn distorted. But he steadfastly resisted programmatic ethical constructions. We know he did not want any human impulse to be misconstrued as a revelation of God—most certainly not in the conscience!—or to be considered as such "good."

The ethical question, What should we do?, remained understandably in the forefront of the discussion. We will see how this question was treated when a foreboding issue arose ten years later. We must try to understand also the reasons for the different decisions and whether there is any help for people of faith in our time as they struggle with the question.

RUDOLF BULTMANN

7

A "DIALECTICAL" CONVERSION TO DIALECTICAL THEOLOGY

BULTMANN'S UNEASY ALLIANCE WITH BARTH

It is appropriate that we consider Rudolf Bultmann last among our six theologians. He joined the ranks of Dialectical Theology and contributed six articles to *Between the Times* over its eleven years, but he was a later convert to the movement and always critical of it in certain respects. He was the first "outsider" to give public approval to Barth's commentary on Romans (in a review that appeared in 1922), but what he approved was the second edition of 1921, not the first (1919), and he stated several reservations. By 1924, however, he identified himself with the movement. Even so, he never surrendered his critical distance. For example, in the same year in which he began to use the first person plural (we) of Dialectical Theology, he published a review of Barth's lectures on 1 Corinthians that, although praising Barth's basic grasp of Paul's thought, was sharply critical of the main thesis. Both in his identity and in his distance from Dialectical Theology, the question of ethics lurked in the background.

Like Barth, Tillich, Althaus, and Hirsch, Bultmann was the child of a minister. His household upbringing, however, unlike theirs, was Liberal. His father was a member throughout his ministry of the "Friends of *The Christian World*," the society that supported the most noted Liberal theological magazine and met annually to hear papers by the leading theological Liberals of the time. Martin Rade, long-time Professor of Theology at Marburg, founded the magazine in 1887 and remained its editor for nearly fifty years. The magazine reflected its editor: Liberal theologically, open and generous to new ideas and to younger theologians, and committed to the social responsibility of the church in the world. Rudolf Bultmann imbibed this spirit in his home and at Marburg, where he completed his theological education and prepared himself for an academic career and where, except for his first five years as a professor, he taught throughout his career. Wilhelm Herrmann, Professor of Theology at Marburg, was the most important influence on him in his formative years. In addition to the themes of Liberal theology, with a strong Herrmannian tinge, he appropriated from Liberalism the critical historical method (which he pressed more vigorously than did his teacher) and an aversion to theological declarations that require for their acceptance a sacrifice of the intellect.

Bultmann chose the New Testament as his special field of study, but from the beginning he was committed to the principle that the historical study of the documents of early Christianity must itself yield theological understanding. As a historian, he was also a theologian and vice-versa.

The First World War affected him deeply and personally. One of his two brothers was killed in action. (The other brother died in a Nazi concentration camp.) He thought the war was "horrible" and revealed "all of the dark, demonic forces of the human heart—all the passions of self-seeking and falsehood, of brutality and hate."[1] In the 1917 sermon from which these citations are taken, there is evidence that the war had drawn Bultmann to a theme that cannot easily be found in Liberal theology. It was the dark theme of the hiddenness of God. The war, he said, had led "us" to "gaze into the abyss of our nature" where "our self appears as a play of strange powers," "into the abyss of life" where "its opposing powers are incomprehensible to us," and, indeed, into "the depths of God" where we "are seized with

---

1. "Vom geheimnisvollen und offenbaren Gott," *Die christliche Welt* 31 (1917), 572–579. The English translation is by Schubert M. Ogden, "Concerning the Hidden and the Revealed God," in *Existence and Faith: Shorter Writings of Rudolf Bultmann* (New York: Meridian Books, 1960), pp. 29, 62.

horror." He spoke of this God as "wholly other than we thought him to be."[2] He set this vision side by side with the sunny recollections of life before the war and proclaimed that both have their source in the mysteriously gracious God who brings redemption in the cross of Christ. These statements do not sound like Liberal theology, but they are counterpoint to it. In the same sermon, Bultmann said it was the duty of humankind "to see to it that nothing as horrible as this war ever again falls over the earth." And he added, "Never before has God expected something so grand from the race" of human beings.[3]

A year and a half after the publication of the first edition of Barth's *Romans* and almost a year to the day after Barth's Tambach lecture, "The Christian's Place in Society," Bultmann read a paper to the Friends of *The Christian World* at Wartburg. His title was "Ethical and Mystical Religion in Primitive Christianity." He defended with minor modifications the position of Liberal theology ("within which I count myself") and ended with a solidly Liberal theme: "In ethical religion . . . there is the creating of life-will, allowing us to reach the mature destiny of those who struggle in obedience to the good, and thus fulfilling our inner life."[4] In it he also alluded twice to Barth's *Romans*. His first comment echoed the criticism that characterized reviews by Liberals: Barth's work is seriously flawed by its unconcern for historical work on the text.

> The modern direction of piety, in its turning away from historical work, has been characterized as Gnosticism. This is correct to the extent that piety wishes to tear the connection with historical forces into shreds, and completely reinterprets history as myth, as appears to me to be the case in Barth's *Epistle to the Romans*.[5]

---

2. Ibid., pp. 25, 26, 29.
3. Ibid., p. 29.
4. "Ethische und mystische Religion im Urchristentum," *Die christliche Welt* 34 (1920): no. 46, 725–736, and no. 47, 738–743. The English translation is in *The Beginnings of Dialectical Theology,* trans. Crim, ed. Robinson, pp. 221–235.
5. Ibid., p. 230.

His other comment was equally critical in spite of a modest word of appreciation: "As much as I welcomed the religious critique of culture in Barth's *Epistle to the Romans,* I can see in the positive aspects he introduces little else than an arbitrary adaptation of the Pauline Christ myth."[6]

The Wartburg conference took place three months after the publication of Gogarten's "Between the Times," and Gogarten and Barth were already in a collaborative relationship. As a matter of fact, two days after Bultmann's paper at the conference, Gogarten read one on "The Crisis of Our Culture" in which he sounded themes of the new movement. In 1920, Bultmann was not yet a part of it.

He began to change his view of Barth in 1922, when he lectured on Romans at the university. In the course of these lectures, he worked through Barth's second edition and decided he had to take it seriously. A Swiss student studying in Marburg who attended Bultmann's lectures wrote Barth that the last six sessions of the course were turned into a "work group" on Barth's commentary, that instead of a critic, Bultmann had become an advocate, and that Bultmann had read a lecture praising the work.[7] This lecture marked a turning point in Bultmann's theological thinking. He published it in *The Christian World*.[8]

It was only a turning point for Bultmann, not yet a conversion. But contrary to his reaction to the first edition, he now thought that Barth, in both his positive representations and his negative contrasts, had given powerful expression to Paul's understanding of faith. He cited one of Barth's descriptions of faith with approval:

"He who recognizes the limits of the world through a contradicting truth, the limits of his own self through a contradicting will, *he who therefore confesses he belongs to*

---

6. Ibid., p. 232.

7. Reported by Barth in a circular letter to his close friends, dated March 26, 1922. *Karl Barth—Eduard Thurneysen Briefwechsel,* vol. 2, p. 62.

8. *Die christliche Welt* 36 (1922): no. 18, 320–323; no. 19, 330–334; no. 20, 358–361; no. 21, 369–373. The English translation is in *The Beginnings of Dialectical Theology,* trans. Crim, ed. Robinson, pp. 100–120. Citations will be from the English translation and will be indicated by page numbers in parentheses following the quotations.

this contradiction and undertakes to base his life on it, he has faith." (106)

Barth had convinced him that this statement was appropriate to Paul. Bultmann now saw that when faith is so understood the No that Barth enunciated so firmly could be distinguished from "the inner-worldly criticism of a defiant, resigned, or despairing pessimism" such as one finds in a Schopenhauer or a Spitteler and which is nothing but a human No from human beings who want the world to be different and thus is actually a human yes (106). Bultmann: "But the No which is decisive for faith is that which is spoken by *God*" (106). In short, Bultmann had come to believe that Barth was fundamentally right in his dialectics of "no and yes."

Of equal importance, Bultmann thought Barth was right in what he rejected on the basis of this understanding. Faith is not a psychological experience; it is not engendered by demonstrable historical facts; and it is not a mystical flight from this world into realms beyond. It can be viewed only as a miracle emerging from the crisis in which we are placed by God, from the paradoxical situation of human life, which (again citing Barth)

> "consists in our being led step by step by the holy demand of God which meets us in the recognized problematic of our existence to the final possibility in which we, looking, perishing, pleading, crying out of deep need, stretch out our arms toward the great unknown, toward the Yes which stands unperceivable over against the No in which we are imprisoned." (106)

It may have been the case that Bultmann was able to affirm so much of Barth in his second edition of *Romans* because he thought he found in it numerous points of contact with the theology of Wilhelm Herrmann. (There is no evidence that Barth thought he was dependent on Herrmann!) At one point, however, Bultmann thought Barth rightly went beyond Herrmann. It had to do with the question, How does one come to faith? Bultmann thought Barth ignored the question. Both thought, so Bultmann surmised, that the question could be answered only by showing what faith means, and to do that rightly points one not to a human possibility (which could answer the question) but to a necessity. Bultmann wrote, in basic identity with Barth and with only a slight leaning toward Herrmann:

> It becomes clear that the possibility of bowing becomes the necessity of bowing, and that the man who is confronted with the question "How do I come to faith?" can find his answer only by taking thought whether and where in his life he meets the reality which he can absolutely bow to and must bow to. . . . The decision must be made by every man for himself. Others can only help him in that they try to say what faith means. (115)

Bultmann had continuing difficulties with Barth, most interestingly at two points. First, though he agreed with Barth that faith is not a discernible psychic experience, he could not understand how one could talk about faith without talking about its appropriation in the consciousness or self-understanding. He recognized that Barth wanted to avoid any talk about faith that made it a human possibility or something people could claim for themselves. Bultmann thought he agreed with Barth in this effort, but he also thought Barth was not entirely clear. He was certain it was not the view of Paul, for whom faith, he said, was a conscious acceptance. "A faith beyond consciousness is most certainly not the 'impossible possibility,' but in every sense an absurdity" (111). He thought one could describe faith as a conscious act without falling into the pitfalls Barth rightly wanted to avoid. In the next few years, Bultmann would identify more closely with Barth, but the difference between them on this point was never resolved. In time it would become a key to their separation. We will see that it also has implications for ethics.

The second most telling point on which Bultmann took issue with Barth in this review essay had to do with the role of criticism in exegesis. Bultmann affirmed Barth's focus on the subject matter of the text, and he thought Barth had "grasped Paul's view of faith in its depths" (119). However, he judged that Barth had done violence to the particularity of Romans and to Paul, indeed to the subject matter, by avoiding criticism, or, as Bultmann preferred to put it, "radical criticism."

> One must measure by the subject matter to what extent in all the words and sentences of the text the subject matter has really found adequate expression, for what else can be meant by "measuring"? In Barth, however, I find nothing of such measuring and of the radical criticism based on it. It is impossible to assume that everywhere in the Letter to the Romans the subject matter must have found adequate expression, unless one intends to establish a modern dogma of inspiration, and something like this seems to stand behind Barth's exegesis—to the detriment of the clarity of the subject matter itself. (119)

An emphasis on radical criticism as the most adequate way to lay hold of the subject matter was characteristic of Bultmann. It led later to a deepening chasm between him and Barth. In the final sentences of this essay, Bultmann argued that the principle of criticism should apply to the text not only historically but theologically as well. First he drew an analogy: just as it is a service to Barth to criticize his commentary because his subject matter is more important than his interpretation of it, so also is this the case with Paul in his letter. Criticism of Paul shows "no lack of respect" for him or what he wrote. Then Bultmann concluded:

> In him [Paul] there are other spirits speaking besides the *pneuma Christou* ["spirit of Christ"]. And therefore criticism can never be radical enough. Such criticism therefore is—it follows from Barth's own basic premise of "measuring by the subject matter"—inseparable from exegesis and real history. Only in such criticism can the historical work attain its final goal, in which it meets the systematic theology which has traveled on another road—reflection on the motives and forces, on the bases of our life. (120)

Little more than a year later (early 1924), Bultmann had identified himself with Dialectical Theology. Having heard that

Bultmann was on the verge of a public declaration, Barth made a quick trip to Marburg with twelve students in order "incognito" to hear Bultmann present a paper on "Liberal Theology and the Latest Theological Movement," which he published shortly afterward in the widely read magazine *Theological Leaves*.[9] In this essay, Bultmann referred to Dialectical Theology using the first person plural pronoun ("we," "our"), and he spoke of it as "the cause" (29, 31). "What a shift!" Barth exclaimed in a letter to Thurneysen, though he noted that Bultmann still bore "a few pieces of egg shell from his past."[10] Barth's assessment was directly on target.

In his lecture, Bultmann expressed his continuing appreciation for Liberal theology's "development of the critical sense, that is, for freedom and veracity" (29). This critical sense, he said, made it possible for him and others from Liberal backgrounds to become and remain theologians. However, he had come to believe that Liberal theology was flawed at several crucial points. It tended to base faith on what it thought it could establish historically without taking sufficient account of the fact that no historical reconstruction of the past can have more than a relative validity. Moreover, it forgot that what it presented as reconstructed history, like all history, consisted of "entities which exist only within an immense inter-related complex" (31). As history, they can be understood only as finite and human, whereas the subject matter of theology is God. With Barth and Gogarten, he affirmed that "there is no direct knowledge of God. God is not a given entity" (33). The varied liberal formulations

> totally lack the insight that God is other than the world, he is beyond the world, and that this means the complete abrogation of the whole man, of his whole history. Their common aim is to give faith the kind of basis which destroys the very

---

9. "Die liberale Theologie und die jüngste theologische Bewegung," *Theologische Blätter* 3 (1924), 73–86. The English translation is in Bultmann, *Faith and Understanding*, trans. Louise Pettibone Smith, ed. Robert W. Funk (Philadelphia: Fortress Press, 1987), pp. 28–52. Citations will be from the translation and will be indicated by page numbers in parentheses following the quotations.

10. *Karl Barth—Eduard Thurneysen Briefwechsel,* vol. 2, p. 227.

essence of faith, because what they seek is a basis here in this world. (40)

These statements situated Bultmann solidly in the dialectical camp.

He thought his rejection of Liberal theology's claim that secular daily work is service to God did the same. In good dialectical fashion, he emphasized that

> no activity *within the world* can be service to God. . . . The one essential is . . . to listen to the "stumbling block" of God's Word, the Word which declares that the world exists in sin and that man in the world can do nothing which can sustain the character of service to God. (41–42)

Even good, dutiful acts that are "worthy of honor and terribly necessary" are not as such Christian because no act can "relate itself directly to God. . . . All forms of community life, the worst and the most ideal alike, stand equally under the judgment of God" (42). This judgment applies as well to all law and government. "All authority stands always under the judgment of God" (44).

However, Bultmann took a step that one does not find in Barth. To say that there can be no direct service of God in this world did not mean for him that there is no service of God.

> Only when I recognize that the work *in itself* does not serve God, only if I undertake it in *obedience* and maintain an inner detachment from it, only if I do it as if I did not [a major theme of Bultmann drawn from 1 Corinthians 7:29–31], can it be the service of God. (41)

He was clear about the foundation for a Christian ethics in faith. To be sure, like Dialectical Theology, he rejected the Liberal premise that specific ethical principles could be derived from faith, but his rejection was different from that of Barth and Gogarten. For Bultmann, the position one took depended on the specific situation and the decision one took in that moment.

In order to understand how this view of human life in the world in faith differed from Dialectical Theology (in a way Bultmann himself apparently did not see in this essay that otherwise was a "confession" for the theology of Barth and Gogarten), we must recall his emphasis on the "consciousness" of the person of faith in his review of Barth's commentary and take note particularly of the final section of this lecture. That section begins with the thesis of Dialectical Theology that "God is not a given entity" (45). "God represents the total annulment of man, his negation, calling him in question, indeed judging him" (46). Bultmann was thus far dialectical. He was also dialectical when he argued that this proclamation of judgment does not result in scepticism or pessimism but rather comes from the realization that "man's fundamental sin is his will to justify himself as man, for thereby he makes himself God" (46).

Bultmann stepped a foot outside Dialectical Theology when he explained the above conclusion with reference to what happens in the person of faith. "To know this judgment is also to know it as grace, since it is really liberation. Man becomes free from himself. And for man to become free from himself is redemption. . . . The knowledge of this truth is called faith" (47). Bultmann talked about the transformation of the person "whom God has put to death and made alive again" (47). He considered this the "true miracle" (49) that is never a possession but rather has to be reclaimed in faith again and again. By this time, he agreed with Barth that faith is not a state of consciousness, but he could not refrain from talking about faith as something a person recognized in him or herself. "Only the man who knows himself to be a sinner can know what grace is. He knows himself as a sinner only in so far as he stands before *God;* therefore he can only know of sin when he also knows of grace" (51). Bultmann obviously thought faith had a discernible effect upon the person. He did not want to place that effect in the consciousness, but it is clear that for him it was something that determined the life of the person of faith in the world.

He thought he was still within the orbit of Dialectical Theology, but at best he was on its edges. In this essay, he spoke of human being as well as of God—and of both simultaneously, a trademark of Bultmann in his developed theology. He concluded in identity and difference with Dialectical Theology by saying: "The subject of theology is God. Theology speaks of God because it speaks of man as he stands before God. That is, theology speaks out of faith" (52).

Bultmann's substantial identity with Barth in the understanding of God and his substantial difference from Barth in emphasizing the effects of faith in the human being are further evident in essays that followed.[11] Over the next couple of years, he developed with clarity and confidence—and with increasing reliance on his interpretation of Paul's letters—an understanding of faith that emphasized the priority and transcendence of God (the Wholly Other) and the transformation of life here and now in faith. In contrast to recognizing the truth of a timeless idea or to being elevated to a realm beyond nature, he understood faith as an event, the source of which could be only the God beyond all things. In response to the proclamation of the gospel, the grace of God, a person is liberated from bondage to the self. Thereby that person comes to understand sin as wanting to make and control one's own life, to be one's own God. Sin, therefore, is not simple moral failing, and one does not come to know sin until one comes to know grace. Because it is an event, faith is never something that is settled once and for all. It has to be reclaimed again and again by the repeated remembering and hearing of the gospel.

Because it liberates by turning one outside oneself and because it does not lift one above history, this life in the world is determined by the love of neighbor, which is an expression of the love of God. But because it takes place in human history ("this side," not the "other side"), it is always marked by failure, but failure does not destroy the relationship with God, nor does it dampen the wish to love. Bultmann returned always to the

---

11. Note especially "Das Problem der Ethik bei Paulus" [The Problem of Ethics in Paul], in *Rudolf Bultmann: Exegetica,* ed. Erich Dinkler (Tübingen: J. C. B. Mohr [Paul Siebeck], 1967), pp. 36–54, originally published in *Zeitschrift für die neutestamentliche Wissenschaft* 23 (1924), 123–140; "Das Problem einer theologischen Exegese des Neuen Testaments" [The Problem of a Theological Exegesis of the New Testament], *Zwischen den Zeiten* 3 (1923), 334–357; "Welchen Sinn hat es, von Gott zu reden?" in *Glauben und Verstehen,* vol. 1 (Tübingen: J. C. B. Mohr [Paul Siebeck], 1933), pp. 26–37, originally published in *Theologische Blätter* 4 (1925), 129–135, translated as "What Does It Mean to Speak of God?" in Bultmann, *Faith and Understanding,* trans. Smith, ed. Funk, pp. 53–65.

metaphor of a relationship, and the sense of relationship with God is received by the person of faith as both a gift and a claim, the two inseparably and coherently together.

The claim, however, because it is like the claim of a spouse whom one loves, cannot be translated into a law or set of laws. To state the claim in the form of rules would damage the relationship (and weaken the sense of claim by giving it prescribed limits). What to do or not to do can be decided only in the specific instance with the understanding that it is never entirely right. One can say only, "I believe, help my unbelief."

To understand faith in this way is to understand why Bultmann insisted that to speak of God is at the same time to speak of human being. One can speak of God only out of the sense of a relationship with God. Thus everything one says about God has its corollary effect in the way one understands oneself. This insistence troubled Barth. In 1925, at a colloquium for theological students in Göttingen, Barth heard Bultmann read an essay on the theological exegesis of the New Testament. Barth thought well of the essay and took special pleasure in the fact that his colleague on the faculty, Emanuel Hirsch, was unsuccessful in undermining what Bultmann said. However, Barth was critical of Bultmann on the point we are now considering. In a circular letter, he told his friends that he thought Bultmann was too "anthropological-Kierkegaardian-Lutheran" and too "Gogartenian!" (more on this later), and he explained what he meant by citing Bultmann: "To speak of God means to speak of human being."[12] Even so, he thought this was ten times better than the current appropriation of Karl Holl (for example, by Hirsch).

One might wonder whether Barth's objection to Bultmann on this point represented a real difference when one reads a 1958 recollection by Barth of the early years of Dialectical Theology. The sentence in question comes from a preface to a collection of letters between Barth and Thurneysen (1921–1925) that Barth prepared for Thurneysen's seventieth birthday. He wrote: "Fortunately, by way of a new understanding of the two natures of the one Jesus Christ, we recognized fairly early that one cannot speak

---

12. *Karl Barth—Eduard Thurneysen Briefwechsel*, vol. 2, p. 306. The letter is dated January 16, 1925.

of man without speaking of God and that one cannot speak of God without speaking of man."[13] It is not difficult, however, to see a difference between Barth and Bultmann on the theme. Barth bases the necessity of speaking about human being when speaking about God and vice-versa on the classic doctrine of the divine and human natures of Jesus Christ. Thus the necessity derives from Christology. Bultmann did not base the theme on the dogma of the two natures of Christ. Invariably, he connected it with the metaphor of a relationship between God and the human being and with the effects of faith in the temporal life of the believer. Later, Bultmann would draw the inference, already implicit in his thinking, that a doctrine such as that of the two natures of Christ has meaning only as an implication of the effects of faith in the life of the believer. Barth, on the contrary, believed that the doctrine was given with the revelation and was to be accepted in faith. To Bultmann, acceptance as such seemed arbitrary, a sacrifice of the intellect, and he steadfastly held that Christian faith does not require such a sacrifice.

Another illustration of the difference between Bultmann and Barth is evident in Bultmann's generally sympathetic review of Barth's 1924 book on 1 Corinthians, *The Resurrection of the Dead*.[14] Barth took the text as a literary unity and found the key to its understanding in the fifteenth chapter, which proclaims the final resurrection. Bultmann, although he was critical on this and that point of exegesis, thought Barth brilliantly recaptured the message of Paul in almost every respect, including (perhaps especially) Barth's resounding emphasis on the eschatological "no" over everything human and this-worldly.

---

13. Karl Barth, "Lebendige Vergangenheit," in *Gottesdienst-Menschendienst* (Zollikon-Zürich: Evangelischer Verlag, 1958), p. 9. Translated in *Revolutionary Theology in the Making,* trans. Smart, p. 67.

14. Karl Barth, *Die Auferstehung der Toten* (München: Christian Kaiser Verlag, 1924). The English translation is *The Resurrection of the Dead,* trans. H. J. Stenning (London: Hodder & Stoughton, 1933). Bultmann's review, "Karl Barth: Die Auferstehung der Toten," was published in *Theologische Blätter* 5 (1926), 1–14. The English translation is "Karl Barth: The Resurrection of the Dead," in Bultmann, *Faith and Understanding,* trans. Smith, ed. Funk, pp. 66–94. References to Bultmann's review will be from the English translation and will be indicated by page numbers in parentheses following the quotations.

At the end of his review, however, he took issue with Barth's main thesis. He pointed to what he called a peculiarity of Barth's work: Barth almost never turned to other letters of Paul as a help in interpreting 1 Corinthians. Bultmann thought Barth could have found support from them in his transformation of what Paul apparently meant by the end time in 1 Corinthians. Paul seems to depict the end as an objective event in time, and Barth changed this conception into what he called, more vaguely, an "eternal future" (92). First, Bultmann noted that Paul could not have meant straightforwardly that the end is an objective event in time because he sees it as an "event in which time stands still and the past is over" (93). He pointed out that even in 1 Corinthians 15, except for "the misleading, polemical section vv. 35–44," there is no picture "of the conditions of life after the resurrection" (93). "Fundamentally there is nothing 'afterwards' " (93). All Paul can say about life after the resurrection, Bultmann noted, is that it is "to be with Christ." Then he cited other passages he thought clarified Paul's meaning (1 Thessalonians 4:17 and Philippians 1:23) and continued:

> The meaning of "to be with Christ" must be determined from what Christ meant to Paul. For that meaning, Rom. 5:1ff., must be mentioned in addition to I Cor. 1:30: "whom God made our wisdom, our righteousness and consecration and redemption." There we have the statement of what Christ means for men, *these* actual men who we ourselves are in our temporal situation. (93)

Bultmann was moving to his main point, which was an understanding of eschatology materially different from Barth's in that it is rooted in a present reality.

> Christ is not the cosmic ground of a future condition of existence, but the historical foundation of our present life. In a certain sense we *are* the resurrected, . . . the "first fruits", . . . a "new creation." . . .
> But this resurrection life is never something objective. It is between time and eternity. In the judgment *of God* we are the justified, and the "final possibility" that this may become a reality in our temporal life is "love." (93-94)

Barth had understood 1 Corinthians 13 (the chapter on love) as eschatological in the sense of a reality God will bring forth at the end of history. Barth thought love cannot be a present reality in this world that is so distant from God; it can show itself here only in the negating contrast of God's "No." Bultmann affirmed God's "No." He concurred that nothing in human history can be identified with the divine reality. But those who come to faith in response to the proclamation of the gospel of Jesus Christ are and want to be (at the same time) new creatures, living their lives in the world in community on the basis of love that they know can never be fully realized in this world.

The conclusion, therefore, challenged Barth's thesis that 1 Corinthians has its unity in the fifteenth chapter (the final resurrection): "Since in the First Letter to the Corinthians the dominant theme is not justification by faith but the temporal life of the believer within time, ch. 13 is the true climax of the letter" (94).

Bultmann's review essay was sympathetic to Barth, but it challenged Barth's basic thesis about 1 Corinthians. In these years, Bultmann was able to identify himself with Barth, but the difference between them was more substantial than he realized.

8

A CONTROVERSY ABOUT
JESUS . . . AND ETHICS

HIRSCH AND BULTMANN

In 1926, both Emanuel Hirsch and Rudolf Bultmann published books about Jesus.[1] They were strikingly different. Differing treatments of Jesus, however, were, if anything, more common in the early part of this century than they are today. A discussion between the authors of these two books was by no means necessary, and it might not have occurred had not Hirsch written a relatively brief review of Bultmann's book in a journal oriented to ministers.[2] Bultmann chose to respond both to the review and to Hirsch's book with a major programmatic essay on Christology.[3] Hirsch then wrote a long essay in reply.[4] The two books are basic documents for understanding their respective authors, but for our purposes their direct engagement in the review and responses is more revealing of the fundamental conflict between them and of their future courses.

The books were indeed strikingly different. Hirsch was confi-

---

1. Emanuel Hirsch, *Jesus Christus der Herr* (Göttingen: Vandenhoeck & Ruprecht, 1926). Rudolf Bultmann, *Jesus* (Berlin: Deutsche Bibliothek, 1926); the English translation by Louise Pettibone Smith and Erminie Huntress Lantero is *Jesus and the Word* (New York: Charles Scribner's Sons, 1934).

2. *Zeitwende* 2, no. 2 (1926), 309–313.

3. "Zur Frage der Christologie," *Zwischen den Zeiten* 6 (1927), 41–69. English translation: "On the Question of Christology," in Bultmann, *Faith and Understanding,* trans. Smith, ed. Funk, pp. 116–144.

4. "Antwort an Rudolf Bultmann," *Zeitschrift für systematische Theologie* 4 (1927), 631–661.

dent that a critical study of the first three Gospels yields a historically reliable account not only of Jesus' sayings but of his life and self-consciousness as well. He tried to show that there was a perfect unity between what Jesus taught, his good deeds, the course of his life, and his inner sense of being the unique Son of God. As evidence for the latter, he relied heavily on the historical accuracy of the stories of Jesus' baptism by John, when Jesus is said to have heard a voice declaring him to be the Son of God, and his temptation by Satan, when Jesus, according to Hirsch, distinguished his Sonship from the Jewish messianic idea.

Bultmann, on the other hand, was thoroughly sceptical of the Synoptic Gospels as historical sources for the course of Jesus' life, and he was convinced that the sources do not permit insight into Jesus' self-consciousness. In continuity with the tradition of the historical-critical study of the Gospels, to which he made notable contributions, he viewed the Gospels as proclamation rather than as historical accounts, and he was convinced that the most we can recover as historical are the basic themes of Jesus' own proclamation.

The different treatments of the sources by these two men led them to different theological conclusions. Hirsch argued that because we can discern a perfect unity between Jesus' teaching, the course of his life, and his self-consciousness, we can confidently take him to be the divine Son of God. He regarded this belief as the basis of Christian faith. In the coherence of Jesus' life, his message, and his claim about himself, we are confronted with the decision about him, and if our hearts respond to the heart of Jesus, we will recognize the will of God for us in our consciences. The way to grace is "that Jesus Christ encounters us and takes our conscience, our heart under his direction. Only in this way do we come to take part in the community of prayer and love in which Jesus stands with the Father and out of which his love flows."[5] In Christ, therefore, eternity enters time and gives it true reality. All of time and history is determined by our decision of conscience about Jesus as the Son of God, and it becomes, therefore, the task of a Christian philosophy of nature and history to explore the specific meaning of this reality for any specific time and place. For Hirsch, the hinge of Christian faith is the decision that acknowl-

---

5. Hirsch, *Jesus Christus der Herr,* p. 77.

edges the heart of God in the heart of Jesus Christ. He was critical of the dogmatic formula about the divine and human natures of Christ, but his theological focus was on the person of Christ.

The person of Christ does not figure at all in Bultmann's study of Jesus. The focus, rather, is on the message of Jesus. The message, however, does not consist of lessons, truths, or maxims that can be affirmed, learned, and applied. It is an address that calls into question the person as such. To hear it is to obey it in the sense of understanding oneself anew as living in the presence of God. The message becomes, in the crisis of decision, an event, the transformation of the self, in which the self is turned outward from itself toward God and neighbor. In the traditional language of theology, then, the hinge of Christian faith is the work of Christ rather than the person of Christ.

Given the sharp differences between these two books on Jesus, it is noteworthy that Hirsch's review of Bultmann's book was not unfriendly. He concluded it by stating that the book was not distant from good churchly preaching. He thought it might affect those who think that critical radicalism has rendered Jesus irrelevant "as a question of conscience having to do with them personally."[6] He said that the last word to Bultmann had to be thanks.

Hirsch did forthrightly state three criticisms of Bultmann. First, he took issue with Bultmann's radical criticism. It was certainly not easy, he thought, for Bultmann to write a book about Jesus. Bultmann doubted the historical accuracy of so much in the Gospels that there is hardly enough material about Jesus left to make a book. Hirsch thought Bultmann stood virtually alone in the extent of his historical scepticism, but he noted with approval that Bultmann, even so, wrote about what material he accepted with total seriousness. "Bultmann understands what remains for him from the words of Jesus as encountering himself in his own existence, as an address directing itself to him personally. I am almost inclined to say, as an appeal to his conscience."[7]

Second, Hirsch thought Bultmann did not and could not achieve the central intention of his book. He thought what Bultmann most wanted to accomplish was a presentation of Jesus'

---

6. *Zeitwende* 2, no. 2 (1926), 313.
7. Ibid., p. 309.

message of the coming of the kingdom such that the reader would be placed in the crisis of decision, called by the claim of God for obedience, led to recognize himself or herself as a sinner, to find forgiveness in God and life in following the will of God, and that the reader would experience all this as an "event." He commended Bultmann for trying to accomplish in all this the highest that a theologian can accomplish—namely, to draw the readers into a question of decision about their own relation to God. But from his point of view, Bultmann presented the claim of God as so encompassing that the human being was left alone, without access to the mystery of God's grace. In this criticism, Hirsch surely had in mind his own emphasis on the believer's relation to the historical Jesus, in whose heart, he was confident, one finds the heart of God.

This difference has illuminating implications for ethics. For Bultmann, Jesus' teaching on the claim of God does not yield applicable maxims, though it is determinative for the whole of one's life. Precisely because God's claim has to do with everything a person is and does, it can never be satisfied. It remains unmanageable. For Hirsch, on the other hand, the implications for human life of the contact of the believer with God through Jesus can be specifically worked out by a Christian philosophy of nature and history.

What one must surmise Hirsch had in mind in his second criticism became explicit in his third. In Hirsch's judgment, this point was the most crucial one. Bultmann, he said, focused on the "word," but he did not consider that words can be given different meanings by different people. As a prime example, he took the word *love* and argued that one can know for certain what that word meant for Jesus only when one knows the inner heart of Jesus himself. He accused Bultmann of holding to the words themselves "as if the published book had fallen from heaven." "One does not bear a word to another the way a dock worker carries a sack where it does not matter whether the sack has iron or coal in it." Rather, bearing a word to another is like "the way an apple tree bears an apple. It is self-evident that the tree can bear nothing else because the same life, the same juice flows in both."[8]

8. Ibid., p. 312.

In short, one must know the tree—that is, Jesus' heart—in order to understand the word. Hirsch thought this point revealed the weakness of Bultmann's historical scepticism. For Hirsch, everything depended on the inner character of the person who bore witness to God's will. Knowing the inner character of Jesus gave access, he believed, not only to the character of God but also to the claim of God upon us in our worldly life as that can be developed for the conscience by a Christian philosophy of nature and history.

Bultmann responded to Hirsch by writing a major programmatic essay on Christology. His purpose was to clarify the meaning of faith in God through Jesus Christ. He tried to accomplish this purpose by contrasting his position with the position Hirsch developed in his book and review. Bultmann was cordial to Hirsch. Several times, he pointed to similarities in their intentions, he noted that they both were dealing seriously with a pressing theological problem, and he denied any personal antagonism between the two of them. However, he viewed the difference between them as insuperable. "My criticism of his position would remain entirely negative if I could give no positive answers to his position."[9] This was strong language, but not overwrought.

Bultmann judged that Hirsch had made the basic mistake of assuming that one could extract the historical phenomenon of Jesus from the Gospel accounts and that the yield of this endeavor would be the object of faith. In this enterprise, he found a wedding of rationalism and pietism. He thought it was rationalistic, because the only way one can relate to a person from the past is to see in that person "a moral demand that is timeless—the recognition of the fact that for us there is a law."[10] Hirsch argued that the effect of Jesus upon us is to make us aware of a moral demand in our consciences, and Bultmann saw no way for that moral demand to be explicated except as it is in rationalism—for example, in a philosophy of nature and history. Bultmann noted that when Hirsch tried to go beyond this form of rationalism he found himself trapped in pietism. Jesus, according to Hirsch, not only presents the moral demand; he exemplifies it in his person. Hirsch tried to

---

9. Bultmann, "On the Question of Christology," p. 130.
10. Ibid., p. 126.

argue the coherence of the teaching, life, and heart of Jesus, and Bultmann cited sentences that had more than a drop of sentimentality. He could not see how such appeal to sentiment, especially with reference to the death of Jesus, set Jesus apart, for example, from Socrates or German soldiers who went to their death in obedient love to the Fatherland.

Most fundamentally, Bultmann argued that it is simply impossible to establish a relation with a person from the past. One can admire, respect, and remember persons from the past, but one cannot enter a relationship of trust with them. They are gone. Bultmann was convinced that Hirsch's basic problem was his historical procedure, and he believed it to be flawed both historically and theologically.

Bultmann solidly affirmed his own strict criteria for determining the historical reliability of texts, the scepticism that Hirsch saw as a serious weakness in him. Of course, insistence on such standards for claims about Jesus would seriously damage Hirsch's position. For Bultmann, however, such insistence opened the possibility for understanding what the Gospel texts are about. They are not historical records of Jesus; rather, they are proclamation, that is, talk about Jesus as the message of the early community. They are gospel, and as such they are our access to gospel. Thus Bultmann also was undisturbed by Hirsch's criticism that he treated the Bible as if it had fallen from heaven. That criticism could mislead if Hirsch were taken to imply that Bultmann held some kind of inspiration theory about the Bible as a whole, but Bultmann even so was eager to admit that for the church's proclamation today, all it has is the book, the gospel. That is what must ever anew be understood and proclaimed.

This point brings us to the nub of the issue. Proclamation accosts the hearer in her or his present, declares that person as standing before God, and poses the question whether the hearer will respond in faith. To respond in faith is not simply to accept a statement or set of statements as true. It is not simply to pledge oneself to follow a moral demand that can be analyzed outside the one spoken to. On the contrary, to respond in faith is at one and the same time to intend the object of faith, God as known in Jesus Christ, and to call the self radically into question. It is to be determined in the totality of one's being and self-understanding by this God whose absolute claim is acknowledged and whose grace is received. Faith, received as a gift, bears within it the critical principle, rooted in self-criticism, and the transformation of the self such that the self is turned outward from itself in love.

Ethics, then, is not the consequence but the corollary of faith.

> The proclamation therefore comes to us each time within our historical existence, not outside it. It proclaims *forgiveness*. It does not detach us from our historical situation but propels us into it. . . . It directs man to his own humanity. For *this* humanity, grace is valid. . . . We are asked whether we will to belong to the new age of love and life, or whether we will to remain in hate and in death. . . . Since the historical fact of Jesus Christ, we are asked: will we listen to God or to the devil?[11]

Both Hirsch and Bultmann were trying to find a way that avoided the arbitrary objectivism of orthodoxy and the contentless subjectivism of late Liberalism, but they steered their ships along radically different courses. Both, however, held their crafts steady, as the years to come would show.

Hirsch's extensive essay "Answer to Rudolf Bultmann" brought the discussion to a close. He claimed Luther and Kierkegaard in support of his own position, and he charged Bultmann with setting himself apart from the community of scholars in his radical historical scepticism and with Barthian arbitrariness in his biblicism. The combination of doubt about the Gospel accounts and, as it seemed to Hirsch, biblical authoritarianism struck Hirsch as impossible. Once again he emphasized the importance of focus on the person of Jesus as Jesus can be known through what Hirsch called "the gospel histories."[12] This time he added that Bultmann—and Barth—had no noticeable personal dimension in their theology, and he observed that praying seemed unimportant to them.

He thought he and Bultmann still shared the view that faith finds its content in the ground that confirms it and that the truth

---

11. Ibid., pp. 140, 142.
12. Hirsch, "Antwort an Rudolf Bultmann," p. 645.

faith lays hold of is available only on the basis of decision, but he argued that Bultmann's reliance on the text as such was a cold alternative for what Bultmann considered his sentimentality. Hirsch was keenly aware that faith is a risk and that anyone could exchange God for a demon, but he thought his way was more firm than the arbitrariness, for example, of Barth or Althaus, who finally rest their cases on the assertion "God has spoken."

Revealingly, he also concluded with reference to ethics. When one finds the most critical truth in the acknowledgment of Jesus as the Son of God, one must believe that there can be no such thing as a double truth. Thus one acknowledges that God is the Lord over all truth, that "God's truth does not want to destroy natural truth but to liberate it from service to the past." Thus "the obedience of faith, in the same way, does not want to destroy natural truthfulness but to extract it from the service of the profane."[13] Thus faith in Jesus as the divine Son of God leads one precisely into the philosophy of nature and history that we have already witnessed in Hirsch's seminal book, *Germany's Destiny*, and that we will see again in his 1933 analysis of the religious situation of that year.

In the years following the end of the war in 1918, Barth, Hirsch, Tillich, Gogarten, Althaus, and Bultmann attained prominence in German theology. They changed the character of the theological discussion. In the course of their work, they entered alliances with and drew battle lines against each other. As the Weimar Republic limped to its grave and the shadow of Hitler stretched across the land, those alliances and battle lines firmed up in some cases, and in others shifted and were formed anew. That fateful story is the subject of Part III.

---

13. Ibid., p. 659.

PART III

"THE GREAT TURNING POINT":
1933–1935

> Many gave the warning, for years gave the warning. That our voices grew fainter is our guilt, our greatest guilt. . . .
>
> Everywhere the same insane faith, a man, the *Führer*, the Caesar, the Messiah will come and work miracles. He will bear the responsibility for the future, master all of life, ease anxiety, eliminate misery, create the new *Volk*, the kingdom of total splendor, yes, transform by the power of his divine mission the old, weak Adam. . . . Do not question. Believe!—ERNST TOLLER[1]

> Whenever they burn books, sooner or later they will burn human beings also.—HEINRICH HEINE[2]

Looking backward, one might well be astonished that the Weimar Republic lasted fourteen years. The time was exceptionally rich in cultural and intellectual activity, but it suffered throughout from political instability. From the first, the Republic was hopelessly divided by a large number of political parties. Several on the far right as well as the Communist party on the far left wanted to do away with the Republic. Parties from the moderate left (the Social Democrats) to the moderate right (several parties) wanted to make democracy work, but there was little gifted political leadership in any party. Over the fourteen years, there were nineteen different coalition governments.

The German economy suffered from heavy reparations pay-

---

1. Ernst Toller, *Eine Jugend in Deutschland* (Reinbeck bei Hamburg: Rowohlt Taschenbuch Verlag, 1963), pp. 8–9. Ernst Toller was a German Jewish writer whose plays were "the sensation of Expressionism" during the Weimar Republic and whose poems and novels were also widely read. He managed to get out of Germany in 1933 and made his way to the United States. On May 22, 1939, he hanged himself in a New York City hotel room.

2. Quoted by Stefan Zweig in *The World of Yesterday* (New York: The Viking Press, 1943), p. 385. Heine (1797–1856) was a German poet of Jewish descent.

ments, the occupation of the Saar region with its rich mineral deposits and heavy industry, and, perhaps most of all, the huge war debt Germany had incurred because the Kaiser had not wanted to raise taxes to pay for the war effort. In the early 1920s, the governments saw no alternative to printing money.

Inflation followed. At the end of the war, the German Mark was valued at nine to the dollar. It lost value steadily except for one year (1920) until 1923, when the bottom fell out of it. In January of that year, the dollar was worth 18,000 Marks, by July, 350,000; in August, 4.5 million; and on November 15, 4,200 billion. Prices rose so quickly that the ordinary German had to spend everything within minutes after being paid, while a few unconscionable entrepreneurs gobbled up businesses by borrowing huge sums they could easily repay in grotesquely devalued Marks.

To this unstable economy and widespread poverty were added the ravages of the worldwide depression in late 1929. In March 1930, three million Germans were unemployed. By December, the number had risen to 4.4 million and a year later to 5.6 million—this in a country whose total population numbered only 56 million.

It is no wonder that no government could establish control over the situation, and it is no wonder that the electorate was fickle in political allegiances. Many voters looked hopefully at anything that was different and held promise for bringing security.

The unlikely and unexpected benefactor of this condition was Adolf Hitler and his National Socialist German Workers Party (NSDAP or Nazis, after the first four letters of the German word for "National"). Hitler's party experienced its first significant victory in the elections in September 1930. In 1928, 809,000 Germans had voted for the Nazis, giving the party 12 seats in the parliament. In 1930, to the surprise of most, 6.4 million Germans voted Nazi, giving the party 107 of the 452 seats, only 36 fewer seats than the Social Democrats won. The Nazis actually won a majority of the seats (230) in the election on July 20, 1932, but because of a couple of rare political mistakes by Hitler, 34 of those seats were lost in the quick election held less than two months later.

Even so, the country was in its worst political crisis. Neither

Papen, the favorite of the aged president, General Hindenberg, nor General Schleicher could manage to govern as Chancellor. On January 30, 1933, Hindenberg, against his wishes, named Hitler Chancellor of Germany and head of a coalition government in which there were only two other Nazis in the cabinet. Papen had urged Hindenberg, who trusted him, to take this action, and boasted to friends, "Within two months we will have pushed Hitler so far into the corner that he'll squeak!"[3] His view was shared by many. Not least because of their snobbery, they could not take "the little Corporal" seriously.

Hitler acted with characteristic decisiveness and speed. While assuring the generals that the army would retain sole authority in the use of armed force, his associates, most notably Goering in Prussia, took control of the police forces and reconstituted them as arms of the party. He effectively blamed the burning of the parliament building on the Communists. The fire occurred on February 27, and before dawn on February 28, four thousand Communist party members and officials along with many others had been arrested. He inveigled an emergency decree from Hindenberg, who had a mortal fear and hatred of communism. He closed down left-wing presses and imposed severe restrictions on others. Finally, although the elections he held in early March did not give the Nazis a majority, he called for a vote on the crucial Enabling Act.

This act, which gave Hitler dictatorial powers, required a change in the constitution. Therefore, it required a two-thirds vote of the parliament. Hitler made extravagant promises to win the support of the center parties, and on the day of the vote (March 23) his agents prevented the eighty-one Communist delegates and twenty-six of the Socialist deputies from attending. He won with fifty-eight votes to spare and became Dictator of the Third Reich.

With deliberate speed, he and his supporters instituted measures to bring all sectors of German society into line with the new regime.

---

3. Quoted by Craig in *Germany: 1866–1945*, p. 570.

9

THE END OF
BETWEEN THE TIMES

BARTH VERSUS GOGARTEN

Immediately after Hitler's accession to power, there was a movement within the German Protestant church to bring it into line with values and policies of the new regime. Friedrich Gogarten identified himself with a wing of this German Christian movement. Not long thereafter, Karl Barth publicly withdrew from *Between the Times,* and the journal came to an end.

The moment was dramatic. For over a decade, the names Barth and Gogarten had been spoken in one breath in theological circles all over Germany and beyond. It was another way of saying "Dialectical Theology."

The break, however, was not entirely surprising. The theological public could have observed developing divergences in their thinking and a less frequent use by each of the plural form of the personal pronoun (we, us, our). In 1929, in a review of Barth's first volume of dogmatic theology, Gogarten had sharply criticized Barth for not having developed a proper anthropology (doctrine of human being)[1]; and in his 1932 recasting of that first volume under the new title *Church Dogmatics,* Volume 1, Part 1, Barth had written a direct and caustic response. What the theological public could not know was that for several years Barth had grown more and more suspicious of Gogarten.

---

1. "Karl Barths Dogmatik," *Theologische Rundschau* 1 Neue Folge (1929), 60–80.

160

We have already noted that even before the first issue of *Between the Times* came out in 1923, Barth expressed a misgiving about Gogarten to Thurneysen. After saying that he was "more than ever convinced that both of us are biting on the same bone," he added that he felt an "element of distrust that somewhere at the bottom of things I have in regard to him."[2]

That "element of distrust" gradually became more clear to Barth. In the years between 1923 and 1933, Gogarten was mentioned more than a hundred times in the correspondence between Barth and Thurneysen. These references reflect not only friendship and theological identity but also a growing distrust by Barth of the direction Gogarten's theology was taking.

Barth's misgivings focused on three points. First, Gogarten, ostensibly from the base of Dialectical Theology, began to write about family, vocation, and State as orders instituted by God upon which one could construct guidelines for a mode of life in the world. Second, Gogarten began to develop the thesis drawn from the contemporary Jewish theologian Buber and reminiscent to Barth of the nineteenth-century sceptic Feuerbach that faith is a sense of relationship between I and Thou. Out of this consciousness of relationship, he correlated statements about God and human being, thus emphasizing anthropology, in contrast to Barth. Third, Barth noticed that Gogarten was developing Christology on the basis of the reconciling effects of Christ in a person rather than on the doctrine of the two natures of Jesus Christ. Barth thought all three of these developments pointed to an underlying proclivity in Gogarten for natural as opposed to revealed theology.

As the years went by, Gogarten, in further contrast to Barth, wanted to deal with the means human beings have for understanding the Word of God. His conviction that faith is fundamentally relational gave him confidence that faith could be explained in a way that human beings could grasp. The gospel, he thought, achieves a discernible coherence because what is said about God has its immediate corollary in what happens in the human being who responds to the gospel. This means as well that the life of the human being in the world is affected in ways we can explore and

---

2. *Revolutionary Theology in the Making,* trans. Smart, p. 122.

describe. Thus theology and ethics are immediately related, and history as the arena in which human beings give shape to their common life has immediate theological import.

As Gogarten became more confident in his orientation, he began to modify his earlier insistence with Barth that God alone is the subject matter of theology, though he remained dialectical. Further, he was uncomfortable with Barth's claim that it is theologically perverse to ask how it is possible for a human being to hear—that is, to understand—this Word of God. God, Barth insisted, not only speaks the Word but also creates the hearing, without reference to what happens in the human being who hears. In 1929, when Gogarten first published criticisms of Barth, he concentrated on what he claimed was the absence of a proper anthropology in Barth. He thought this lack isolated God so severely that God has no accessible and comprehensible word to the human situation. He believed that Barth based his theology on an arbitrary doctrine of revelation that in turn led him "phenomenologically" to bracket human being and to talk about God as God is in Godself. In contrast, Gogarten thought one could talk about God only as God meets human beings in their concrete situations, only as God is understood in relation to human beings.

Barth's response in his *Church Dogmatics*, Volume 1, Part 1, was typical of his polemical eloquence. He stated that Gogarten's complaint was "comforting" to him and that he would "regard it as a great disgrace really to do what Gogarten luckily has discovered I have not done." Theology, he asserted, should never concede "the Church's lack of independence in life and thought over against the world, the primacy of the questions which the world has to put to the Church over the questions which the Church has to put to herself."[3] For Barth, the sole, the first and final reality for the church is the revelation of God, and anything that modifies that exclusivity dilutes the freedom of God in God's Word.

Gogarten, meanwhile, was developing further the points that distinguished him from Barth. In exploring the implications of the thesis that faith is fundamentally a sense of relationship, he

---

3. Karl Barth, *The Doctrine of the Word of God,* trans. G. T. Thompson (Edinburgh: T. and T. Clark, 1936), pp. 143, 144.

thought he saw a comprehensible identity between the commands to love God and to love the neighbor. From this he inferred that a fundamental thrust of the gospel is to bind human beings together in mutual responsibility for each other. He found the most serious violation of that claim of God in the pervasive individualism and sense of autonomy in contemporary western liberal society. Thus he grew increasingly disenchanted with the Weimar Republic. Further, in emphasizing the bondedness of human beings to each other, he began to emphasize the priority of the *Volk* over the individual, though he made it clear, in contrast to others, that by *Volk* he did not imply blood or racial kinship. He took the fateful steps of (1) deducing the necessity of lordship in society from the Lordship of Christ in faith and (2) deciding that the claim of God can show itself in the ordering of a *Volk* in the State.

Although he hedged his convictions by emphasizing the ambiguity of everything human, he took the dreadful steps of welcoming the advent of the Third Reich and joining the German Christian movement. Theologians, he insisted, cannot persist in polite indifference to the political events of the day. In these events, he claimed, they face their most weighty task. In that critical time, he thought the proper task of theologians was not so much to be negative and protesting but positive. The claims of *Volk* and State today might be mistaken, he asserted, but they were not as bad as those of cultural Protestantism. This conviction was his main reason for joining the German Christian movement. Further, he was convinced that the power would rest with the German Christians, and he believed it was better to participate in the forums where the decisions would be made. One must take *Volk*, State, and law seriously in order to be able to criticize them when they transgress their limits.[4] Gogarten wrote this explanation to Georg Merz, the managing editor of *Between the Times*, after Barth publicly withdrew from the journal.

Barth titled his open letter of resignation *"Abschied"* (Departure, Parting). He explained that he was resigning from the journal not only because of his growing disaffection with the trend of Gogarten's thought but especially because Gogarten had joined

---

4. *Zwischen den Zeiten* 11 (1933), 552.

the German Christian movement. He said he felt betrayed by Gogarten's movement toward natural theology as it was evident in his affirmation of a knowledge of God apart from the revelation in the Word of God. After the fact, he said, Gogarten's acts are not surprising. He thought they were related to Gogarten's Roman Catholic (!) and neo-Protestant tendencies and were more harmful than those of the theologians in the liberal Harnack-Troeltsch era. Worst of all, Gogarten now stood with Emanuel Hirsch, and Barth made it clear that he did not stand with Hirsch. He stated that he could not work with a German Christian or anyone close to that movement or with anyone who identified in any way with those who supported a proposed church law that would exclude from church ministry all persons of non-Aryan origin.[5] Barth believed he had to withdraw from the journal. Not to be heard at all is better than to be heard with one ear while Gogarten was being heard with the other. The difference between himself and Gogarten, he wrote, was irreconcilable.[6] The time "between the times" was over.

Three and a half months earlier, on June 25, 1933, Barth had announced the beginning of a new time in a typically bold and direct essay that he titled "Theological Existence Today!"[7] More than anything else written in this time, this essay coalesced the opposition to the German Christian movement and gave initiative to what issued a year later in the Confessing Church with its justly famous Barmen Declaration, which Barth wrote.

In his essay, Barth began by noting that he had frequently been asked if he had anything to say to the present church situation. His answer was crisp and clear: "I endeavor to carry on theology, and only theology, now as previously, as if nothing had happened" (9). He warned that theological professors must not abandon their

---

5. Gogarten also opposed the so-called "Aryan paragraph." The support of the paragraph by the German Christians, together with a ridiculous mass meeting in November 1933 in which it became clear that the German Christians wanted to disclaim the origins of Christianity in ancient Israel and the Old Testament, led Gogarten publicly to sever his relation with that movement. We will look more carefully at the Aryan paragraph in Chapter 15.

6. "Abschied," *Zwischen den Zeiten* 11 (1933), 9.

7. Translated by R. Birch Boyle (Lexington, Ky.: American Theological Library Association Committee on Reprinting, 1962). The citations that follow will be indicated by page numbers in parentheses.

vocation by "becoming zealous for some cause" they think to be good (11). Then he turned to premises on which he thought the whole church ought to be able to agree.

> One is, that there is no more urgent demand in the whole world than that which the Word of God makes, viz., that the Word be preached and heard. . . . Further, it is the unanimous opinion within the Church, that God is never for us in the world, that is to say, in our space and time, except in this His Word, and that this Word for us has no other name and content but Jesus Christ, and that Jesus Christ is never to be found on our behalf save each day afresh in the Holy Scriptures of the Old and New Testaments. One is not in the Church at all if he is not of a man with the Church in these things. (11–13)

He explained what he meant: "Where the Bible is allowed to be Master, theological existence is present: and where theological existence lives, it is then possible for Church reform to issue from the Church's life" (30). Further: "When it is recognised that *He* [Jesus Christ] and *He alone,* is the Leader [*Führer*], there is the possibility of theological existence" (46).

He acknowledged that some fellow members of the Reformed Church (Calvinist, Barth's tradition) and even some with whom he had collaborated and some who passed as students of his had joined the ranks of the German Christians. He summarized the tenets of the German Christians and then wrote:

> What I have to say to all this is simply said. I say, absolutely and without reserve, NO! to both the spirit and the letter of this doctrine. I maintain that this teaching is alien, with no right, in the Evangelical Church. . . . I have a request to make to my various theological friends also, who find themselves shifted into being in a position to say Yes! to this teaching, having been "duped" or tricked by some sophism. I ask them to take note from me, that I feel myself utterly and finally divided from them. (50)

With respect to the church in the State, he made careful distinctions:

> The Church believes in the Divine institution of the State as
> the guardian and administrator of public law and order. But
> she does not believe in any state, therefore not even in the
> German one, and therefore not even in the form of the
> National Socialist State. The Church preaches the Gospel in
> all the kingdoms of this world. She preaches it also *in* the
> Third Reich, but not *under* it, nor in *its* spirit. (51–52)

And with respect to membership in the church, he was unmistakably clear:

> The fellowship of those belonging to the Church is not
> determined by blood, therefore, not by race, but by the Holy
> Spirit and Baptism. If the German Evangelical Church
> excludes Jewish-Christians, or treats them as of a lower
> grade, she ceases to be a Christian Church. (52)

He concluded:

> The liberty that has to be preserved is *liberty:* and by liberty I
> mean the sovereignty of the Word of God in preaching and
> theology. . . . Of course something has to be done; very much
> so; but most decidedly nothing other than this, viz., that the
> Church congregations be gathered together again, but aright
> and anew in fear and great joy, to the Word by means of the
> Word. (72–73, 77)

It is a mark of the consistency of Barth that his resistance was
exclusively theological and ecclesiastical. Not everybody understood it that way. Some theologians, especially outside of Germany, took his theological position to be a political rejection of
the National Socialist State, not just an opposition to the movement in the church to support it. In December of 1933, in the
foreword to the fifth issue of *Theological Existence Today,* which
by then had become a publication series, Barth corrected his
friends on this point. It is difficult, he commented, to understand
the church situation in Germany from the outside, but one
damagingly misconstrues the church opposition if one takes it to
be the symptom of resistance to the present-day regime in
Germany. He stated clearly that he himself was not a National

Socialist, but he insisted that the battle he was waging in this journal had nothing to do with his political view. There have been, he wrote, some denunciations of him to the authorities, but he has been allowed to do what he must and wants to do. Hitler, he added, has indicated that he does not intend to impair the independence of the church. Barth wrote that he resisted the tendency in National Socialism to seek shelter in theology, but he did not object to its ordering of State and society. If his objection were political, then he would be acting like the German Christians—that is, politically. "That is precisely what one cannot and may not do!"[8]

The issue from the beginning for Barth was the freedom of the Word of God in the church. He opposed Gogarten because he thought Gogarten was introducing alien themes that compromised the absolute priority of the Word of God. When Gogarten joined the German Christian movement, Barth believed it was due precisely to the alien themes Gogarten had introduced into theology. He decisively severed all relations with Gogarten, and he just as decisively resisted the German Christians who were trying to bring the German Protestant church into line with the new regime. The source of his break with Gogarten, the source of his resistance to the German Christians, was consistently theological, not political.

One must believe that Barth concurred with his friend Thurneysen in a comment Thurneysen made as he resigned alongside Barth from *Between the Times*. Thurneysen wrote that it seemed to him that what the German Christians were doing was exactly the same from the right side as what the Religious Socialists had done from the left side:

> The straight and good way of the Church, however, is neither the one nor the other. . . . She only walks well when she holds herself blindly and simply to the Word of her Lord. That way, however, in the issue before us now, is sufficiently unambiguous: she gives to the State what belongs to the State

---

8. Karl Barth, "Vorwort," in *Theologische Existenz heute,* no. 5 (München: Christian Kaiser Verlag, 1933), p. 9.

without any skimming or reservation—then, however, to God what belongs to God.[9]

That statement irrepressibly reminds one of the maxim so frequently used in our time and others to shield conservative and reactionary politics from theological critique: Religion (theology) and politics must not be mixed. Moreover, the position Barth himself set forth repeatedly in 1933, as the church struggle began to take place, does not ease one's apprehensions about this connection. Even so, it would be a disservice to Barth to press the association without further comment.

Eberhard Jüngel, one of the most thorough and insightful interpreters of Barth, has written that for Barth, theology could not be a predicate of politics but politics is rightly a predicate of theology.[10] The point is subtle but clear enough. In my judgment, it is correct to say that political convictions did not serve as presuppositions of Barth's theological arguments, though that judgment has been passionately disputed. Barth's theology can no more be explained by his political preference for Social Democracy than can his later theological dispute with Emanuel Hirsch be explained by noting, as did Hirsch, that he was a Swiss "outsider." Not only did he state his own intentions in this matter without any touch of equivocation, but the most evident and straightforward interpretation of what he wrote confirms his stated intentions. Certainly, this is the case over the years we have reviewed, and it continued to be the case through the revocation of his German citizenship and his expulsion from the country in 1935.

If it is clear from his writings in this crucial time and in his activities in the church struggle that politics was not a presupposition for his theology, it is not so clear that politics was a predicate of his theology. Theologically, he seems to have been exclusively concerned with the purity of the church's message and unwilling to address purely political issues.

From the beginning, we have noted Barth's relentless impulse to think of God in contrast to the world. His view of God as the

9. Thurneysen in a concurring postscript to Barth's "Abschied," p. 549.
10. Eberhard Jüngel, *Karl Barth, a Theological Legacy,* trans. Garrett E. Paul (Philadelphia: The Westminster Press, 1986), pp. 41, 104.

Wholly Other, his intense and unyielding sense for the judgment of God on everything human, and the dominant position of eschatology in his theology gave his opponents cause to criticize his theology for not yielding a positive theological ethics. "A plague on both your houses," they argued, is unhelpful as an answer to the pressing ethical question. Gogarten thought such an ethical indifference was the inevitable result of Barth's speaking about God objectively rather than in relation to human beings.

On the other side, as we have seen, Barth often asserted the contrary. His stunning 1919 lecture at Tambach on "The Christian's Place in Society" is a primary example. Nowhere, however, did he set forth theological foundations for ethics more concisely and clearly than in a 1926 lecture to an ecumenical conference on home missions meeting in Amsterdam. The lecture was published in *Between the Times*.[11] His title was "Church and Culture." In this address, he vigorously emphasized the dialectical themes that led his critics to charge him with ethical indifferentism, but in a tightly structured conceptuality developed through eight theses, he showed how the dialectical themes support and demand vigorous activity in the world.

He defined the church as the community instituted by God, a community of sinful people who in faith and obedience live from the Word of God. Culture he understood as the task set forth by the Word of God, the task of determining what it means to be human as that should be realized in the life of this world. Thus the theme "Church and Culture" signified the question that can be answered only in the hearing of the Word of God, the question about the meaning of this task for every person.

The heart of the essay follows in Barth's discussion of what one sees from the standpoints of creation, reconciliation, and redemption.

First, from the point of view of creation, culture is the promise given originally to human beings of what they should become. Because the church is the community of sinners who know about reconciliation, it does not forget that the God who has given reconciliation to sinners in Jesus Christ is also the Creator of humankind. It also knows that the kingdom of Christ does not

---

11. "Die Kirche und die Kultur," *Zwischen den Zeiten* 4 (1926), 363–384.

begin with the incarnation, but that the incarnate Christ is also the divine Word (the creating *Logos*) who fills heaven and earth and who in his act of reconciliation puts powerfully into play God's rightful claim upon human beings. That rightful claim is that the human being belongs to God. It includes not only the claim that God originally placed on human being but also God's original promise. "Reconciliation in Christ is the resuscitation of the lost promise. It renews the point of view of creation with its great 'Yes' to human being with its reasonableness of reason."[12] So the church is bound together with culture in the promise it has rediscovered in Christ's reconciliation.

From the point of view of reconciliation, Barth saw culture as the law of God in view of which the sinner sanctified by God has to exercise his or her faith and obedience. It is always the sinner, and thus the one absolutely distinguished from God, who lives in the world under this law. Moreover, the reconciled person is invisible to the world. Both of these themes are characteristic of Barth from *The Epistle to the Romans* on. But here he clearly stated that the norm for human activity for those who are reconciled is the law, and the law refers to humanity as such. Gogarten considered "humanity" an "ideal" and rejected it because he thought it implied the autonomous individualism characteristic of Anglo-American democracy. Barth, on the contrary, claimed that "the command of the positive revelation here comes precisely together with the command of natural right or justice."[13] This law demands realization. It posits a higher and lower, a better and worse, of activity, all of which, of course, has fallen into sin.

The content of that law is always and without remainder culture, as Barth has defined it. It has to do with human beings in their corporate life and mutual responsibility. The law does not tell us it can be accomplished, and the obedient person, who knows himself or herself as a sinner, knows it cannot be accomplished. But obedience never asks whether it can achieve what is required; otherwise, it would not be obedience. One does what one must without calculation. Barth concluded his presentation of this thesis with the comment: "Woe to the church when it does not

---

12. Ibid., p. 373.
13. Ibid., p. 375.

proclaim this obedience. It would betray the Gospel with the Law, itself with culture."[14]

In contrast to reconciliation, Barth understood redemption to be the future and final eschatological event. Thus the point of view from redemption is the far side of human history. From that point of view, culture is the limit God has set for human beings on the other side of which God makes everything new in the fulfillment of the promise given in creation. Like most of his critics, Barth was willing to talk about the new creation, but for him one could speak about it only in faith, that is, eschatologically. Here the utter difference between God and human being comes into play again. Human beings do not bring forth the kingdom of God. That kingdom is the promise of God and our hope in God. Anything we do stands between promise and fulfillment and thus is under judgment. Barth's position does not lead to ethical indifferentism. He understood that reconciliation and the demand of God require human beings to be human with and to each other. He must have thought the application of this directive would be self-evident to anyone who took the revelation seriously.

In view of the clarity of this essay, it is not astonishing that Barth insisted in "Theological Existence Today!" that we must undertake theology "as if nothing had happened." The doing of theology is always pertinent to the ethical question no matter what the current situation may be, and it remains always the same task. In this essay, as less clearly in other places, he had coherently, from his point of view, argued in effect that theology yields politics or, to use Jüngel's felicitous phrase, that politics is a predicate of theology.

What is astonishing is that Barth did not in 1933 and the months following use what he had developed in this essay (and elsewhere) to make a judgment about the political situation. He may have considered such a judgment self-evident. Even so, it is the case that in 1933 he addressed politics as a predicate to his theology only with reference to ecclesiastical affairs.

Gogarten, on the other hand, showed no such reluctance. Moreover, at least with respect to his intentions, Jüngel's apho-

---

14. Ibid., p. 376.

rism about theology and politics in Barth seems to apply as well and more explicitly to Gogarten. Even before 1933, Gogarten was speaking and writing about political issues, most thoroughly in his book *Political Ethics*.[15] In this 1932 work, he consistently inferred what he said about politics from his basic theological themes, but the position to which he came clearly favored National Socialism.

There are ambiguities about his orientation. We have already seen that in his response to Barth's departure from *Between the Times* he explained that he identified himself with the German Christians because he thought that was where he could exercise significant influence and because one needed to be on the inside and take them seriously "in order to be able to stand against them in the name of the gospel if they overstep their boundaries."[16] However, Gogarten apparently was no darling of the right-wing movement. There is evidence that before Hitler was named Chancellor in January of 1933, students oriented to National Socialism had protested Gogarten's teaching, and colleagues in theology called for his dismissal because he did not conform with the *volkisch* movement. Further, some have reported that Gogarten's books would have been burned in 1933 had not the director of the Protestant theological library prevented students from taking them off the shelves.[17] We know that in late 1933, after the notorious rally of German Christians at the Sport Palace in Berlin, Gogarten publicly distanced himself from the German Christian movement. Further, in 1936 he signed with several others a ringing criticism of the radical German Christians in Thuringia.

On the other side, his five books and eight articles between 1933 and 1937 give support to his at best qualified Yes to the Nazi regime. His alignments were consistent with his writings. In 1933,

15. Friedrich Gogarten, *Politische Ethik: Versuch einer Grundlegung* (Jena: Eugen Diedrichs Verlag, 1932).
16. From Gogarten's letter to Georg Merz, editor of *Zwischen den Zeiten*. Merz quoted Gogarten's statement in the response he wrote to Barth's "Abschied." *Zwischen den Zeiten* 11 (1933), 552.
17. Karl-Wilhelm Thyssen, *Begegnung und Verantwortung: Der Weg der Theologie Friedrich Gogartens von den Anfängen bis zum Zweiten Weltkrieg* (Tübingen: J. C. B. Mohr [Paul Siebeck], 1970), p. 223. Thyssen reported these items on the basis of conversations with Gogarten, and the dean of the Protestant faculty at that time, Lonicer, confirmed them to Thyssen "in all points."

he joined the editorial board of a new journal, *German Theology,* which began publication in 1934. All of his colleagues on the board supported the new regime, and some of them—for example, Heinrich Bornkamm, Gerhard Kittel, and Emanuel Hirsch— announced their unqualified and "joyous Yes" to "the great turning-point." The journal announced as its intention "to embrace all circles that attend to the obligation that comes from the gospel and from the turning point in Germany's fate brought about by National Socialism to struggle for an ecclesiastically responsible, reality-oriented Protestant theology that is bound to the *Volk.*"[18]

After 1937, Gogarten fell silent. He published nothing more until 1948, three years after the Third Reich and Germany were destroyed.

Gogarten's private and more comprehensive orientation to the Third Reich is a puzzle that likely will never be solved, but the development of his theology and of his political theology until 1937 is a public record. We have already noted the emergence of three themes that gave Barth pause. We need now to trace the development more fully and to test its coherence.

When the world of yesterday, the modern world that culminated in the Great War, fell apart for Gogarten, he came to believe that the problem with that world had been the ideal of individual autonomy and further that there was a fundamental contradiction between individual autonomy and Christian faith. Karl Barth's *Epistle to the Romans* was for him the breakthrough to the authentic theological recovery of Christian faith because it took the subject matter of theology, God, with unyielding seriousness. Consequently, it revealed the life and death crisis in which human beings stand. Individual autonomy is the symptom of radical sin because it does not acknowledge the chasm between God as the Wholly Other and human beings. Faith is the acknowledgment that God is Lord and that one is, in all one's self-initiated willing and acting, characterized to the core of one's being by sin. This is the case both with the good things we attempt and the evil we do. Sin is not a moralistic category. It has to do

---

18. Reported in *Theologische Blätter* 13, no. 1 (January 1934), 27.

with not recognizing the absolute Lordship (*Herrschaft*) of God. That is what disobedience to God means, and on that disobedience God must and does pronounce a deadly No.

God's Yes can be heard only in Jesus Christ, who reconciled sinful human beings to God. To be reconciled means as sinful persons to be justified or made whole by grace through faith. In faith, they acknowledge the Lordship of God, submit themselves to the authority of God, and recognize themselves as sinners. The dialectic of God's Yes and No is not Yes to this and No to that, but No to the human being as such and Yes to the human being as such.

Thus far we see a basic identity between Gogarten and Barth. Looking backward, however, we can detect nuanced differences in emphasis that would have been all but unnoticeable at the beginning. Whereas for Barth the dominant image for God was the "Wholly Other," for Gogarten it was "Lord" (*Herr*). Consequently, for Barth the dialectic of Yes and No was propelled primarily by the sharp contrast he drew between time and eternity, whereas for Gogarten it was more strongly propelled by the total claim that God, the Lord, has on human beings as expressed by "the law," which demands absolute obedience. The obedience is absolute in the sense that it demands the whole self of the human being rather than specific acts. Thus it is not first of all what a person does that alienates her or him from God, but what a person is (i.e., a person who wants always to be autonomous).

If we reflect about the apparently modest difference between a preference for speaking of God as "Wholly Other" and a preference for "Lord," we can project theological tracks that grew more distant from one another. We can see how Barth moved to an understanding of theology as the knowledge of God given in God's self-revelation. Theology, most properly, is dogmatics, the object of which is God, and the dogmatician must strive to protect the elaboration of the self-revelation of God from adulteration by human elements. The entrée to dogmatics, which is also the first act of faith, is the acceptance of God's self-revelation. Even the acceptance of the revelation is God's act.

On the other hand, we can see how Gogarten's emphasis on the Lordship (*Herrschaft*) of God pointed already to thinking of God in relation to human beings. Lordship means to be Lord over something—in this case, over the whole of creation and most particularly over human beings. We can also see how each image for the divine conjures up immediately a corresponding conception of the human being. To know God as Lord means, at the same time, to know oneself as subject. To know the absolute claim of God means, at the same time, to know oneself as a person who stands under that absolute claim and is hopelessly at odds with it. The movement of thought is not from the knowledge of a universal human condition, known by revelation, to the application of that human condition to oneself. Rather, it is an understanding of the self that is immediately bound up with belief in God and by inference applies to the whole human race.

Further, to have faith in the grace of God in Jesus Christ is to have one's consciousness transformed such that one understands oneself as a sinner who is accepted by God—that is, received into a life-giving relationship with the almighty Lord. Thus Christian faith transforms the life of the person in the world. It has discernible effects immediate in human life that are no less discernible because the person so affected knows herself or himself as still unqualified for God's grace and able therefore to receive it only as a gift. The proclamation of the grace of God in Jesus Christ invites one to receive one's life as a gift from God. Faith, then, is an event in the life of the person who so responds to the proclamation, but it is taken as a miracle in the sense that the person can understand it only as a gift of God. Faith is not a miracle in the sense that one accepts the self-revelation of God and asserts that this acceptance is itself the action of the Holy Spirit.

This way of Gogarten, then, does not develop theology as the knowledge of God explicated in the form of dogmatics, but rather as history—that is, the descriptive internal history of the encounter between God and human beings in the world and of the ensuing character of the life of the person of faith in the world. That life in the world can be nothing other than the wish, coming from the basic determination of the self in faith, to live for the other, which is the antithesis of individualistic autonomy. Faith and ethics, therefore, are inseparably bound up with one another: the command to love God is, at the same time, the command to love the neighbor.

As the 1920s neared their end, Gogarten began to develop the inferences yielded by his understanding of faith. Faith in Jesus Christ is an event. That is, it is historical. Therefore, God is concerned for human history. Faith in Jesus Christ means to understand oneself as alienated from God, characterized by radical sin. Therefore, all human beings are guilty of radical sin. Faith in Jesus Christ leads one to understand oneself as subject to the Lordship of God. Thus all are subject to the Lordship of God. Just as one comes to see oneself as a creature of God, so God is the Creator of the human race, indeed, the whole world. This world, then, is alienated from God and is under the power of sin, which shows itself as the autonomous rejection of all authority. By providence, God has graciously built into creation restraints on the unbounded exercise of that autonomy so that human beings might be prevented from wantonly destroying each other. This gracious ordering of creation is displayed in the family, the people (*Volk*), and, above all, the State. These are "Orders of Creation," but unlike other thinkers who spoke about the Orders of Creation, Gogarten saw them as Orders of Sin (that is, orders ordained to restrain sin) recognizable as such only in faith. Faith, then, leads one to affirm these Orders, to give God thanks for them, and to work in the world for their enhancement. It is the role of the State to preserve and enhance the life of the *Volk,* and it can do this only by the exercise of authority and coercion—that is, Lordship. The enemy of the divinely given Order of the State is the same as the antithesis of faith: individualistic autonomy. On the basis of this conviction, Gogarten came to despise Franco-Anglo-American democracy, the abstract Enlightenment ideal of Humanity, and, specifically, the Bill of Rights. Thus he became convinced that the Weimar Republic was hopeless. On the basis of it, he came to the conviction that Germany's hope lay in the establishment of an authoritarian State that would be both National and Social, and on this basis he gave an at least qualified Yes to the assumption of power by Adolf Hitler.

Martin Buber, probably the most creative and influential Jewish theologian of the twentieth century and a contemporary in Germany of Gogarten, pointed to a fatal flaw in Gogarten's thought. In a little book, *The Question to the Single One* [the

Individual], Buber dealt briefly with Gogarten's *Political Ethics* of 1932. Buber developed this book from an address he gave to students from the three German-speaking Swiss universities at the close of 1933. His book was published in Germany in 1936, "astonishingly," as Buber put it, "since it attacks the life-basis of totalitarianism."[19] Buber commented about Gogarten's work:

> I do not see how his [the person's] being unredeemed can be broken off from its dialectic connexion with redemption . . . and used separately. Nor do I see how the concept of being evil can be translated from the realm of being "before God" into that of being before earthly authorities, and yet retain its radical nature.[20]

If one understands faith as relational, an event in the life of the human being, it is legitimate and purely descriptive to note that persons of faith will extend what they want to say about God in relation to themselves, to God in relation to all others and to the world. But these extensions (all human beings are characterized by radical sin; God is Creator and Lord of the world, and so forth) do not then become truths independent of the relationship known in faith, and no further inferences may be drawn from them.

Consonant with Buber's analysis, we may also observe that when Gogarten took the step of establishing the inferences of faith as truths independent of the relationship and from which further inferences may be drawn, he lost the dialectic. That is, he lost the principle of criticism with reference to the Orders of Creation. Although now and again he exercised a measure of caution, the way by which he arrived at what he said about family, *Volk,* and State as Orders of Creation did not require him constantly to see them as ambiguous, that is, not only as given by God for the well-being of human kind (the Yes) but also as susceptible to perversion by human beings (the No).

As we have noted, Gogarten fell silent in 1937, two years before Hitler invaded Poland, launching the Second World War. He

---

19. Martin Buber, *Between Man and Man,* trans. Ronald Gregor Smith (Boston: Beacon Press, 1955), p. vii.

20. Ibid., p. 77.

published nothing for eleven years. After 1948, books and articles again flowed from his pen, and he once again became one of the more influential voices in Protestant theology, not only in Germany. His postwar theology shows continuity with themes he developed earlier, but the extension of the general inferences he drew from faith as relational is missing.

10

THE DEHN AFFAIR

A CLASH BETWEEN BARTH AND HIRSCH

The infamous "Dehn affair" poignantly illustrates the instability of German society and the destabilizing tactics of German "patriots" and Nazi-oriented young people in the years immediately preceding 1933. It is also the prelude to the public clash between Karl Barth and Emanuel Hirsch.

Günther Dehn was a Lutheran pastor who, in the 1920s, became relatively widely known for his concern about social structures that led to oppressive poverty. For a number of years, he was pastor in a tenement district of Berlin. In his judgment, only socialism promised a structural solution to the plight of laborers. He was a member of the moderate Socialist party. One remembers the statement of Walter Benjamin, a gifted Jewish literary critic of the time: "It was a great advance in my understanding when for the first time poverty dawned on me in the ignominy of poorly paid work."[1] Dehn recognized that ignominy and firmly believed that the Christian gospel impelled believers to work for structural changes in society that would alleviate it.

He was present for the Tambach Conference in 1919 at which

---

1. Walter Benjamin, *Schriften,* vol. 1 (Frankfurt am Main: Suhrkamp Verlag, 1955), p. 632. Translated by Hannah Arendt in her introduction to Walter Benjamin, *Illuminations* (New York: Schocken Books, 1969), p. 29.

179

Barth spoke on "The Christian's Place in Society," and he experienced this lecture as "a great liberation." "In my mind's eye I saw at once a really free church—free because it was bound solely to God in God's revelation."[2] From that time on, he read Barth avidly and in his own way appropriated Barth's theology.

In 1928, Dehn was invited to lecture in the Ulrich's Church in Magdeburg at a meeting on "The Church and the Reconciliation of Peoples (*Völker*)." His assigned topic was "The Christian and the War." What he said evoked an uproar and was not forgotten by those who did not like what he said. His basic theme was that the message of the Bible is peace but that we who hear the message are sinners. He referred to the teaching on the Orders of Creation (which he called "unorders") and criticized them as egoistic, giving unwarranted encouragement to nationalistic feeling and, especially, to the armaments industry. The transformation of this faulty world will come only at the end of time as God's eschatological act, but to place one's final hope in God does not mean that Christians should and can do nothing in the meantime. Christians should try to view the past war as nonpartisan observers following the rule that what Germans claim for themselves they must grant also to their opponents. Above all, that means they should not romanticize the war or give it a Christian face. Along the way, he noted that those who were killed were also trying to kill others. To draw a parallel between Germans who were killed in action and the deaths of Christian martyrs is therefore impossible. He defended Germany's role in the war as self-defense, but the position he developed was a moderate pacifism. Most of all, he wanted to overcome militarism. In the ensuing discussion, a young woman in the audience accused him of calling Germany's fallen

---

2. Dehn, *Die alte Zeit, die vorigen Jahre,* p. 221. It is interesting to note that the Tambach Conference was not Dehn's first meeting with Barth. In his candidate year before ordination, Dehn and a good friend and fellow candidate had traveled to Switzerland to visit points of ecclesiastical interest. In Bern, they were invited to dinner at the home of Professor Fritz Barth. Dehn was seated for dinner next to Professor Barth's son, Karl, who was a theological student. Dehn recalled that he would gladly have discussed Swiss ecclesiastical and theological issues with Barth, but Barth was interested in nothing beyond activities in his student fraternity, the Zofinga. Dehn, who was opposed to student fraternities, was unimpressed with Barth. "At that time there was no indication of future greatness." Ibid., p. 143.

heroes "murderers," and others vilified him for not having dealt with the "lie" about Germany's war guilt.

The reaction to his speech was so strong that the local church consistory felt it had to review the matter. Although it chose not to discipline Dehn, it did suggest that he was in collusion with the leftist press that had given a lot of publicity to the issue, and it expressed sympathies for those who had been offended by what Dehn had said.

About two years later, at the end of 1930, Dehn was invited to be Professor of Practical Theology at Heidelberg. The faculty was unanimous in its support of the appointment until a right-wing journal objected and printed material that tried to damage Dehn. The dean of the Heidelberg faculty asked Dehn for a clarification of the proceedings in Magdeburg. After Dehn's account was reviewed, six of the seven faculty members voted that Dehn was unsuitable to teach German youth.[3]

The following year, Dehn was invited to a similar position on the faculty at Halle. The faculty there had not included Dehn on its list of acceptable candidates, but the Minister of Culture, who had the authority to make the final appointment, sent the list back to the faculty asking for someone who had a sense of identity with the proletariat. The faculty thought Dehn had not sufficiently distinguished himself with scholarly publications but agreed that Dehn would not be unbearable.

When his appointment was made public, resistance began. The Higher Education Group of the National Socialist German Student Union published a flyer against him. The university senate forbade further student action, but two weeks later the students demonstrated against Dehn. Dehn was put on leave for his first semester. That was in the spring of 1931.

In the fall of 1931, as Dehn was prepared to begin his teaching, action against him intensified. Students threatened to leave Halle, objecting to Dehn and to what they called "police action" against themselves. The president of the university and the university senate stood behind Dehn. Students from several associations clamored more loudly.

---

3. The one who continued to support Dehn was Martin Dibelius, Professor of New Testament and Bultmann's closest colleague outside Marburg.

Dehn was scheduled to give his first lecture on November 3 at five in the afternoon. Opponents packed the lecture hall and refused to let him speak. The president came with the police. He rescheduled the lecture for the next day at eight in the evening, hoping that only those who wanted to hear Dehn would take the trouble to come. The president was present and threatened disciplinary measures against any who disrupted. The lecture took place. However, the nationalistic student federations vowed to continue their demonstrations until Dehn was gone, and various organizations began to demand the president's resignation.

A few days later, the nontenured younger instructors announced their support for the students who objected to Dehn. They criticized these students for their methods but praised their motivations. Students from Halle and other nearby universities poured into Jena and held a mass demonstration against Dehn and the Minister of Culture, and vowed to keep up their resistance until Dehn resigned. The theologians in Halle, meanwhile, maintained neutrality but asked for a second Professor of Practical Theology.

In the middle of that same month (November 1931), Karl Barth, Karl Ludwig Schmidt, the editor of *Theological Leaves,* and Professors Martin Dibelius, Otto Piper, and Georg Wünsch published a statement in support of Dehn.[4] A few days later, a second professorial declaration in support of Dehn came out in *The Christian World.* Among others, it was signed by Rudolf Bultmann and Hans von Soden, the dean of the theological faculty in Marburg. The statement indicated that the Marburg faculty was unanimous in its support of Dehn.

The furor died down, and Dehn was able to lecture in peace. But a few weeks later, just before Christmas, he published a collection of documents on the Magdeburg incident. A postscript he wrote for the collection rekindled the flames. Among other things, he said that distorted idealism is demonry, and he declared that fanatical love of the fatherland, tinged with pseudoreligious coloring, would lead the country to perdition. Student opposition became more vocal and disruptive, and the students were now fully joined by a group of the younger instructors. Professors from

---

4. Wünsch later modified his support "on theological grounds."

various parts of Germany entered the fray against Dehn. The church, under the leadership of Bishop Otto Dibelius, remained silent.

The Minister of Culture agreed to appoint a second Professor of Practical Theology as an alternative to Dehn. Dehn was then able to lecture in the spring and summer of 1932 without disruption, but he was denied the right to preach in the university church. At the conclusion of the summer 1932 semester, Dehn was given a year's leave of absence. In the course of that year, Hitler gained total power. Günther Dehn was one of the first professors to be dismissed by the new regime.[5]

Among the professors from other universities who supported the objections to Dehn was Emanuel Hirsch. With a colleague in theology at Göttingen, Hermann Dörries, he published a statement on January 27, 1932. They declared that they had thus far stayed out of the affair because as outsiders their intervention could only be disruptive. Nor did they intervene when Dehn's colleagues imposed a truce that properly censured the unruly conduct of the students but did not add a word of understanding for "the passionate Yes to *Volk* and freedom which stood behind the students' objection."[6] However, now that Dehn had broken the truce, while the students, with one exception, maintained their academic discipline, Hirsch and Dörries felt impelled to speak out. They made two points.

First, they said that one cannot consider the Dehn case under the rubric of academic freedom. Dehn was not proposed by the faculty. The Minister of Culture returned the faculty's original list with no critique whatsoever of the names on that list on the grounds of academic incompetence. Moreover, the Minister of Culture disregarded faculty objections to Dehn on the ground of academic incompetence. In such a situation, it is not possible to

---

5. In giving this account of the "Dehn Affair," I have drawn on the essay by Ernst Bizer, "Der 'Fall Dehn,' " in *Festschrift für Günther Dehn,* ed. Wilhelm Schneemelcher (Neukirchen: Verlag der Buchhandlung des Erziehungsvereins Neukirchen Kreis Moers, 1957), pp. 239–261.
6. The Hirsch-Dörries declaration was published first in the German university newspaper of January 31, 1932. It was republished in the magazine *Deutsches Volkstum* (1932), 285–286.

view the objections of the students as a breach of academic freedom. On the contrary, the students were appealing to the right of self-government by German academicians.

Second, in view of the present-day ethical confusion about the war question on the part of the German people and German Christians, no theological professor can be denied the right to speak to the issue in an effort to clarify consciences. That right cannot be denied even to Dehn, "who comes to an ethically false conclusion." But one can require the pacifist Dehn to acknowledge that the nation, its freedom, and its fragile condition are values sanctified by God and that these values call forth the total surrender of heart and life. Further, one can demand that he avow the passionate will to freedom in our *Volk* that is "enslaved and shamed by power-mad and avaricious enemies." The German youth have opposed Dehn because they miss in him this acknowledgment and this avowal. They asserted that the postscript Dehn appended to his recent work proved them right. In that postscript, he called their Yes to *Volk* and freedom demonry and urged resistance to it in the name of God. He has thereby destroyed any effectiveness he might have had as an educator of young German men.

Hirsch and Dörries ended their statement by proclaiming their unity with the youth and their thanks to them for the new hope they were giving Germany in the precarious situation of "our *Volk*."

Karl Barth entered the fray with an article in the *Frankfurter Zeitung* of February 15, 1932, "Why Not Fight the Battle Along the Entire Line? The Dehn Affair and Dialectical Theology."[7] He began by noting that a few months earlier, he and others had declared their support of Dehn "both personally and substantially." As the affair grew more intense, he noticed that the objections to Dehn were exclusively political. He decided that he, as a born Swiss, though he had lived in Germany for ten years, should stay out of the controversy to avoid misunderstanding.[8]

---

7. See p. 6.
8. When Barth was given a regular professorial appointment in Münster, he was also awarded German citizenship. He did not, however, surrender his Swiss citizenship.

But recently, he added, the affair has taken a new turn that has impelled him to enter the discussion. He referred to the declaration by Hirsch and Dörries. He put two questions to his former Göttingen colleagues: (1) If you really want to fight about the Dehn case, should you not conduct your battle on a much broader front? Should you not acknowledge that the underlying issue is theological and has specifically to do with Dialectical Theology? (2) If you want to take the matter seriously, should you not rise above the passions of the moment and conduct your battle on the basis of theological science? He ended this introduction with the comment: "I hope evermore that one will permit even the born Swiss—he has nevertheless lived these past ten years in Germany—at least these questions." Then he explained the questions.

First: Your enemy is not only Günther Dehn! Barth noted that what seemed to raise the greatest outcry in Dehn's Magdeburg address was the connections Dehn had made between murder, capital punishment, killing in self-defense, and killing in war. Barth said he himself first made these connections in lectures on theological ethics at the University of Münster in 1928, lectures he repeated at the University of Bonn in 1930. In neither case was there an uproar, even though he was aware that among the 250 listeners at Bonn were a good many National Socialist and similarly oriented students. Why has Dehn been singled out rather than he himself? Barth claimed that Dehn was only following his (Barth's) theological line of thought. The issue, he insisted, has to do and must have to do with the theology Dehn represents. That, he said, is the theology that has been given the tag "Dialectical Theology" or "Theology of Crisis." The remarks Dehn made that offended some can be understood only in connection with that theology. It is, therefore, he added, improper to attack Dehn and things he said rather than to deal with the grounding of these remarks in Dialectical Theology. Dehn, he asserted, is perhaps not at all the one you want to meet in battle. Barth directed this challenge to Hirsch and Dörries. Because they are theologians, he reasoned, more is expected from them than a focus on Dehn as a person and on a few of his statements abstracted from their contexts.

Second: Let the discussion be passionate but scientific![9] If the old and the young opponents of Dehn, he began, are to fulfill his first request, then they must be open to his second question. If it is to be a theological battle (i.e., with Dialectical Theology), then it has to be conducted in the sphere of scientific theology. If so, the statements by Dehn that raised such an outcry should not be the focus but (1) his arguments for them, (2) their grounding in his theology, and (3) Dialectical Theology as such. It is the latter that should be tested for the claim to truth that Dehn made for his statements. Barth insisted that only in this scientific way can one make a negative judgment about Dehn's address or his later publication. He observed that no one, including Hirsch and Dörries, had yet done that. All of them, he observed, have focused only on catchwords.

He boldly quoted: "The barbarians plunder the whole field of slaughter. Must it be?" Then he called to mind a particularly barbaric statement Hitler had recently made against "theoreticians," which students republished in the newspaper of Halle University, and commented: "If that statement is taken seriously by the Halle students and the professors who defend them, then I consider myself to have been slapped on the mouth." It would mean, he said, that all discussion is at an end. He could not believe that was what those who oppose Dehn intended. He could not believe that for them the only important matter was—here he repeated a piece of the citation from Hitler—"that no one take the power away from us." Such could not possibly be the case with those who oppose Dehn if they are willing to trace to the foundation what it is in Dehn that bothers them.

So, he challenged, let the discussion take place passionately but scientifically in order to show that even in theology "we can distinguish black from white." Everyone, he said, needs to see that it requires really difficult work to put together a truly comprehensible case for or against Dehn.

Then he concluded his article: Is it thinkable, he asked, that the

---

9. In Germany, the terms "science" and "scientific" have a broader reference than they have in English-speaking countries. They refer to any rigorous intellectual discipline, therefore also to work in what we call "the Humanities," and therefore also to work in theology.

students who raised no outcry at my lectures on theological ethics understood that hard, scientific work is required to make a case and that one simply does not flay away at catchwords? Is it possible that the further course of the Dehn affair might proceed from the same understanding? Then he referred specifically to his former colleague, Hirsch, with whom he feared he could agree neither theologically nor politically, but he expressed his hope that for both Hirsch and Dörries, theology was the primary interest and not politics.

A week and a half later, Hirsch responded in the right-wing journal *Deutsches Volkstum,* edited by his friend Wilhelm Stapel.[10] He objected to Barth's implication that he and Dörries had agreed entirely with the students. He pointed out that they had distinguished between the students' methods and their spirit. He denied that either the students or he and Dörries were motivated by "party politics." He and Dörries had foresworn all party affiliations, and the students had various political persuasions.

He chided Barth for thinking they opposed Dehn because he was an advocate of Dialectical Theology and suggested that Barth was too touchy and polemical on the matter. It is not, he said, Dehn's mode of theology that has convinced them that Dehn could not be effective as a teacher of German youth. He insisted that he and Dörries affirmed the freedom of theology.

Hirsch thought Barth's Swiss identity was a more serious problem. Hirsch considered this identity Barth's "national decision." He had no objection, but he was convinced it made Barth incapable of understanding the German situation. "You have never had to understand sympathetically a German mother who earnestly had to consider the possibility that the bones of her son had been cast by some Belgian farmer into the manure heap." Hirsch was enraged that Barth had charged fallen German soldiers with having broken the commandment not to kill.

Hirsch then addressed Barth's two points. First, the theological foundations on which Barth and Dehn base their position on the war

---

10. "Offener Brief an Karl Barth," *Deutsches Volkstum* (1932), 266–272.

issue. Hirsch pointed out that Dialectical Theology had been discussed repeatedly, not least of all by himself. He thought Barth was guilty of an overweening sense of self-importance. Not only has Barth's Romans commentary become only a vague memory, but there are Dialectical Theologians who have developed political ethics that are like the political ethics of Althaus or himself.[11] "It is a falsification of the facts when you assert that Dehn's case has to do finally with Dialectical Theology." It has to do rather with two one-sided theologians, one a Swiss and the other a person of limited powers who has made an affair for theology and the church.

Second, with respect to Barth's demand that the issue should be discussed scientifically, Hirsch reminded Barth that he had done precisely that in his book *Germany's Destiny*, that he had been affirmed by many, and that others had also written scientific works in theology sympathetic to the plight of the German *Volk*. Dehn, he said, had not only ignored that body of literature but had produced nothing scientifically substantial of his own. He cautioned Barth to protect himself from "hangers on." He reminded Barth that Christian faith has to do with the totality of one's life in the presence of God. That radical character of faith, he thought, leads one to question whether objective scientific criteria are appropriate for all issues. In any case it leads one to know that one must always make a decision about the divine claim with respect to one's own particular life situation. He and Dörries, he added, are entirely willing to affirm the freedom of "all truthful theological thinking" on the issues raised in this affair, but they set as a condition that any theologian who deals with them must be existentially engaged and bound up with the German *Volk*.

Hirsch took note of the statement by Hitler that Barth had quoted. He granted that if such a statement had been made by a theologian, he would have been horrified. What Barth failed to

---

11. In the summer of 1931, Hirsch and Paul Althaus published a joint statement in which they complained of the "murderous politics" and the "war" being waged against Germany by its enemies. They warned, "The end of this frightful war in the midst of peace that has been continuing now for twelve years can, if it is kept going only a little longer, bring about the destruction of our *Volk*." The statement was reprinted by Karl Ludwig Schmidt in *Theologische Blätter* 10 (June 1931), 177–178. Schmidt commented that he held the Hirsch-Althaus statement to be "theologically, politically and humanly" impossible.

consider, however, was the statement's context, the necessity to resist intellectuals who are alienated from the *Volk*. Barth should have the circumspection to notice how close he was to those detached intellectuals. We, he concluded, are right to insist on engagement and to learn from our youth about the Yes to the German *Volk* and their freedom.

Barth's answer and a final reply from Hirsch were published together a month later in *Deutsches Volkstum*.[12] Barth insisted that what he had written made personal references out of place. He referred to his effort to be a good German as well as a good Swiss and pledged to leave such considerations aside. He expressed his astonishment that Hirsch had entirely overlooked the main subject of his article and repeated the thrust of what he had written, quoting his last sentence: "I hope, however, that your and my primary interest belongs to theology and not to politics." He found nothing in Hirsch's statement that dealt either explicitly or implicitly with theology. On the contrary, he charged that Hirsch's passion lay entirely in his political confession of faith, and he gave several illustrations of his point.

Barth said he should have known better than to expect Hirsch to answer theologically. He should have known from Hirsch's works, which he had read, that Hirsch could do nothing but continue to insist on the identity of theology and politics, to claim that obedience to God means to have an "existential connection with the German *Volk*," and not to acknowledge any "over and beyond," not God, not gospel, not church, not even law, which might stand over against the Yes from however pure a human will. He said he should not have expected from Hirsch a theology that in the face of politics does not become politics but remains theology. Hirsch's thought, he claimed, was the necessary consequence of following the presupposition of Karl Holl's interpretation of Luther. He said he would not again make the mistake of expecting Hirsch to discuss an issue in a genuinely theological way.

Perhaps, he added, he might dare to make that mistake again

---

12. Barth, "Antwort an Emanuel Hirsch," and Emanuel Hirsch, "Antwort von Emanuel Hirsch an den Herausgeber," *Deutsches Volkstum* (1932), 390–394 and 394–395.

even at the risk of Hirsch's scorn. He might remind Hirsch that genuine theological passion begins where passions such as those that surround the Dehn case end, and he might challenge Hirsch with the thesis that genuine theological passion can serve, finally, the interest of politics or even "the life necessities of the German *Volk*."

Although Barth had written his response in the form of a letter, addressing Hirsch as his "colleague" and ending it with a friendly greeting and "Yours, Karl Barth," Hirsch could not bring himself to address Barth directly. He wrote an answer in the form of a letter to the editor, Wilhelm Stapel, indicating that he would not have responded at all except for Stapel's request. What he wrote was entirely on the personal level.

He considered Barth's letter final proof of his claim that Barth, a Swiss, who has not put himself in the position "of us imperial Germans," not only cannot understand a German Christian in the present situation but, now he must add, does not want to understand. If a German Christian does not see things as Barth sees them, he charged, then Barth no longer takes that person seriously as a theologian and a Christian. He said he could no longer honor Barth when Barth sees in all his theological work only a mask for a German politician. He had asked Barth not to confuse the Swiss perspective on German affairs with his dialectical theological theses and not to mix Dialectical Theology with international hypotheses. He wanted to warn Barth against the misuse of religious and Christian categories in opposition to the Germans' affirmation of freedom and *Volk*, but that is exactly what Barth did. Then he wrote, Barth "is thereby only making a moment of German theology and the church out of the limits of his powers," the same cutting comment he had made about Günther Dehn. He repeated that only German theologians and Christians can judge the matter and declared that he stood firm in spite of all attacks on his Christian or theological or even human honor. He pledged that he would give himself to his post as a professor of theology, try to serve his church, and lay the German reality at the feet of God, come what may.

"The Dehn Affair" was a dismal moment as the Weimar Republic expired and the Third Reich sprang to life. The Barth-Hirsch exchange was a depressing addendum to it.

11

ON MEMBERSHIP IN THE SOCIALIST PARTY

BARTH VERSUS TILLICH

When Barth entered the fracas over Günther Dehn with his article in the *Frankfurter Zeitung,* he did not request that the battle take place without passion, only that the passion be centered on theology rather than politics. Barth himself was indeed passionate about theology, and it shows in all his printed works. It is likely that no other theologian has ever used such a variety of printed devices to indicate emphasis: italics, capitalization, spaced letters, and the frequent use of the exclamation point. Even so, although he seemed quite definite about every point he made theologically, he had sufficient circumspection to realize that he might not have gotten things right. When his German publisher urged him to permit a second printing of *The Epistle to the Romans,* he chose instead to rewrite the whole book, and after he published a first volume of *Christian Dogmatics in Outline,* he set that project aside and started anew with the *Church Dogmatics,* which over its long course of many volumes had more than a few new turns. But if he was unsure about his ability properly to lay hold of the subject matter, from beginning to end he had no doubt about the subject matter itself. The subject matter of theology is God as God is revealed in Jesus Christ. That revelation is recorded in the canon of Holy Scripture and witnessed to in the proclamation. There is and can be no other grounding for theology.

Therefore, from the beginning Barth was suspicious of Paul

Tillich. He thought Tillich was too attentive to culture, and he was convinced that the secular realities Tillich looked at, listened to, and participated in had substantive impact on his thought. Tillich was too philosophical, permitting philosophical reflections and categories to have substantive impact on his theological position. Tillich spoke of himself as "standing on the boundary" between religion and other phenomena, and was given to hyphens (as in "religious-social") and the copulative "and" (as in "religion and culture"), which Barth considered a perversion of genuine theology.

Tillich, on the contrary, was more generous to Barth. He criticized Dialectical Theology because in his judgment it did not get the paradox right and was not dialectical at the crucial point, namely, at the point of its own "position" or basic assumption.[1] Even so, he affirmed some of its major themes as a necessary antidote to the aridity of the old Positive (conservative) theology and the unrealistic optimism of the academic or scientifically dominant Liberal theology of the previous century. He thought of himself as a sympathetic friend and friendly outsider.

Although Tillich was generous to those in whom he found points of contact with his own position, in his thought he showed a remarkable facility for what we might call "the bear hug." That is, he appropriated others into his own conceptual view, affirming the others in ways that sometimes led the others to have trouble recognizing themselves. That observation does not diminish Tillich's stature as a theologian. Without question, he was, with the other five we are considering, among the most gifted and creative theologians of the time.

From the beginning of the post–First World War period, Tillich differed from Barth in that his circle of friends and co-workers consisted of people in the arts and in disciplines other than theology. He edited a religious-socialist journal, and his co-workers in the circle of the journal were, for the most part, not theologians. His closest colleagues at the University of Frankfurt, where he was Professor of Philosophy (Philosophical Theology, in Tillich's understanding), were Jewish.

---

1. See Chapter 5, esp. pp. 107–111.

We have noted that Barth, as a young pastor in a Swiss industrial village, joined the Social Democratic Party and was active in the Socialist cause. When Barth was called to Göttingen as Extraordinary Professor of Reformed Theology (less, not more than Professor *Ordinarius*) in 1923, he did not join the corresponding party in Germany. In 1933, Tillich had been a member of the Social Democratic Party in Germany for a few years, and he had been a leader of a group of Religious Socialists for even more.

When Hitler gained total power over Germany, he instituted repressive measures against the parties to the left, including the Social Democrats. He shut down their presses and severely confined their activities. The Social Democrats expected further repressive measures and reprisals against those on the party lists and, as a policy, recommended that all those who held government positions should resign from the party and destroy their party cards. Tillich, following party discipline, resigned; Barth, who had joined the party during the Dehn affair a year earlier, not only resolutely refused to resign but made his membership public. This divergence between Tillich and Barth evoked an exchange of letters that became public only after the Second World War.[2]

Tillich learned about Barth's decision to remain in the party during a visit with Karl Ludwig Schmidt, the editor of *Theological Leaves*. Schmidt also reported to Tillich that Barth had said about him, "Concerning the ideology of Tillich I am simply stubborn." Tillich wrote Barth. He referred to the comment and observed that Barth had made it in connection with the question of continuing membership in the Social Democratic Party. He pointed out that Barth's position on the issue was not only in opposition to his own but to that of the party as well. He told Barth the party did not want to lose its people who held official positions. Having Socialists in official positions, he explained, is more important to the party than party membership, and the party in fact is on the verge of liquidation. Tillich said his resignation had nothing to do with his "ideology" but was rather the policy and tactic of the party itself. He said he was not alone. All of his friends

---

2. The correspondence was published in *Evangelische Kommentar* 10 (1977), 111ff.

in Frankfurt and elsewhere agreed that party membership should not be made a decisive issue in the present situation. Again, he insisted, it was not a matter of his ideology but a purely tactical measure. Should the situation seriously deteriorate, then it might be necessary to stand firmly and publicly as Socialists.

Tillich hoped his letter would help Barth to see that his act was not ideological. At the end of the letter, he said he could understand Barth's position and would welcome a discussion with him on the whole matter. He noted that he would be in Berlin later in the week, where he hoped to inform himself better, and he suggested a meeting with Barth after he returned. Tillich's letter was dated March 29, 1933.

Barth responded on April 2. He said Tillich was right to connect his "obstinacy" with Tillich's "ideology." The question of continuing membership in the party was, he said, a different question for Tillich than for himself. Admitting that he had not heard the position of the party, he pointed out that the "ideology" of which he spoke was then not only Tillich's private "ideology" but that of the position, perhaps the main position, of the party. He granted Tillich the right to hold that ideology, but he wanted expressly to state that he himself could not.

He explained that membership in the SPD did not mean for him the adoption of the Socialist idea and worldview. He held any such idea or worldview to be as such incompatible with the exclusivity of the Christian confession of faith. Thus, he added, he himself had no necessary internal relation at all to "Marxism." As an idea and worldview, Marxism was as equally close and equally distant to him as the prevailing nationalism. Neither could evoke from him fear or love or trust.

He declared that membership in the SPD for him was a purely practical decision. Of the various possibilities in the present, he found the SPD best because it was the party of the working class, of democracy, of nonmilitarism, and of a conscious but rational affirmation of the German *Volk* and State. Because he did not want to leave the responsibility for this party entirely to others but to accept his own share, he joined it. Up until then he had had neither the impulse, the time, nor the request to be publicly active, and apparently it would remain that way, but not necessarily.

Then he pointed to a difference between them on the question of academic freedom. He said that a prohibition to make a confession of socialism in his teaching would be meaningless to him. His own presuppositions would not allow him to promote socialism in his teaching. On the other hand, if the State were to set limits on the subject, for example, in teaching theological ethics, then he would have to resist and take the consequences.

He considered the freedom for a purely political decision something else entirely. In this regard, being publicly recognized as a member of the SPD, in distinction from the "idea" of socialism, was important to him. That has to do, he said, with his life in the world, and "anyone who does not want me in that respect cannot have me at all." He would no longer be credible to himself or to others ("even to theologians") if he allowed a decision to be imposed on him in his role as a citizen that did not correspond to his political convictions. He distinguished himself from Tillich, who, he claimed, held an esoteric, private, and mystifying theory of socialism on which to fall back, whereas his own socialism was exoteric, purely a matter of political persuasion, and therefore not susceptible to regulation by the party book. If the Prussian State that took him in as he was in 1921 was no longer pleased with him, it knew many ways to send him away. "However, it cannot do everything. For example, it cannot coerce a free person to become something other than what that person is." He added: "I want to tell you that I dearly wish there were in Germany a few other free persons with a bit of renown who were so responsible in relation to this pitiful, little party book that they had to remain in the party, thus proclaiming to the State: It simply won't work."

Barth did not fault Tillich for the action he had taken, but he did fault him at another point: "that your presupposition does not reside in a proper theology (*without* esoteric Socialism)."

He did not respond to Tillich's request for a meeting.

This exchange between Tillich and Barth is discouraging. It shows how difficult it was to establish coalitions in those dark days. We cannot overlook a touch of myopia in Barth. He was so intent on explaining why it was necessary for him to identify himself publicly as a member of the SPD that it did not occur to him to explain why he had waited a decade to join nor to take note of the fact that Tillich was more broadly and for a longer time recognized as a Socialist than he. That oversight was unfair.

In the exchange, however, we do see Barth's consistency. Although the issue between him and Tillich was quite different from the issue in the Dehn affair, there is nothing in what he wrote to Hirsch about that case that does not cohere with what he wrote to Tillich about party membership. In it we can also see the subtlety of the theological implications for politics in the mind of Barth. There could be no possibility of a political theology for him, but theology did imply for him a preference for the working class, democracy, and nonmilitarism, for example. As a citizen, he thought the Social Democratic Party affirmed those preferences more than any other party. In joining the party, however, he affirmed only that much. He did not affirm the political philosophy or "ideology" that stood behind it. He was obstinate about Tillich for precisely the same reason that he was obstinate about Hirsch: Although their thinking moved in diametrically opposite directions politically, neither, in his judgment, worked from presuppositions that resided "in a proper theology."

12

THE BARMEN DECLARATION
AND THE ANSBACHER COUNSEL

BARTH VERSUS ALTHAUS

Our Protestant churches have greeted the German turning point of 1933 as a gift and miracle of God. . . .

It is simply the case that in relation to the *Führer,* in being commanded to sacrifice themselves, in the traces of the call of the hour and their responsibility to obey this call Germans who had forgotten about faith . . . have experienced a reality they can only call "religious." Shall we theologians tell them that all this has nothing to do with God, that God speaks only through the biblical witness of Jesus Christ? . . . We cannot and need not do that.[1]

Paul Althaus wrote this enthusiastic endorsement of Adolf Hitler in the early fall of 1933. His castigation of theologians who deny that God can be experienced in historical events and who insist that God can be known only in the revelation of Jesus Christ was directed above all at Karl Barth.

In those years, Althaus was the most prominent exponent of what he called God's *Uroffenbarung* ("primal revelation"), and on the basis of that premise he developed more thoroughly than others the doctrine of the divine Orders of Creation: marriage,

---

1. Paul Althaus, *Die deutsche Stunde der Kirche,* 2nd ed. (Göttingen: Vandenhoeck & Ruprecht, 1934), pp. 5, 7. Althaus gave this essay the title "Das Ja der Kirche zur deutschen Wende" (The Yes of the Church to the German Turning Point).

Volk, civil law, the State, economic relations. He was convinced that the acknowledgment of God's primal revelation was essential to sound theology. Therefore, he was certain that Karl Barth presented in his Christocentric theology the most serious threat to the proper understanding of Christian faith.

We must not suppose that Althaus was a blindly ideological Nazi. As a matter of fact, he was acknowledged as one of the most thoughtful, generous, and circumspect theologians of the day. Barth employed the vigorous dialectic of Yes and No; Althaus used the more cautious dialectic of "on the one hand . . . on the other." But, if Althaus was certain that Barth's major emphasis was on the No such that he was unable to distinguish better from worse in this world, we may observe that Althaus, whether he intended it or not, gave the stronger emphasis to "on the other hand." On the one hand, *Volk,* though it begins with blood purity, has nothing to do with blood in its development, and a *Volk* can assimilate alien strains. On the other hand, however, he charged the church to support measures against the marriage of Germans to non-Germans, and he could speak of "the natural bondedness and love [of the *Volk*] that draws German blood to German blood." On the one hand, he could criticize German anti-Semitic "Pharisaism" and insist that the problem of the degeneration of the *Volk* was due to evil rather than to the influence of an alien race. But, on the other hand, "the church must . . . have an eye and a word for the Jewish threat to our being as a *Volk.*" He found this threat in business, the press, art, and literature. On the one hand, it is not a matter of the hatred of Jews, of blood, or of religious faith, because "on these points one can come to agreement with serious Jews." It has to do (on the other hand) with "a quite specific mutilated and undermining big city spirit whose bearer, above all, is the Jewish *Volk.*"[2] On the one hand, he argued that though the Orders are given by God, they can be perverted by people. Consequently, we must exercise criticism of the shape the Orders actually take. On the other, "the first word, even so, is obedience."[3]

---

2. Paul Althaus, "Kirche und Volkstum," in *Evangelium und Leben: Gesammelte Vorträge* (Gütersloh: C. Bertelsmann, 1927), pp. 119, 130, 131.
3. Paul Althaus, *Theologie der Ordnungen* (Gütersloh: C. Bertelsmann, 1934), pp. 12, 14.

It is all but certain that Althaus did not intend his "on the one hand . . . on the other" to be taken with anything but a balanced emphasis. After reading Althaus's 1927 address to the East Prussian church convention, Barth wrote him about it, partly, to be sure, with his inevitable caustic edge, but also irenically. In that letter, he said, he found everything

> that impresses me about you and is at the same time ominous: your capacity to be open on all sides and to be carried away by your enthusiasm, which, from my point of view, is also the capacity to swallow and approve entirely too much for me to be able always to hear the totally clear sound of your own trumpet.

Klaus Scholder, the most thorough historian of the churches and the Third Reich, judged that this address by Althaus in 1927 gave "theological legitimation to the foundations of the *völkisch* movement."[4]

Because of his fundamental conviction that theology has to do with the self-revelation of God in Jesus Christ as recorded in the canon of the Bible and witnessed to in the church's proclamation, Karl Barth thought that any allusion that could be taken as an affirmation of revelation outside of what is directly related to Jesus Christ (thus "natural" or "general" revelation) had to be fought with every fiber of his being. That is why he reacted so virulently to Gogarten's criticism that he had not developed a proper anthropology. It is why he wrote his famous (or notorious) tract *"Nein!"* ("No!") in response to the essay by his erstwhile collaborator Emil Brunner on "Nature and Grace." It helps to explain his intransigence to Tillich and his total opposition to Hirsch, and it helps us to understand why he expected Bultmann to go with the German Christian movement in 1933. The theology of Paul Althaus was not the least cause of his abhorrence of natural theology. With less passion but no less conviction, Althaus and his colleague at Erlangen, Werner Elert, thought Barth's theology was the most serious distortion of Christian faith in that time.

The difference between these theologians is nowhere seen more

---

4. Quoted in Klaus Scholder, *The Churches and the Third Reich,* vol. 1: *1918–1934,* trans. John Bowden (Philadelphia: Fortress Press, 1988), pp. 112, 113.

clearly than in the justly famous Barmen Declaration, which Barth drafted, and the Ansbacher Counsel, which Elert wrote and Althaus revised.

The Barmen Declaration was accepted at a meeting of representatives of both Calvinist and Lutheran traditions in Barmen on May 30, 1934. Shortly after Hitler was given power in 1933, an emergency league of pastors had been formed to combat the German Christian movement and the State's movement to bring everything in Germany into line with the goals of the Third Reich. The Barmen Declaration served this "Confessing Church" throughout the twelve years of the Third Reich. It has been adopted since then by other churches as one of the standard confessions of the church. Karl Barth wrote the first draft, which was only modestly revised by those who were present at Barmen. In a dark and perilous time, it reflects the mind of Karl Barth with clarity and power:

> Jesus Christ, as he is testified to us in the Holy Scripture, is the one Word of God, whom we are to hear, whom we are to trust and obey in life and in death.
> We repudiate the false teaching that the church can and must recognize yet other happenings and powers, images and truths as divine revelation alongside this one Word of God, as a source of her preaching. . . .
> We repudiate the false teaching that there are areas of our life in which we belong not to Jesus Christ but another lord. . . .
> We repudiate the false teaching that the church can turn over the form of her message and ordinances at will or according to some dominant ideological and political convictions.[5]

The Ansbacher Counsel, written by Werner Elert and agreed to by Althaus, after his two revisions, was published on June 11, 1934. It consisted of eight affirmations. After stating that the church, as the locus of the work of the Holy Spirit, is bound to the Word of God [the Bible], it affirmed:

---

5. John H. Leith, ed., *Creeds of the Churches,* 3rd ed. (Atlanta: John Knox Press, 1982), pp. 520–521.

2. The Word of God speaks to us as Law and Gospel. . . .

3. The Law, "namely the immutable will of God" . . . encounters us in the total reality of our life as that reality is given in the light of God's revelation. It binds each person to the station in which he is called by God, and obligates us to the natural Orders to which we are subjected, such as family, *Volk*, race (*i.e.,* blood relation). . . .

4. The natural Orders, however, do not inform us about the demanding will of God. They are grounded in their connection with our total natural existence, but they are, at the same time, the means through which God creates and preserves our earthly life. Whoever in faith is certain of the grace of God in Jesus Christ experiences also in these orders "unvarnished divine goodness and mercy." . . .

5. In this acknowledgment as believing Christians we are grateful to God the Lord that God has given to our *Volk* in its need the *Führer* as the "pious and trusted governor" and wants to provide good government in the National Socialist State. . . . We therefore consider ourselves responsible before God to work with the *Führer* in our calling and estate.

Then they set forth the task before the church.

6. The church has a threefold relation to the natural Orders. First, it must proclaim the Law of God. . . . That means grounding the Orders in their majesty. . . .

Second, her members themselves are subordinated to the natural Orders. . . .

Third, the church itself bears marks of the Orders which adhere to the natural Orders. . . .

7. Because of the mutability of the relation to the concrete Orders in the third sense the church is given the task of examining its own order. . . .

8. The fulfillment of this task in the church of our day should also serve our theological work and our ecclesiastical effort.[6]

---

6. Gerhard Niemöller, *Die erste Bekenntnissynode der Deutschen evangelischen Kirche zu Barmen,* vol. 1: *Geschichte, Kritik und Bedeutung der Synode und ihrer theologischen Erklärung* (Göttingen: Vandenhoeck & Ruprecht, 1959), pp. 144–146.

The Ansbacher Counsel was overshadowed by more strident and aggressive assertions in support of the Nazi regime and its policies by persons and groups in one or another part of the German Christian movement. Even so, its influence was not negligible. Althaus and Elert were moderately conservative, widely respected German theologians. In their statement, they did not seek to found a church movement, and the circle they formed around the Counsel was short-lived. The Counsel, however, was a public document, and it can only have encouraged conservative and moderate church people to support Hitler. Moreover, it could be used by German Christians who were not so moderate. Perhaps more than any other statement, it helps us to see how serious and well-meaning theologians who had deep feeling for what they considered the plight of their people could be duped into the uncritical support of Hitler in his early years. The episode must be frightfully unsettling to moderate and conservative Christians of every time and place. It is a pathetically modest credit to the irenic Althaus that four years into the Nazi regime he realized he had made a terrible mistake. After 1937 he fell silent.

In contrast, the Barmen Declaration had an astonishing influence, given the totalitarian power of the Nazi regime. It was the only ecclesiastical option for those who resisted "the great turning point." Indirect as it was in its No to Hitler, it was the only formal theological statement of resistance around which significant numbers of ministers and churches could rally. It was the confession that gave the Confessing Church its name. For those pastors, theological students, and local parishes, it was the statement that had to hold together an unwieldy coalition. Given the fact that it was so thoroughly the expression of one man's theology for a coalition that included a relatively broad spectrum, it served remarkably well. In spite of substantive theological differences and in spite of the oppressive circumstances in which it tried to do its work, the Confessing Church wove a fabric of constancy that should never be forgotten.

13

ON THE LOYALTY OATH

A CONFLICT BETWEEN BARTH
AND BULTMANN

On the night of November 11, 1933, Barth and three of his colleagues at Bonn met with Bultmann and two of his colleagues in Bultmann's home. The purpose of the meeting was to discuss the critical situation in the church, but the discussion also led Barth to change his mind about Hans von Soden, Bultmann's closest colleague and collaborator in the Confessing Church struggle. Barth had been suspicious of von Soden because of what Barth judged to be his liberalism. "In a way quite surprising to me," Barth wrote to Bultmann, "I was enchanted by Mr. von Soden. I would very much like to speak further with him."[1]

The meeting also brought about a reconciliation between Barth and Bultmann. Barth confessed that he had expected Bultmann to join the German Christian movement and that he now realized he had been mistaken. Months later, when the trust between these two had grown strong, Bultmann admitted to Barth that Barth's confession had wounded him deeply. "Since then it has continued to gnaw at me and has remained the thorn for my testing (an allusion to 2 Corinthians 12:7)."[2]

Barth tried to ameliorate the offense. He explained why he had miscalculated. He said he had been misled by both a general thesis

---

1. *Karl Barth—Rudolf Bultmann Briefwechsel: 1922–1966,* ed. Jaspert, p. 138.
2. Ibid., p. 151.

and a quite specific point. The general thesis derived from Barth's judgment about everything he classified as natural theology. He thought anyone who affirmed knowledge of God outside of God's self-revelation not only could become a German Christian but, at some moment along the way, would. He admitted he was wrong about the actuality in Bultmann's case, and he apologized. He added, however, that Bultmann needed to explain why his openness to philosophy and to talk about God outside of God's self-revelation did not leave him open to making common cause with the German Christians. Barth pointed to Bultmann's interest in the philosopher Heidegger, who not only had joined the Nazi party, but, as rector of the University in Freiburg, had given an unmitigated endorsement of the Third Reich. Barth also stated that he had, not without justification, thought of Bultmann and Gogarten as being "in the same pot."[3] Barth asked to be instructed on these points.

Bultmann suggested that Barth read a couple of his recent publications. These, he thought, would enlighten Barth about what Barth called his "fundamental theology," and they would evoke discussion on particular points. "But there is no hurry. In these days one has, if not more weighty, then certainly more pressing things to do than to engage in intra-mural discussion."[4] Bultmann was right about the importance of the pressing issues of the moment and the need for mutual trust and common strategy with respect to them.

The period after the important meeting in Bultmann's home on November 11, 1933, was the time when Barth and Bultmann were closest to one another. Von Soden was drawn into this circle, as was Barth's Bonn colleague, Ernst Wolf. The correspondence between Barth and Bultmann over these months reflects warmth and especially a mutual sense for the priority of the public issues. In early May of 1934, Bultmann, von Soden, and their colleague Heinrich Schlier met with Barth and Wolf at Barth's home in Bonn. Together they produced a vigorous declaration on the confession and constitution of the church for which they managed on short notice to win the support of thirty-five professors of

---

3. Ibid., p. 153.
4. Ibid., p. 154.

theology. The declaration was published in pamphlet form on May 23. When representatives of both Reformed (Calvinist) and Evangelical (Lutheran) churches met at the Synod of Barmen and unanimously approved the Barmen Declaration, von Soden was among the 139 delegates, and he was elected to its Central Committee. From the beginning, both he and Bultmann were members of the Confessing Church, even though they had misgivings about the unyielding Barthian imprint on the Confession.

"Intra-mural" differences paled in the face of events that called for a united front. Professors in all disciplines, including theology, were being summarily transferred or dismissed. In November, Barth himself was suspended from teaching, and proceedings against him were instituted. The cause of Barth's suspension was his position on the oath of loyalty to Hitler that was required of all university professors. (In Germany, professors were, and are today, civil servants employed by the State.) The position he took led von Soden and Bultmann, with a sense of urgency, to take issue with him. However, they kept their intramural conflict private.

Barth received notice of his suspension and of the legal process that threatened dismissal on November 26, 1934. On November 27, he wrote to Bultmann. He said a story would be published that day announcing his suspension and giving as the reason his refusal to sign the prescribed oath of loyalty to Hitler. He wanted Bultmann to know that the story in the press did not correspond to the facts. He had not refused to sign the oath. He had insisted only on the insertion of a clause. He enclosed a copy of the oath with the clause he added underlined:

> I swear: I will be true and obedient to the Führer of the German Reich and *Volk*, Adolf Hitler, *in so far as I responsibly can as a Protestant Christian,* observe the laws and conscientiously fulfill the duties of my office, so help me God.[5]

Barth asked Bultmann to inform von Soden.

Five days later, on his return to Marburg from a meeting of

---

5. Ibid., p. 155.

confessing pastors, von Soden wrote Barth. He said the news of Barth's suspension had been a terrible blow to him, "both because of my special personal participation in your work and because of the major significance it has for the battle of the Confessing Church." He acknowledged differences between them that he dared to hope did not endanger their personal relation or their common struggle for the church. He asked Barth, in the confidence of his personal bond with him, to permit him "to express a serious scruple with your decision."[6] He said he could not understand, on the basis of Barth's own theology, why Barth had insisted on inserting the clause. The clause, he argued, requires the State to acknowledge abstractly and in advance what can only happen in a particular instance. But on theological grounds, Barth denies that the State has the capability to recognize such an instance. The reason is that the clause has meaning only for a Christian. For a Christian, however, the reservation is self-evident, but a Christian can invoke it only at the moment when the conflict between obedience to God and obedience to the State becomes critical. To insist on making such a stipulation in advance of a crisis will necessarily appear to the State as a refusal of the oath. Von Soden indicated that he could understand Barth's act if Barth had simply refused in principle to take an oath of loyalty to a human being. In Germany, he explained, there was a long tradition of such oaths. Because of such precedents, von Soden said he thought a refusal to take this oath was theologically mistaken. He was confident the State would not accept the oath with the insertion. If the State permitted it for Barth, it would have to allow others to specify their own reservations of whatever sort.

He thought that this kind of oath had to be interpreted in the way the one to whom loyalty is pledged understands it. With that sense of things, one can accept or reject the oath. To accept it does not mean that one pledges oneself never to break it. It does, however, mean that if one must in conscience violate the oath, one must be prepared to face the consequences. Actually, the oath, von Soden insisted, changes in no way the already existing conditions of professors' employment. Disloyalty to the State has always been a cause for dismissal.

---

6. Ibid., p. 269.

Von Soden told Barth he was prepared to be corrected if he was wrong and asked Barth to instruct him. At the same time, he asked Barth to consider how his action affected those who shared his reservation but who, believing it to be self-evident, had signed the oath. He also asked Barth to consider the damage his action did to the much needed solidarity in the struggle of the Confessing Church. (Barth had not consulted with others.)

Von Soden referred to the report in the Basel, Switzerland, newspaper under the headline "Alarm in the Confessing Church" and wondered about the source of the account. The paper reported that the Confessing Church might found its own school of theology. Von Soden did not see how that statement could have come from the leadership of the Confessing Church. Certainly, he, as a member of the Central Committee, had not been consulted. "One ought not to play with the foundation of theological education for the church before the time calls for it." Such a time would come, he wrote, when Christian theology could no longer be taught in the university. That was not yet the case.

> The duty of theology, as of university professors overall, will always be, to a high degree, the exercise of criticism toward the institutions of both State and Church, and we are agreed that this criticism is not more securely insured by an ecclesiastical authority over the faculties than by the authority of the State. Should, however, it come to the place where the State universities give up or no longer recognize the theological faculties, let it be when and because the State no longer allows the faculties to fulfill the mission given to them in their subject matter and not because the professors do not like the duties they are asked to perform according to laws that are applicable to all.[7]

He pleaded with Barth to reconsider his decision.

The next day, Bultmann also wrote Barth and indicated his full agreement with von Soden's letter. He not only believed the State would not allow the insertion; he was convinced that it could not. He, too, was certain that Barth's reservation was implicit for every Christian, and he, too, believed that such a reservation should be

---

7. Ibid., p. 272.

exercised only in a specific situation of conflict. The State, he said, cannot guarantee our reservation in advance. "The longer I think about the issue, the more I lament your step, with all respect for your integrity and courage, which I scarcely need to mention." Bultmann was concerned that Barth's act would make more difficult or spoil in advance "a discussion between State and Church about the legitimate, or illegitimate, meaning of the totalitarian claim of the State, which someday may be necessary." Like von Soden, he asked Barth to reconsider his action, "but with little hope."[8]

Barth answered von Soden two days later. He thanked him for his good letter and said he would answer it point for point. First, he could not be content with the thought that in the case of a conflict it would be self-evident that a Protestant Christian could obey God first. Second, he saw a difference between this oath and others he had taken in the past. Third, he could only interpret this oath as 100 percent National Socialist. Therefore, fourth, he could view it only as an intention of the signer to swear allegiance to Hitler, body and soul. He said he had made an issue of the oath because he was convinced that if the State allowed his insertion, it would thereby acknowledge that it is an "authority" only in the sense of Romans 13, that is, with no jurisdiction over the soul. On the other hand, he thought that if the insertion were disallowed, then it is clear that the Nazi State is anti-Christ. He sent a carbon copy of his letter to Bultmann.

In time, Barth did reconsider his position. Leaders of the Confessing Church, both Lutheran and Calvinist, urged him to do so and promised their support. Fifteen days after Bultmann wrote his letter to Barth, Barth wrote to the rector of the University of Bonn. He indicated his willingness to sign the oath without the insertion. Nevertheless, two days later the local government in Cologne announced his dismissal. At Bultmann's urging, he appealed to a higher court in Berlin where, in contrast to the provincial court, all the judges were legitimate jurists. As Bultmann expected, that court reversed the lower court and reinstated Barth. It imposed a relatively modest fine—one-fifth of

---

8. Ibid., p. 157.

his salary for one year. That was June 14. Eight days later, however, the Minister of Education, acting on his own authority, proclaimed Barth's dismissal with no right of appeal. Two days later, Barth was appointed Professor of Theology at Basel in Switzerland, a post he held until his retirement.[9]

---

9. The dismissal of Barth from his professorial position was a serious blow to the Confessing Church. As we have seen, he had written the Barmen Declaration and was a powerful theological presence in the movement. However, the Confessing Church was, given the difficult circumstances, well-organized and had a number of gifted and devoted leaders. Its work continued throughout the years of the Third Reich. Its parishes, ministers, and lay people were the most important witness to a Christian faith that would not be "brought in line" with the Nazi regime.

14

"WHAT IT'S ALL ABOUT"

TILLICH VERSUS HIRSCH

Nineteen months before Barth's dismissal, Paul Tillich was suspended from his position as Professor of the Philosophy of Religion at the University of Frankfurt. Professors at the Union Theological Seminary in New York City pooled a percentage of their salaries in order that Tillich might be offered a one-year Visiting Professorship there. It was a generous act of solidarity with a fellow theologian in Germany who had seen his books thrown on the fire in Frankfurt on May 10, 1933. In addition to being generous, it was a stroke of genius. Tillich taught at Union Seminary until the late 1950s. Although he had achieved considerable stature in Germany, his fame in the United States became even greater. Along with a few others at the seminary, he brought it to one of its periods of greatest distinction in theological education.

Richard Niebuhr, Professor at the Yale University Divinity School and a brother of Reinhold Niebuhr, who was instrumental in bringing Tillich to Union Theological Seminary, introduced Tillich to the American theological public with a 1932 translation of Tillich's 1926 book *The Religious Situation of the Present*. This book contained, partly explicitly and partly implicitly, most of the categories Tillich had developed in connection with his leadership of a Religious-Socialist circle in Germany. By means of these categories, Tillich looked at the broad range of human culture and tried to uncover its deeper religious meaning.

The German theological public would have found nothing in the book that was surprising or new. In several books and many articles, Tillich had developed the categories he used to try to make sense of history and culture. He advocated socialism with a religious foundation as the most promising structure of society at the time, and he believed cultural and historical forces were emerging such that the present was especially ripe for the new structure. Tillich was not a politician, but he was an accomplished religious-philosophical theoretician for socialism as well as for Christian faith.

In 1932, when Richard Niebuhr was translating *The Religious Situation,* Tillich was writing his most vigorous book in support of socialism. His work was also a stinging criticism of what Tillich called "political romanticism" and the values most highly prized by the Nazi movement. In characteristic fashion, he praised the Jewish tradition and its contributions to German life and culture.

The book came out just as Hitler came to power. It is not surprising that it was confiscated and suppressed shortly after its publication and thrown on the fire heap in Frankfurt. Nor is it surprising that Tillich was on the first list of professors to be suspended from their teaching posts by the Nazi regime, though it came as a shock to Tillich. In addition to his published criticisms in *The Socialist Decision* and elsewhere, he had been all but uncontrollably outspoken in his distaste for National Socialism and in his support for Jews.[1] What was surprising was Tillich's good fortune in being invited to Union Theological Seminary at just the right time.

After his suspension, while he was wondering about his future and then preparing to come to the United States, his close friend and intellectual comrade from student days, Emanuel Hirsch, was writing a book utterly different from Tillich's *The Socialist Decision,* but reflecting, at least on the abstract level, their conceptual kinship. Moreover, the title he selected could only

---

1. Cf. Wilhelm Pauck and Marion Pauck, *Paul Tillich: His Life and Thought* (New York: Harper & Row, 1976), pp. 125ff. The Paucks report the following incident: "During a summer in Kampen, Tillich and his friends entered a local bar for a nightcap. Other patrons, already less sober, asked him, 'Professor, can you tell us whether there are any Christians in the world any more?' Tillich shouted in reply, 'No, not a single one. The only Christians in the world today are Jews!' " (126).

remind readers of the book by Tillich that Richard Niebuhr had translated. Hirsch gave his book the title *The Spiritual Situation of the Present in the Mirror of Philosophical and Theological Reflection.*[2]

Hirsch hailed "the great turning point" in German history brought about by the National Socialist movement, and he did so with carefully constructed categories of thought. "Horos" (boundary, limit) referred to the boundary beyond which human beings cannot go in their historical life. "Nomos" (law) stood for order, that which constitutes the possibility of life and thought. "Logos" (word, rationality, the term used in the first chapter of the Gospel of John for Christ as Creator and by the ancient Stoics to designate the pervasive power of reason in the world) signified the living Spirit that expresses itself in the world.

The substance of Hirsch's position is clear. Faith in the God of Jesus Christ has to do with our historical life, even though we can never absolutely identify anything in this historical life with the divine life. What happens in this world both is and is not the movement of the divine Spirit. (Hirsch foreswore all utopianism.) Even so, the only way we can recognize the divine Spirit is in and through our historical life, in what happens here and now. Thus we properly focus on the problems of ethics and call for engagement in the common life of our *Volk*. The movement of the divine Spirit can be recognized only through conscience as it is formed by the gospel in recognition of the *Volk* as its effective locus. We are called to decision.

Logos stands for the divine power in history. Nomos represents the special forms of life and thinking perceived in their unique

---

2. Emanuel Hirsch, *Die gegenwärtige geistige Lage im Spiegel philosophischer und theologischer Besinnung* (Göttingen: Vandenhoeck & Ruprecht, 1934). Citations will be indicated by page numbers in parentheses in the text.

Hirsch provided a superscription for each part of his book. These superscriptions were taken from Goethe, Novalis, Stefan Georg, Wandersmann, Rilke, and Eichendorff. Hans Georg Gadamer, one of the most prominent postwar philosophers in Germany, who was a student in Marburg in 1933, makes this comment about the poet Rilke and the Nazi era: "It was his great time. For whenever one was hit in the face by the bombastic linguistic usage from 'the dictionary of the inhuman' it turned out to be the highly cultivated mannerism of the Rilkean language." The quotation is from Gadamer's autobiographical book *Philosophische Lehrjahre*, pp. 117–118.

character for a particular *Volk* by conscience. Horos points to the extremity that beckons us but also makes us realistic, that is, makes us aware of the beyond we cannot reach. Our task is to seek the boundary where the supraworldly and the worldly touch each other, the furthest point in the development of the community of conscience, the *Volk* called to be itself under the claim of the gospel of God.

Every *Volk*—and thus also the German *Volk*—is an individual entity with its own character, or Nomos. It is the role of the State to unfold the peculiar characteristics of the *Volk* and to see that its necessities for life are fulfilled. We must, however, be careful never to put the fatherland in the place of the eternal. We must not make an idol of any earthly form. We must embrace both historical realism and political theology.

For this task we need help. Great personalities or leaders, persons who are prepared both to take daring risks and to accept responsibility for their actions, can help us to understand the times and to solve the questions of conscience. We recognize these men only by decision.

Communism thought it found the key to the reality of the common life, but it did not. Marxism, after all, is secularized, atheistic Judaism, and Jews are the only people who cannot become Christian without ceasing to belong to their *Volk*. But we Europeans are tied to Christianity, especially we Germans. Every German who has caught the spirit now sees a new age and new possibilities. The Third Reich has revealed to us the mystery of the boundary (Horos) of all thinking and willing and of all the laws of our *Volk*. In this revelation we find our freedom.

> Theology must deal with the question of *what it means* that God is Lord of the *Volk* as well as of individuals, that man is a sinner who lives out of God's forgiveness, that God calls us to serve the eternal in the temporal with all our power and skill and honor. (142)

We must understand what that means *today*.

> Jointly with the consciousness of the holy limit [Horos] of human being, the ultimate and highest, which becomes fate

213

for the whole of human being, is effective in National Socialism. (143)

In short, now is the *Kairos* (Tillich's term for the time that is ripe for something new and creative; Hirsch did not use the term).

Tillich read Hirsch's book in New York City. He wrote a response in the form of an open letter to Hirsch, which he asked Karl Ludwig Schmidt, editor of *Theological Leaves* who also was on the first list of suspended professors, to publish.[3] It was a difficult letter to write, he noted, because of his close friendship with Hirsch over so many years. However, he said he had to write it because (1) Hirsch had taken over Tillich's own categories, those of Religious Socialism, and (2) Hirsch had misused them.

A. James Reimer, in his long book on the debate between Hirsch and Tillich, focuses primarily, as did Hirsch and his supporter, Hanns Rückert, on the first point, and he construes the point, as did Hirsch and Rückert, as a peevish accusation of plagiarism.[4] Reimer's heading for the section in which he deals with Tillich's letter is "A Charge of Plagiarism in Tillich's Open

---

3. Paul Tillich, "Die Theologie des Kairos und die gegenwärtige geistige Lage. Offener Brief an Emanuel Hirsch, Göttingen," *Theologische Blätter* 13, no. 11 (November 1934), 305–328. An English translation of Tillich's letter by Victor Nuovo and Robert P. Scharlemann was published in *The Theology of Paul Tillich,* ed. James Luther Adams, Wilhelm Pauck, and Roger Shinn (San Francisco: Harper & Row, 1985), pp. 353–388. Citations from the letter are from the English translation and are noted by page numbers in parentheses in the text.

4. A. James Reimer, *The Emanuel Hirsch and Paul Tillich Debate: A Study in the Political Ramifications of Theology,* Toronto Studies in Theology, vol. 42 (Lewiston/Queenston/Lampeter: The Edwin Mellen Press, 1989). Reimer seems to have a bias against Tillich. In any case, he repeatedly construes (or misconstrues) Tillich's thought in such a way as to show what he considers its weaknesses. In his treatment of Tillich's open letter, he speculates that Tillich responded to Hirsch because his "reputation was at stake," and he judged the letter to be an "outburst" (334). One might think that something like a bias led Reimer unconsciously to mistranslate Tillich at a not insignificant point. About the open letter he wrote, "What concerns Tillich most of all, is the implication that in his [Hirsch's] employment of these categories [i.e., the basic concepts of Religious Socialism] Hirsch may have brought them to their deepest meaning" (256–257). In a footnote Reimer cites, with an error in transcription, the German he has misunderstood: "dass deine Verwendung dieser Kategorien sie um ihren tiefsten Sinn bringst" [sic]. Properly: "Your use of these categories robs them of their deepest sense."

Letter." Tillich indeed made the claim that Hirsch had appropriated without acknowledgment the major categories of Religious
Socialism's analysis and construction. If one takes this point by
itself, in abstraction from the context of the letter as a whole, it is
weak, if not ridiculous. Categories of thought are not copyrighted.
One makes a judgment about their use not on the basis of their
origin but on the basis of their coherence and power to illuminate
the problem or issue under consideration. Moreover, as we have
seen, Tillich and Hirsch drew from more or less the same sources
for their thinking, and at the time of their closest friendship, their
acquaintances observed that they could not distinguish between
their positions. Is it any wonder then that the structure of thought
Hirsch developed in *The Spiritual Situation of the Present* struck
Tillich as identical with the structure of thought he had developed
for Religious Socialism?

That construal of Tillich's open letter to Hirsch, however, is all
but utterly false and irresponsible. Tillich stated his intention
clearly in his second paragraph:

> You used every crucial concept of your adversaries, against
> whom you have struggled for fourteen years, and whom now
> you appear to have vanquished. I could rejoice in this as
> proof of the spiritual power of the intellectual labor of our
> Religious Socialist movement, by which even its victorious
> enemies must live. But two things disturb my joy. First, you
> deliberately conceal your agreement with Religious Socialist
> categories; second, in using these categories, you deprive
> them of their deepest sense. (354)

Tillich did think Hirsch had violated "intellectual veracity"
(354) by not even hinting at the similarity of his structure of
thought to that of Tillich and the Religious Socialists, and he
chided Hirsch about it for two paragraphs. Then he wrote:

> But enough of this! I must consider what is at issue. Two
> closely related tasks lie before me. One is to show how you
> have taken up the basic concepts of Religious Socialist
> thought, especially the *Kairos* doctrine, and, at the same
> time, by eliminating their prophetic-eschatological elements,
> have twisted or emptied them, and the other is to present an

actual critique of your theological method through a discussion of your basic attitude as well as various particular solutions. (355–356)

The accusation that Hirsch had borrowed basic concepts from Religious Socialism was, primarily, a "set up." What Tillich wanted to show was that Hirsch had used these concepts without seeing their inherent "prophetic-eschatological" dimension (i.e., the critical principle). In short, Emanuel Hirsch, arguably the most gifted mind in German theology in the twentieth century, was faulted by Tillich for not thinking his categories through to their conclusion! Tillich's basic charge was that Hirsch had overlooked the critical power of the *Kairos* doctrine and had transmuted it into an enthusiastic affirmation of a finite event, the Nazi victory. *"You have perverted the prophetic, eschatological Kairos doctrine into a sacerdotal-sacramental consecration of a current event"* (363. Tillich's emphasis).

That statement takes us a little more than one-fourth into Tillich's letter. In the remainder, he makes a number of points. Among them two stand out and represent most of the others as well. First, Hirsch's view that the present moment is decisive and that anyone identified with the German *Volk* and with a sense of identity with their destiny must decide for Hitler negates the critical power inherent in the concept of *Kairos*. Tillich wrote: "You are impelled not by the realism of faith but by an unbroken enthusiasm that deprives you of critical insight and critical utterance" (365). He added:

> When we first joined the socialist movement it was at once clear to us that, at one decisive point, we must enter as uncompromising critics and revisionists. Intrinsic to every prophetic-eschatological movement is the danger of utopianism. Utopianism, however, is the absolutizing of a finite possibility. At the end of every utopian enthusiasm stands disappointment and doubt. (366)

Tillich's second point was that Hirsch, in using the basic concepts of Religious Socialism, deprived them of their deepest meaning. What he meant by this claim might give pause to those in our own time who, in the laudable cause of fostering diversity in expressions of Christian faith, emphasize the distinctiveness, if not revelatory power, of the experience of particular groups. Tillich's point was that Christian faith is not necessarily what a particular group (in this case, the German *Volk*) experience it to be. The experience of a person or group is certainly the mode by which Christian faith is appropriated, but the meaning of that faith is beyond, even over against, particular experience.

Tillich did not mean to imply that revelation is a concept of objectifying thinking, a set of statements that convey reliable knowledge about the Unconditioned.

> It is revelation only as an actual revelation for someone. But—and this is the other side—when it does take place, that is, when it is actualized correlatively, it is exclusive. There can be no other revelations beside it but only other situations from which one enters into the revelational correlation. Every new situation changes the correlation but does not change the revelation. If I wanted to express the matter without using the word "revelation," I would speak of the place from which our existence gets its meaning, a meaning that is unconditioned and exclusive, simultaneously sustaining and directing. Revelation is that to which I am conscious of being unconditionally subject as the final criterion of my thinking and acting.
>
> The *Kairos,* the historical time, can thus never of itself be a revelation. It can only indicate the entering of a new correlation of revelation. It designates the moment in which the meaning of revelation discloses itself anew for knowledge and action, in which, for example, the final criterion of truth over against a temporal constellation is visible anew, as, say, the cross of Christ over against capitalistic or nationalistic demonry. (372)

What Tillich missed in Hirsch he held to be essential to Christian faith. He thought Hirsch had surrendered the ancient Jewish-Christian principle of criticism for sacramental, sanctified enthusiasm.

That movement by Hirsch is what Tillich thought violated the insight of Religious Socialism. To speak in a specifically Christian way, the cross of Christ, which turns all human expectations upside down, is the fundamental criterion for human thought when it has been "grasped" by the power of the "Christ." Tillich's point is that nothing finite can yield a revelation of the Unconditioned. Although our only access to the Unconditioned is our finite perception, we must never release that finite perception from the critical principle, that is, from the principle upon which we understand and assess all human phenomena.

Throughout his letter, Tillich addressed Hirsch in the familiar form of "you" (German: *du*), a mode of address used only between close friends, and he signed the letter accordingly, "Your Paul."

Hirsch was so angered by what Tillich wrote that he could no longer speak directly to him. He responded in an open letter to his friend, Wilhelm Stapel, a lay theologian and publisher who was one of Hitler's most outspoken supporters.[5] He accused Tillich of having written nothing more than a political pamphlet, answered him almost point for point with typical acidity and brilliance, and attacked him forcefully and most especially on the charge of having borrowed his basic categories. His letter is substantive, and we are already acquainted with the substance of his view. Restating his major thesis, he wrote:

> Precisely the God who makes me free in his love places me in a specific earthly-historical life with his law and a sense of duty. . . . The freedom of the conscience from the law in relation to God is the unconditional sanctification of service in fulfillment of the law.[6]

In this, he said, we are different from the Marxists. Tillich had said that nothing earthly can be sanctified and holy, but the gospel, Hirsch insisted, teaches us that anything earthly can become holy. We have seen the Horos, the ultimate boundary, in what has transpired in Germany. Therefore, now is not the time for the critical word; it is the time for the helping and clarifying word. The

---

5. Emanuel Hirsch, *Christliche Freiheit und politische Bindung: Ein Brief an Dr. Stapel und andere* (Hamburg: Hanseatische Verlagsanstalt, 1935).

6. Ibid., pp. 38–39.

divine love does not begin with criticism but with an unconditional and enthusiastic Yes. He ended the letter, "Heil Hitler."[7]

Shortly thereafter, the exchange came to an end with Tillich's brief essay *"Um was es geht"* (What It's All About).[8] In short, Tillich stated, it is all about one thing only—the critical principle. He acknowledged that originality or plagiarism has nothing to do with the substance of the matter. The substance is the critical principle. One must in faithfulness to the Christian message, which itself can be understood only by critical reflection, maintain the dialectic.

> Whoever is convinced that the understanding of the past has decisive significance for the meaning of the present and the formation of the future must with both passion and distance keep careful watch over the development of our historical consciousness.[9]

Hirsch had tried to identify Tillich with Karl Barth and to base the identity purely on political convictions. Tillich denied the charge. He acknowledged that he stood with Barth insofar as Barth represents the prophetic criticism of the demonized sacramentalism of the German Christian theology with which Hirsch was sympathetic, but unlike Barth, Tillich wanted to be thoroughly critical and to think his way critically to a theology of politics that is adequate to the responsibility of the Christian in the world.

Tillich concluded his statement:

> A theology that allows its historical right to be curtailed in the face of a political—or any other—total view of reality has mutilated itself. In that moment when politics grounds itself metaphysically, this grounding must be subjected to responsible theological criticism.[10]

---

7. Ibid., p. 48.
8. *Theologische Blätter* 14, no. 5 (May 1935), 117–120.
9. Ibid., p. 118.
10. Ibid., p. 119.

Indeed, that is what it is all about. Tillich made his point without ifs or buts, and Hirsch should have granted it. The thorough and pervasive exercise of the critical principle was one of those points of identity between those two friends that they had talked about on long walks and written about in long letters and that had led mutual friends to say they could no longer tell them apart in their thinking. After all, Hirsch was, by his own admission, one of "those theologians who through theology—and to be sure, precisely through a theology that is critical and does not shy away from any question—were saved for theology."[11]

But in 1933, by a decision of his conscience, by a leap of faith, he made one fateful exception to the exercise of the critical principle and gave way to uncritical enthusiasm. Thus, in his response to Tillich he prefaced his "Heil Hitler" by saying, "Now is not the time for the critical word; the divine love does not begin with criticism but with an unconditional and enthusiastic Yes."[12]

Ernst Toller, the author of the first superscription at the beginning of Part III, was right. Human life and destiny is always endangered when prophets of whatever sort demand, "*Frage nicht, glaube!*" Do not question. Believe!

In 1948, Tillich returned to Germany for the first time since 1933. Germany was destroyed, and its people were destitute. In the midst of a busy schedule of lectures and consultations, he made a special effort to call on Hirsch. Wilhelm and Marion Pauck, Tillich's fine biographers, describe the meeting:

> Hirsch stood waiting for Tillich in his Göttingen garden. He was almost entirely blind, very old, his hair uncombed. The two men talked of their work, Hirsch's family, his blindness, the loss of a son in Yugoslavia. Hirsch still clung to his belief that Hitler had been sent to create a unified German nation. His forced retirement and reduced pension caused by his Nazi sympathies embittered him. Despite all, he had continued to be enormously productive, a feat Tillich admired. Their

11. "Meine theologischen Anfänge," *Freies Christentum* 3, no. 10 (October 1951), 2.
12. Hirsch, *Christliche Freiheit und politische Bindung,* p. 48.

farewell was particularly moving for Hirsch, who wrote Tillich later in the year how often he thought of their meeting, and thanked him for the gifts he brought: a bottle of wine, two bars of chocolate, and a piece of soap.[13]

13. Pauck and Pauck, *Paul Tillich: His Life and Thought*, p. 214.

15

BULTMANN AND THE STRUGGLE

For a number of years, especially after 1945, the dominant theological alternatives in Germany were Barth and Bultmann. As we have seen, however, in the late 1920s and early 1930s these two shared some common basic themes, even as they came more clearly to see their differences. Bultmann also had affinities with the theology of Tillich. He maintained a distance from Tillich's constructive categories, but he was close to Tillich's appropriation of justification by grace through faith. Also one recognizes in him Tillich's Protestant principle, although Bultmann rang that bell more insistently.

Most intriguing, in Bultmann we find common points with Hirsch, Althaus, and Gogarten. The points of identity with Hirsch are the least significant and are purely formal. They both held firmly to the heritage of historical criticism from Liberal theology, though Bultmann was more radical and consistent in employing it. Also, Bultmann shared with Hirsch (and many others) the conviction that Christian faith has to do discernibly with human life in the world. While acknowledging these formal points of agreement, we must observe that not only in the 1920s but also at the beginning of the Third Reich and throughout its twelve years Bultmann lost no opportunity to criticize Hirsch, directly on technical or scientific theological grounds and indirectly for his anti-Semitism. As we have seen, Paul Althaus developed more thoroughly than others the doctrine of God's primal revelation in the Orders of Creation and used this doctrine to defend compliance with the Nazi regime. Bultmann also affirmed the Orders of Creation doctrine, but as we will see, he turned it against Althaus and others who used it in support of the Third Reich. With Gogarten, Bultmann shared the fundamental theological conviction that to speak about God is at the same time to speak about human being. That is, we can speak about God only by talking about God's relation to human beings and the effects of this sense of relationship in human beings. When Gogarten identified with the German Christian movement and affirmed the Nazi regime, Bultmann did not give up on him. Bultmann, who wrote more than anyone else against the early anti-Semitic policies and activities of the Nazi regime and its supporters in the Protestant church, quoted Gogarten in his affirmation of the Jews. There is reason to believe that the confidence and friendship of Bultmann was no small factor in moving Gogarten to distance himself from the German Christians and in saving him for creative theological work after he realized what a mistake he had made about the Third Reich.

A brief review of Bultmann's understanding of the fundamental importance of the crucifixion and resurrection for faith will illustrate some of the themes that made his theology distinctive. He quite rightly saw that the statement "Jesus died on the cross" is a straightforward historical statement whose affirmation requires no act of faith at all. What requires an act of faith is to say that the Jesus who died on the cross is the Christ and that the crucifixion is God's decisive salvific act. That confession, however, goes beyond a historical claim, and it is impossible authentically to make that confession by relying on what one supposes is a historical account. One is able to make the confession only when in response to the proclamation something like a crucifixion happens to oneself and becomes radically constitutive of the self. Martin Luther was getting at the same thing when he said that when one responds to the gospel with faith, God breaks the curvature of the self in upon the self. In this connection, Galatians 2:19b–20 was important to Bultmann: "I have been crucified with Christ. It is no longer I who live, but Christ who lives in me; and the life I now live in the flesh [that is, here and now in this world] I live by faith in the Son of God who loved me and gave himself for me" (RSV).

As a good historian, Bultmann recognized that the statement "Jesus Christ was raised from the dead" cannot be a historical statement like the statement "Jesus was crucified." There are no canons of human understanding that allow one to make a historical judgment about a reputed resurrection.

In the early 1960s, the San Francisco *Chronicle* published a story about the "death" of a Buddhist nun in India. A couple of days after she had been pronounced dead by a physician, as her body was being carried to the funereal pyre, she sat up. She said she had been to the gates of hell and was alive again. The reporter did a credible job—no explanations or interpretations, only the facts. The story did not report a resurrection but the claim of a resurrection. A common response to this item was scepticism, and for good reason. To accept as true without question the report of a resurrection requires a suspension or sacrifice of the intellect.

It is, of course, possible to accept the resurrection of Jesus Christ by an arbitrary act of will, but Bultmann insisted that Christian faith does not require a sacrifice of the intellect. How, then, can it be possible for a Christian to say that Jesus Christ was raised? Bultmann thought the only possibility was the same condition that could lead a person in response to the Christian proclamation to say that the cross of Jesus is the decisive salvific act of God, that is, the sense not only of dying with Christ but also of being raised, as it were, with Christ to new life here and now. The confession that Jesus was raised, then, however the resurrection may have taken place—which one cannot know as one knows historical events—is a corollary of new life, of the liberation of the self from the self in response to the proclamation of the gospel.

Bultmann, therefore, insisted that every statement about Christ (Christology, a doctrine about Christ) is, *at the same time,* a statement about human salvation (soteriology, a doctrine of salvation) and, as a corollary, every statement about God (theology, a doctrine about God) is, *at the same time,* a statement about human being (anthropology, a doctrine about humankind). It means that Christian theology and Christian ethics are identical in their foundation, and the life of the Christian in the world can be set forth so that people can understand it.

We have seen that Barth was suspicious of Bultmann's view. He thought the way Bultmann correlated God and human being implied a natural theology, and Barth was convinced that natural theology negated the gospel and would lead inevitably to the support of Hitler's policies in the church. Thus he thought Bultmann would join the German Christians.

Like most others, Bultmann did not sense the enormity of what was to come when Hitler was given power in early 1933. Hans-Georg Gadamer, later one of the most distinguished philosophers in Germany, was at Marburg and belonged to the "Bultmann Greek group," a small circle that gathered on most Thursday nights at Bultmann's home to read classical Greek texts, after which they would smoke, drink, and share university gossip and jokes. Gadamer reports that they were unprepared for 1933 and that none of them had read *Mein Kampf*. They generally followed the liberal press and were not alarmed, even about the anti-Semitic rhetoric. "Until June 30, 1934 we all basically believed that the spook would soon disappear."[1]

Even so, Bultmann considered the new political situation in 1933 sufficiently grave that he decided it was necessary for him to speak about it as he began his opening lecture of the summer semester on May 2. In that lecture, he proved himself knowledgeable about the Nazi ideology and about the political theology that affirmed it. The basic theme of the lecture, in both method and substance, was fundamental to Bultmann's theology. At a time when already many, including students, were eager to denounce critical voices as enemies of the State, he not only urged his students to criticize the State theologically but took the further step of publishing his lecture in the widely read *Theological Leaves*.[2]

---

1. Gadamer, *Philosophische Lehrjahre*, p. 51. Gadamer commented, "We would learn otherwise. Especially the theological faculty . . . stepped forward actively against the anti-Semitism."

2. "Die Aufgabe der Theologie in der gegenwärtige Situation," *Theologische Blätter* 12, no. 6 (June 1933), 161–166. English translation: "The Task of Theology in the Present Situation," in *Existence and Faith*, trans. Ogden, pp. 158–165. Citations from this lecture will be taken from Ogden's translation and indicated by page numbers in parentheses in the text.

He began: "Ladies and Gentlemen. I have made a point never to speak about current politics in my lectures, and I think I also shall not do so in the future. However, it would seem to me unnatural were I to ignore today the political situation in which we begin this new semester" (158). To address the political situation "as theologians," however, does not mean to defend a political point of view. Rather, it means to disavow both "the 'happy yes' . . . that is spoken all too quickly today" and "a resentful criticism" (158). The first task of the theologian is to reflect on "the relation of faith to nation and state, or the relation between the life of faith and life in the political order" (158). Basic to this relation is faith's orientation to "the God who is Creator and Judge of the world and its Redeemer in Jesus Christ" (158–159). Bultmann related everything he said to this twofold theme, and his hearers and readers could have construed what followed only as a most sober warning and a negative judgment of the new regime and its enthusiastic reception by many.

Dealing with the theme of God the Creator was dangerous. We have seen that Paul Althaus (and a good many others) had coupled this theme with a novel understanding of Luther's statements about the Orders of Creation in support of their decision to hail Hitler's advent as "the great turning point" in German history and destiny. Althaus argued that God had created the world such that human beings find their lives in families and a *Volk*. The *Volk*—in this case, the German *Volk*—is thus ordained by God, and obedience to God requires us to foster the common life of the *Volk* with its special character. In their development of this doctrine, Althaus and the other "political theologians" rejected communism because of its internationalism, and western capitalism because of its individualism, and they called for fostering the purity of the *Volk* (*Blut und Boden*, "blood and soil").

Bultmann affirmed the Orders of Creation doctrine. He observed that we are not persons in the abstract but in specific situations. Much of what we are and have is given, for example, our sex, our family, our nationality. Our relationship to these orders is first of all a positive one. As members of a nation, we share a common destiny and are responsible for a common future.

That recognition, however, is only the beginning of thought about God the Creator with respect to our being placed within a given people. We dare not understand God the Creator as simply immanent in this or any other order. We dare not understand any phenomenon within this world as unambiguously sacred. Our relation to the Orders of Creation, including *Volk* and nation, is therefore positive precisely because it is critical. God is both Creator and Judge of the world.

God's creation is good, but it is subject to perversion by us. The Orders, to be sure, are given by God, but they present us with possibilities both for "free and noble action *and* temptations to act slavishly and meanly" (161). In a direct attack on the enthusiasm that was welling throughout Germany at that time, Bultmann said:

> No state and no nation is so unambiguous an entity, is so free from sin, that the will of God can be read off unambiguously from its bare existence. No nation is so pure and clean that one may explain every stirring of the national will as a direct demand of God. . . . In a day when the nation has again been generously recognized as an ordinance of creation, the Christian faith has to prove its critical power precisely by continuing to insist that the nation is ambiguous and that, just for the sake of obedience to the nation as an ordinance of creation, the question must continue to be asked what is and what is not the nation's true demand. (162)

In the present situation, Christian faith must be a "critical power" and "prove its essentially *positive* character precisely in its *critical* stance" (162). It is able to do this because it knows God not only as Creator and Judge but also as Redeemer. It knows not only about sin, the human inclination selfishly to pervert all gifts, but also about grace. Grace, the gift of God's love, frees a person to love. The Christian is liberated from a bondage to self and to the world as given and achieves a positive critical stance by being freed to love the neighbors to whom he or she is bound by the common ties of humanity.

The positive service of Christian faith to the nation, therefore, is to exercise unremitting criticism of self, others, and nation based on the rigorous understanding of justice we find in the prophets and Jesus and in love for other people.

A half century later, we look back upon the Nazi rule of Germany and recall how through its rhetoric and propaganda it distorted the German language, reduced words to banality or made them stand for their opposites (a dangerous trend also in the United States today), and how by shouting and repetition it gave "the big lie" the aura of truth. Thus it is poignant when Bultmann referred to a recent Nazi student demonstration in which the slogan was "We want to abolish lies!" The slogan, he said, is good, and then he added, "But it also belongs to lying to hide the truth from oneself" (162). Then he commented on three recent developments in order to illustrate Christian responsibility to the nation.

The first seems relatively insignificant, but it uncovers something quite serious. The new Marburg city council, in its enthusiasm for the new regime, had already acted to rename some streets and squares for Nazi leaders. Bultmann said that such approbation in advance of the struggle to fulfill the task is light-minded and contradicts the critical stance of Christian faith. Christian faith and uncritical enthusiasm are incompatible. That statement directly contradicted Hirsch, who thought the new situation called for the helpful and clarifying word, not the critical word. "The divine love," Hirsch wrote, "does not begin with criticism and reservation. It pours itself totally into our life."[3]

Second, Bultmann warned against the growing practice of denouncing people to the authorities. (Many are well aware of the horrible role the denunciation of others played during the McCarthy era in the United States and always plays in any totalitarian police state.) To inform against others, Bultmann said, poisons the atmosphere. Referring again to the motto Nazi students had flaunted, he wrote: " 'We want to abolish lies'—fine, but it also belongs to this that one respects the free word, even when it expresses something other than what one wishes to hear. Otherwise one educates [people] to lie" (165).

Finally, he protested against the defamation of persons who are different from oneself, and he made his protest specific. "As a

---

3. Hirsch, *Christlicne Freiheit und politische Bindung*, p. 44.

Christian, I must deplore the injustice that is also being done precisely to German Jews by means of such defamation" (165).[4] This defamation, he said, is a demonic distortion of the intention to serve truth and country.

Then he brought his lecture to an end:

> If we have correctly understood the meaning and the demand of Christian faith, then it is quite clear that, *in face of the voices of the present, this Christian faith itself is being called into question*. In other words, we have to decide whether Christian faith is to be valid for us or not. . . . And we should as scrupulously guard ourselves against falsifications of the faith by national religiosity as against a falsification of national piety by Christian trimmings. The issue is either/or! (165)

Even as Bultmann gave his lecture, the church struggle was beginning. One of the first moves of the Nazi-affirming German Christian movement was to introduce the "Aryan paragraph," a new church law that would exclude from church ministry any person of non-Aryan origin and any person married to a person of non-Aryan origin. For well over a century, it had not been entirely unusual for Jewish persons in Germany to be baptized into a Christian church. In many of these cases, the motivation was social, to open possibilities that were barred to Jews who had not been "assimilated" and baptized. In some cases, there was, apparently, genuine conversion. Some ministers in the Protestant churches, therefore, were Jewish in descent. Some who were not were married to Jews. The "Aryan paragraph" was proposed by church leaders sympathetic to the Nazi regime as a way of bringing the church "into line" with the regime. The regime had already instituted such a law barring "non-Aryans" from civil service positions. A group of pastors in Hesse asked the theological faculties at Erlangen and Marburg for their opinions about the proposed new church law.

---

4. In the August issue of *Theological Leaves,* Martin Buber quoted with appreciation from this part of Bultmann's lecture in an open letter he wrote to Gerhard Kittel, who did not share Bultmann's view. "Offener Brief an Gerhard Kittel," *Theologische Blätter* 12, no. 8 (August 1933), 249.

Paul Althaus drafted the Erlangen statement. By unhistorical appeals to the New Testament and by pathetic appeals to the requirements of the German *Volk,* it supported the exclusion of Jews from church leadership.

The Marburg statement was supported unanimously by the faculty. After arguing the universality of Christian faith, that makes all people brothers and sisters without respect to race, it denounced the church law and concluded: "If these statements are taken with theological seriousness, then a political or ecclesiastical-political binding of church proclamation or a restriction of the rights of non-Aryan Christians in the church is not permitted."[5] The dean, Hans von Soden, signed the statement for the faculty. Bultmann wrote it.

In addition, Bultmann wrote a position paper that dealt specifically with the understanding of the Bible on the issue "The New Testament and the Race Question." He circulated the paper throughout German universities asking for the signatures of New Testament scholars. Twenty-one professors signed it, though three later withdrew their names. In the paper he drew on the New Testament to argue that race played no role in the church in its beginnings, and he dealt specifically with the passages that others had brought to bear in support of the exclusion of Jews from church ministry. The statement concluded: "It is therefore our view that a Christian church may absolutely not surrender this point of view [namely, the full inclusion of non-Aryans in the German church]."[6]

Bultmann sent the position paper to all central church offices and members of the National Synod, and he published it in *Theological Leaves.*

Georg Wobbermin, a colleague of Hirsch in Göttingen, wrote an extensive essay, countering the Marburg faculty's statement and Bultmann's position paper and defending anti-Jewish mea-

---

5. "Gutachten der theologischen Facultät der Universität Marburg zum Kirchengesetz über die Rechtsverhältnisse der Geistlichen und Kirchenbeamter," *Theologische Blätter* 12, no. 10 (October 1933), 294.

6. "Neues Testament und Rassenfrage," *Theologische Blätter* 12, no. 10 (October 1933), 296.

sures on the basis of what he called "existential psychology."[7] Wobbermin explained that the value of the method of existential psychology is that by taking account of the specific situation, it makes psychology useful for theology. In their concentration on the New Testament, the Marburg statement and Bultmann's paper overlooked the concrete situation and thus Luther's insight that no one understands the Word of God until that person experiences it. When one takes the present situation into account, the anti-Jewish measures are not only justified but appropriate.

First, Wobbermin noted that the church, in establishing the measures that excluded Jews from ministry, did not necessarily expound its own view but simply took up the view of State law instituted through "the National Socialistic German freedom movement" (357). Neither of the statements took account of the fact that the church was only trying to bring itself into line with the State. He wrote: "If the provisions of the Aryan paragraph that stand in question here are to be so decisively and radically denied in the context of the church, as both pronouncements want it, then the error must lie deeper" (357). He meant that the civil laws themselves must then be in error, and he taunted Bultmann and his Marburg colleagues to be consistent and carry through on this point. He wanted to represent them as having attacked the State.

He emphasized that the Jewish question was above all a race question. "It belongs to the great service of Adolf Hitler that he has raised this fact to the consciousness of broad circles" (358). The situation in Germany, he claimed, was a quite special one, and he explained that that was why foreigners had such difficulty at the present time understanding Germany. Because the present-day German Jewish question was an issue of race, the New Testament is irrelevant. The New Testament knows nothing, he conceded, about race or racial issues. The statements in question, he added, did not sharply argue that the New Testament actually excludes racial issues. It may be true that race has no bearing in

---

7. The article appeared under the editor's heading, "Zwei theologische Gutachten in Sachen des Arier-Paragraphen—kritisch beleuchtet," *Theologische Blätter* 12, no. 12 (December 1933), 336–359. Citations from Wobbermin's article will be indicated by page numbers in parentheses.

the individual's relation to God, and it certainly is the case that communion between all the Christians of the world is an aim of the international ecumenical movement, but the Aryan paragraph deals exclusively with a specific problem in the human sphere.

Wobbermin asked rhetorically if this human sphere with its concrete historical relations and distinctions could be understood to have no significance at all before God and if the church was not permitted to attach significance to it. He considered the answers to these questions self-evident and chastised Bultmann for disagreeing. Further, he thought Bultmann's statements were arbitrary constructions with no relation at all to the New Testament. In support of this judgment, he pointed to Paul's distinction between men and women and to Paul's prohibiting women from speaking in the church.

In conclusion, Wobbermin said the anti-Jewish measures were not really a matter of taking away rights or of punishment. They were, he insisted, only a matter of focusing on a critical situation. He admitted that the results could be tragic in individual cases, and he said that he, too, would experience pain in certain cases. Then, however, he claimed that the critical situation was caused precisely by "Jewish-cultural-Bolshevistic literati" (359) who threatened the German spiritual life and the church in the most severe way, and he pointed out that in some universities already 50 percent of the assistants and instructors were Jews. The church must contribute to the common German task, no matter how depressing it might be.

Bultmann responded to Wobbermin in an essay, "The Aryan Paragraph in the Context of the Church."[8] It was printed immediately following Wobbermin's piece. He said he would treat the Aryan paragraph only with reference to the church, not with reference to the State. He defended what the Marburg faculty and his New Testament cosigners had declared as appropriate judgments. He pointed out that for Wobbermin there seemed to be no question that civil laws can simply be transferred to the church.

---

8. "Der Arier Paragraph im Raume der Kirche," *Theologische Blätter* 12, no. 12 (December 1933), 359–370. Citations will be indicated by page numbers in parentheses.

"For us there is no doubt that this should *not* happen" (360). Church laws must correspond to the essence of the church. The Erlangen faculty, though its position differed from that of the Marburg faculty, agreed at least on that point.

The question for Bultmann was whether the Aryan paragraph was bearable in the church. For him the answer was simple, and he put it in the form of his own rhetorical question: "Does the proclaimer of the gospel in the church speak out of his being as a member of a *Volk* or out of the spirit of Christ?" (362). Then he commented, "Were I a non-Aryan or a not-purely-Aryan Christian, I would be ashamed to belong to a church in which I could, to be sure, listen but in which I had to keep silent" (362).

In this connection, he took up the question of sex and argued on historical-critical and exegetical grounds that Paul not only did not prohibit women from speaking in church but recognized no distinction of any kind in the church with respect to any church function. Both theologically and on the basis of the New Testament, Bultmann affirmed the ordination of women and their service as pastors. Later in his essay, he argued on the same grounds, with a side glance at the United States and in criticism of another supporter of the Aryan paragraph, that there is no valid barrier to blacks being pastors of white congregations.

In a way that reminds us of what he said in his opening lecture earlier in the year, he wrote:

> The things that are given us by nature are both limits and
> questions. They conceal curse with blessing. No Christian
> existence is possible in a simple, unambiguous "ethical"
> affirmation of what is given by nature, neither the particular
> gifts of the individual . . . nor social ties of whatever sort. . . .
> Only a rationalism blind to reality can isolate a natural order
> like biological determination in its significance for human
> community. Racial identity as a purely given fact contains
> absolutely no unambiguous direction for human action. (364)

It needs to be noted that although Bultmann indicated at the beginning of his essay that he would speak only about the church and not the State, his last point, as he stated it, has universal application.

Once again, he argued that not all the mores and orders of the *Volk* are bearable within the church. Racial exclusiveness is unbearable, and thus the Erlangen declaration and Wobbermin's position are not only false but heretical. The Aryan paragraph simply contradicts the truth of the church of Christ.

Wobbermin, working out of his so-called "existential psychology," stated that he wanted to avoid the Jewish destruction of the "German spiritual life." Bultmann commented: "If Luther had been an existential psychologist of religion there would have been no Reformation. Luther split the German spiritual life in two!" (366). The German spiritual life, he continued, is a historical phenomenon that is as ambiguous as any other historical development with its possibilities both for good and for evil.

Then, picking up on Wobbermin's taunts, he addressed Wobbermin directly:

> But I want to say to you, Colleague Wobbermin, you who reproach us for paying no attention to the concrete historical situation: I think we see it. We see it in all its ambiguity, and what we see gives us no comfort! And we believe that in this discord we must direct ourselves to the word of our Lord and not cast a sidelong glance at the so-called "unity of the German spiritual life." . . . Only under the criticism of the word of God and in constant tension with it can a true *Volk* consciousness, conscious of its limits as well as of its value and its task, develop. . . . If the church in the "New Empire for *Volk* and State" wants to bring blessing, it can do so only if unflinchingly and soberly it fulfills its proper mission, only if it never forgets that its critical task holds it constantly in tension with the consciousness of the *Volk*. (367, 368, 369)

Of the three theologians under consideration who saw the demonic character of "the great turning point" from the beginning, Bultmann was the only one who remained in Germany for the duration of the Third Reich. He was not free from harassment, but he was not dismissed. Marburg was a small university town far from Berlin. Although the town was governed by Nazis, the university had a sizable contingent of both professors and students who were not sympathetic with the regime, especially in the theological school. It tells us something about conditions, at least in the state of Hesse, of which Marburg is a part, that as late as 1944 Bultmann, who was entirely open about his membership in the Confessing Church, could be elected to the Hessian Protestant Church Council. During the dark years until 1945, when the United States army liberated Marburg, Bultmann continued to develop and apply the understanding of Christian faith he had already established.

A key to that understanding was his conviction that faith and life cannot be separated from one another. Throughout these years, he organized and led a "Theological Work Group" of pastors and teachers of religion whose purpose was to discuss how the bond between reflection about Christian faith and the actual life of the pastor and teacher could be maintained under the difficult conditions of the regime. In 1942, when the last teacher of religion in the local high school was conscripted, Bultmann himself took on the responsibility, and he continued it outside the school after Nazi authorities forbade the arrangement. He was an active member of his parish. He often preached, but when he was not preaching he served as deacon, receiving the offerings of the parishioners as they left the church service.

In his speaking and writing, he pressed the implications of his understanding to but not beyond the limit to which he thought he could go without being silenced. A sampling will suffice.

In 1935, the Minister for Science forbade theological professors from taking a position on the church struggle and, above all, from participating in theological examinations for ministerial candidates who were in the Confessing Church. The Minister also prohibited closed meetings of the Marburg faculty. Bultmann wrote the Minister:

> Because the intellectual work of theology has its grounding and purpose in the Protestant Church and because there can be no question that the Church has meaning and implications for both the people and the State, it is utterly impossible for the theological teacher in his instruction not to take a position on the ecclesiastical events and regulations of the present. Otherwise he would sunder the relation between intellectual work and concrete life which grants intellectual life its right in the first place. For since the current differences among

ecclesiastical parties are based on different conceptions of church doctrine, working toward a fundamental clarity in all questions pertaining to Christian doctrine . . . can by no means be separated from taking a position on the current ecclesiastical disputes even should I not make them the major subject of my lectures. It is equally impossible to represent a definite view in academic instruction and not to draw out the consequences of such a view for practical life.[9]

Frequently, Bultmann addressed issues pertaining to the State, especially as some connected their thinking about the State to the revelation of God in nature and to the Orders of Creation doctrine. In 1936, in an essay, "The Sermon on the Mount and the Justice of the State," he referred to the radical demands in the Sermon on the Mount where Jesus is reported to have used the formula "You have heard what was said to those of old . . . , but I say unto you . . . ," and contrasted them with the claims of the State.

The meaning of these antitheses is simply that the demand of *God* is set over against *justice* [that is, what the State declares to be "right"] and law. . . . God demands *more* than justice demands and can demand. . . . The meaning of justice [as God's claim] for them [the Prophets] is that it checks man's self-will and binds the life of the community with ordinances that protect each person from the oppressions of others. . . . With the idea that [prophetic] justice receives its meaning from the demand of love there is also given a criterion for criticizing and further developing positive justice [that is, provisions for justice in the State].[10]

In a special issue of *Protestant Theology* in 1941, Bultmann wrote on "The Question of Natural Revelation."

Where do we get our criterion for what is essentially German, if we assert the existence of such a thing? . . . *Every*

---

9. Cited by Erich Dinkler in "Rudolf Bultmann als Lehrer und Mensch," *Kirche in der Zeit* 14, no. 8 (August 1959), 259.

10. "Die Bergpredigt Jesu und das Recht des Staates," *Forschungen und Fortschritte* 12 (1936), 101–102. The English translation is from *Existence and Faith,* trans. Ogden, pp. 202–204.

phenomenon of history is ambiguous, and none reveals God's will in itself; and now more than ever *every historical phenomenon of the present* is ambiguous. . . . *The essential nature of the German people* is *not* present *as a clear criterion* by virtue of which we may clearly judge the rightness of our action.[11]

Most striking in relation to the topic of the State in that awesome situation was the essay Bultmann contributed to a volume for Karl Barth on his fiftieth birthday in 1936. Bultmann wrote on the apparently innocuous topic of "Polis [State] and Hades [the underworld] in Sophocles' Antigone."[12] The classical play deals with the conflict between Creon, the ruler of Thebes, and Antigone, who defied Creon's decree forbidding the burial of her brother, Polynices, who had tried to overthrow the tyrant. Haemon, the son of Creon, was in love with Antigone. Bultmann noted that Antigone appealed to the *nomoi* ("laws," the term used by Hirsch in his 1933 "joyous yes" to Hitler) and to *dike* ("righteousness"), both given by the gods. The ruler, of course, has the right and the power to proclaim the laws, but in this instance Antigone saw a conflict between a law proclaimed by Creon and justice. "She was obliged to trespass against this [Creon's] proclamation, for to obey it would have meant obedience prompted by the fear of men, for which she would not have wished to be answerable to the gods" (23). Bultmann commented that Antigone knew that her view was relative, but she dared to believe Creon's position was also relative. "The power from which true law is derived and by which all human law and its statutes is given" (25) has a relative status. Therefore, "she honors the gods when she trespasses against Creon's command" (25).

Without comment from Bultmann, the words of the tyrant had an unmistakably contemporary ring:

---

11. *Offenbarung und Heilsgeschehen,* Beiträge zur evangelische Theologie, no. 7 (1941). The English translation is from *Essays Philosophical and Theological,* trans. Greig, p. 105.

12. "Polis und Hades in Sophocles Antigone," *Theologische Aufsätze, Karl Barth zum 50. Geburtstag* (1936), pp. 78–89. The English translation is from *Essays Philosophical and Theological,* trans. Greig, pp. 22–35. Citations are from the English translation and are indicated by page numbers in parentheses.

CREON: Am I to rule for others, or myself?
HAEMON: A State for one man is no State at all.
CREON: The State is his who rules it, so 'tis held.

. . . .

Whomever the State
Appoints, must be obeyed in everything,
Both small *and great,* just *and unjust alike.* (Bultmann's emphasis)
(29, 30)

In Bultmann's analysis, Sophocles' play made its own point: The laws instituted by a State are ambiguous and must be measured by the transcendent standard of justice.

National Socialism had an uncanny appeal to hosts of Germans. It was much more than a political program. It rooted itself in a comprehensive ideology and was nourished by mystic impulses. A good many writers expounded the worldview and tried to evoke its mystique. Works of art from the German past were drawn into their service. The musical dramas of Wagner, the poetry of Rilke, and the novels of Hermann Hesse were immensely popular. Also, theologians and preachers tried to appropriate the worldview and mystique in their expositions of Christian faith. In these years, Bultmann continued to argue, as he had already in the 1920s, that Christian faith is neither a worldview nor a form of mysticism. On the contrary, he taught that Christian faith is an event in response to the proclamation of Jesus Christ in which a person is turned outward from the self and both called and freed to live here and now in behalf of others in the consciousness of living in the presence of the God of grace and justice.

The most base and tragic aspect of the Nazi worldview and its mysticism was its emphasis on "blood and soil" and its anti-Jewish racism. We have already seen that Bultmann objected to the defamation of the Jews and to the proposed Aryan paragraph in the church in 1933. In 1936, he wrote an essay that took Alfred Rosenberg to task. Rosenberg was probably the worst and certainly the most popular Nazi ideologue. In 1930, he published *The Myth of the Twentieth Century*. By 1938, this book had gone through 142 printings. Bultmann wrote on "Jesus and Paul" and referred to Rosenberg [who thought Jesus was not a Jew] at the start:

According to Alfred Rosenberg, the "great personality of Jesus" has "been misused" by ecclesiastical Christianity. "Whatever its original form, the great personality of Jesus Christ was immediately after his departure burdened and amalgamated with all the rubbish of Near Eastern, of Jewish and African life."[13]

Rosenberg argued that the apostle Paul was a chief originator of this debasement of Jesus. Bultmann carefully and thoroughly argued that one cannot take Jesus without Paul, that the proclamation of Paul coheres essentially with the message of Jesus. Bultmann pointed out that the legal prescriptions Jesus claimed had been superseded were not specifically Jewish.

> Rather, they are demands of justice such as everywhere spring from man's moral consciousness: the prohibition of murder and manslaughter and of adultery and perjury; the law regulating divorce; the *jus talionis* [the law of punishment in kind]; and the demand for national solidarity. . . . God demands more than justice. (189)

> For Jesus, just as for Paul, God stands beyond the world as Creator and Judge, and this world itself is perverted and fallen under the domination of evil powers. . . . Thus whoever finds Paul offensive and uncanny must find Jesus equally so. For what Paul expressly says, namely, that the gospel is a scandal, is exactly what is shown by Jesus' proclamation, ministry, and destiny. (193–194)

> It [the message of Jesus and Paul] asks us whether we are prepared to understand the meaning and goal of our life not in terms of our own world-views and plans, but on the basis of the Christian proclamation that encounters us as the word of God. (201)

In a 1936 essay, he added in the same vein: "The Christian doctrine of the state may not attempt to reduce the latter . . . to a

---

13. "Jesus und Paulus," *Jesus Christus im Zeugnis der Heiligen Schrift und der Kirche.* Beiheft 2 zur *Evangelische Theologie.* The English translation is from *Existence and Faith,* trans. Ogden, p. 183. Further citations are from the English translation and are indicated by page numbers in parentheses.

nationality that is constituted by the divine powers of blood and soil."[14]

The Jewish issue also evoked further conflict between Bultmann and Emanuel Hirsch. In 1936, Hirsch published two books on the Gospel of John. Bultmann wrote a long review essay of these books that came out the following year.[15] In detail, Bultmann argued that Hirsch's fundamental thesis was absolutely wrong. He quoted Hirsch's statement of the thesis: "Between Christianity and Judaism, between faith in the living Word that liberates and Jewish service which means bondage, there is an irreconcilable opposition" (123). He devoted most of his essay to undermining Hirsch's basic thesis that the Gospel of John contrasts the freedom of faith with Jewish legalism. It is the case that in John the "Jews" are the stereotyped opponents of Jesus. Bultmann put the term "Jews" in quotation marks and argued that for John it was simply a synonym for "the world" and that the theme of the Fourth Gospel is the fight of the Redeemer over against "the world." He thought Hirsch's most unfortunate thought was that the Gospel was like a Greek tragedy. Hirsch came to this conclusion because he thought it was impossible that "it could have been written by a Semite" (131). Bultmann claimed that we can know nothing of the author, but he put forward a considerable amount of research that pointed to the origin of the Gospel in the world of Semitic gnosticism, and he observed, "Hirsch has sovereignly ignored" (132) that research. He charged that instead of dealing with the evidence, Hirsch was "from beginning to end" determined by the one-sided view that Jesus' struggle was against Jewish legalism and messianism, "against the Jewish essence that [Hirsch thinks] has infiltrated or wants to infiltrate the Christian churches" (133).

In 1940, Hirsch published a book on *The Resurrection Accounts and Christian Faith*. Bultmann again reviewed Hirsch's work.[16] In

---

14. "Der Sinn des christlichen Schöpfungsglaubens," *Zeitschrift für Missionskunde und Religionswissenschaft* 51 (1936). The English translation is from *Existence and Faith*, trans. Ogden, p. 223.

15. "Hirschs Auslegung des Johannes-Evangeliums," *Evangelische Theologie* 4 (1937), 115–142. Citations are indicated by page numbers in parentheses.

16. *Theologische Literaturzeitung* 65 (1940), 242–246.

his book, Hirsch found the deeper content of the original Easter faith in the freeing of the disciples from the Jewish faith. Bultmann commented that this view was very one-sided, "above all when he does not take into account that in the early Easter faith the Old Testament-Jewish faith in God as the Lord of history, who leads history to its goal, is maintained, indeed, that that [early Easter] faith is in no way comprehensible without this [Jewish] faith."[17]

The following are a few excerpts from Bultmann's sermons in those years, which, together with his teaching, gave students the courage to take up the preaching office in the days of the church struggle.[18]

June 7, 1936, speaking about outcroppings of evil in the world that lead people to ask how God could allow them:

> Do we take it so much for granted that we ourselves could never be guilty of these atrocities, that the thought or question never occurs to us whether every man who partici-
> pates in evil is not in part responsible for what the massed forces of evil are doing on this earth?[19]

May 9, 1937, talking about the Christian attitude to nature:

> We know very well those misleading voices which in our time declare: it is in nature, in its infallible courses and eternal energies, that God reveals Himself to us. . . . We cannot doubt as Christians that we must not follow such teaching. . . .
> He [the nature mystic] feels that a divine energy and a sacred will are expressed in his blood, and in the impulses to which it gives rise. God lives within him, he thinks, inasmuch as he belongs to the community of his people [Volk] with its natural roots in race and soil, and its solidarity flowing from oneness of blood and one sacred energy throbbing within it.

---

17. Ibid., p. 243.

18. The comment was made by Erich Vellmer in *Gedenken an Rudolf Bultmann*, ed. Otto Kaiser (Tübingen: J. C. B. Mohr [Paul Siebeck], 1977), p. 10.

19. Rudolf Bultmann, *This World and the Beyond: Marburg Sermons,* trans. Harold Knight (New York: Charles Scribner's Sons, 1960), p. 19. Further citations from this book are indicated by page numbers in parentheses.

God in the race, God in man! For Christians it is a matter of course that a belief such as this violates the majesty of God, and the Christian recoils in horror from the consequences to which such a blasphemous doctrine leads. (37, 43–44)

May 15, 1938, in dealing with a text from John:

The very existence in the world of the Christian Church is a protest against the world; a protest against the presumption of the world to be able to impose ultimate duties and obligations. . . .

The Christian faith (and not it alone) knows, or can know, . . . that the struggle between right and wrong, between truth and falsehood in world history is never decisively closed, but lasts as long as earth remains. Savagery that had apparently been mastered breaks out afresh one day; crimes of wanton wickedness, the like of which had long been forgotten, dare to sully human civilization once more. Again and again it happens that right is crushed and innocence is trampled under foot, truth is suppressed and falsehood is enthroned. . . .

And the Christian knows that even the most ardent readiness for sacrifice does not in itself prove the rightness of his cause. (63, 65–66, 69)

From December 11, 1938:

To-day we hear voices loudly raised and in no uncertain manner, to declare that such a hope [the messianic hope for deliverance from oppression] is not only a childish dream but is actually pernicious and morbid, since it incapacitates people to perform the work that is required to be done; and that for these reasons it should be fought and conquered by all possible means. And in this struggle which is now engaged, it is being said: what is the origin of such a hope? It originates with Israel and the Jews! with Jewish prophets and dreamers! All that is essentially foreign to our own way of life.

We must not allow ourselves to be led astray by such voices even if the picture they draw were true. But it is not true. (102)

242

PART IV

THE UNCERTAIN PRESENT

"How can one look out for something one can't see? . . . One can't calculate everything in life."—HANS FALLADA[1]

He knew nevertheless that here on earth we have all to go our ways on crutches.—HERMANN BROCH[2]

In 1946, one year after the devastation of Europe and the Holocaust ended in the unconditional surrender of Germany, Hans Fallada wrote a gripping novel about an elderly Berlin couple during the war years. After their son was killed in Hitler's war, their feelings of abhorrence for the Nazi state surfaced. In their simple way, they decided to do something about it. They began writing criticisms of the regime on small cards. Each day, the husband would travel to a section of the city and deposit cards in apartment houses so that the tenants would be sure to find them. It was, one would think, an ineffectual form of resistance, but it preoccupied a good part of the Berlin Gestapo for two years.

The suspense of the novel is in the juxtaposition of the couple's activity with the work of a shrewd detective who wove a net from a few clues and many inferences and slowly pulled it around his prey. Surprised to find that his catch was only a simple, elderly couple who, once caught, spoke honestly and straightforwardly about what they had done, except for each trying to protect the other, the detective was almost converted to their cause. The course of the affair, however, was by that time out of his control. The old man was decapitated, and the old woman died in her cell in a bombing raid.

---

1. Hans Fallada, *Jeder stirbt für sich allein* (Reinbeck bei Hamburg: Rowohlt Taschenbuch Verlag, 1964), p. 233. The novel was first published in 1947.
2. Hermann Broch, *The Sleepwalkers,* trans. Willa Muir and Edwin Muir (New York: Grosset & Dunlap, 1964), p. 340. The original German edition appeared in 1931.

Fallada titled his novel "Everyone Dies for Himself or Herself Alone,"[3] a flip of the well-known conceit "Everyone lives for himself alone." Although the old man often repeated the title sentence, his character, his wife's character, and what they accomplished without calculation or awareness displayed the fallacy of it.[4]

At an ominous moment in the story, the old man said, "How can one look out for something one can't see? . . . One can't calculate everything in life."[5] No one can ever with certainty see what is coming, nor is it possible to look out for what one cannot with certainty see. In any case, one cannot calculate how to deal with the diabolical specter whose shape is different every time and everywhere it appears.

To live in this world is to live in an uncertain present. That does not mean that this or any other present is moving into dark times comparable to the darkness of Nazi Germany. It does mean that in this present time, as in any future present time, a cloud, the harbinger of an encroaching darkness, could be on our horizon. If so, it would be difficult for us to recognize it for what it is, and we can rely on no formula or calculation to help us. Hermann Broch's character in *The Sleepwalkers* was right: "He knew nevertheless that here on earth we have all to go our ways on crutches."[6]

But however helpful it is to know that, those who are concerned about Christian faith want to know more. They want to know whether in the always uncertain present there are in Christian faith understandings of God, self, and world that help one to recognize the demonic before it shows itself boldly and whether Christian faith helps one find the courage to name it for what it is and to say "No!"

No historical study can answer these questions definitively for this or any other present. Every present must struggle with the theological question for itself, and every past effort is dated. But

---

3. *Jeder stirbt für sich allein.* Happily, *sich* in the German language is not gender specific.

4. One is reminded of Romans 14:7 (translating from the German version of Luther): "For no one of us lives to him- or herself, and no one dies to him- or herself."

5. Fallada, *Jeder stirbt für sich allein,* p. 233.

6. Broch, *The Sleepwalkers,* p. 340.

Christian faith has a history; and with imagination, people concerned about it can not only understand that history better, they can also make judgments about it and appropriate it, with whatever modifications, in working their way to answers, however provisional they may be, for their time and place. What we have recalled can be particularly helpful, because from where we stand it was so clearly a dark time and because we can see that living into it, as our six theologians had to do, it was as uncertain a time as our own.

If our recollection is to be helpful for our time, we must move from the history of theology (recounting as best we can the course of theology in the past) to historical theology (hazarding judgments, yes and no, about that past). In this way, we are on the way to being theologians, that is, daring to say what authentic Christian faith means and does not mean, implies and does not imply, here and now.

*   *   *   *   *

One is tempted to explain Emanuel Hirsch by reference to the effects his special experiences and particular formation likely had upon him personally. Psychological allusions are an all but involuntary mode of explanation in our time, and Hirsch provides ample data for such speculations. In 1914, he wanted to serve his country as a soldier, but he was rejected because of his poor eyesight and his weak physical stature. Surely, we are inclined to think, having to stay on the home front intensified his patriotism and accounts for the astonishing discipline he maintained in filling the shoes of two professors at the university in Bonn during the First World War before he formally qualified himself as a professor. He called this work his "war service." The news he read and his own inclinations would have led him to believe that German soldiers had in fact not broken the time-honored rules of warfare by killing Belgian civilians and that the German surrender had in fact come about because of "a stab in the back," a conviction not unlike that held by a good many with respect to the defeat of the United States in Vietnam. A good bit of further data could be added to encourage us in this explanation. But psychology is not theology, and our question is theological. Moreover, Hirsch intended his position to stand or fall on the basis of its theological coherence, and we must take him in the way he wanted to present himself.

Hirsch was a formidable theologian. He mastered not only the documents of the origins and traditions of Christianity but also philosophy and everything else that came into his purview. Above all, he was a systematic theologian no one interested in theology could ignore. He based his theology on four premises: (1) The power of the God who created the world pulses through the creation drawing or enticing history to the more complete fulfillment of its purposes. (2) Faith in this God has to do with historical life. It is not simply an individualistic doctrine of personal salvation. The demand of God is that we take responsibility for corporate well-being in the world. (3) The specific claim of God, because of the limitations of our life, has to do with one's particular time and place, and it can be known only through the conscience, by the risk of decision. (4) The courage to live boldly and responsibly under the claim of God is given by the conviction that God justifies the sinner by grace rather than by the sinner's fallible works.

He drew these premises from the biblical accounts of God's dealings with Israel, from what he took to be the personality and message of Jesus, and from the proclamation of Paul. These premises were truths for him on the basis of which he developed a theology of history that tried to illuminate the historical situation of the time and to give guidance to those who struggled in their consciences about what to do. It is of the essence of Christian faith, he was convinced, that it yields answers to the ethical question.

Like Althaus and Gogarten, Hirsch saw a fundamental contradiction between the sense of corporate responsibility given by Christian faith and the radical individualism that had developed in the western democracies. He was especially critical of appeals to serve "humanity." As an ideal, "humanity" seemed to him so abstract and vague that it could not yield realistic ethical guidelines. On the contrary, a *Volk,* he thought, is not at all abstract or vague. It can elicit a sense of identity and consequently a willingness to sacrifice everything for the good of the larger whole, thus overcoming egoistic individualism. He believed that identity with the *Volk,* willingness to sacrifice, and transcending self-centeredness cohere with and are sanctified by Christian faith in God.

In the 1920s, Hirsch was certain the German *Volk* faced its most severe crisis. Germany was an impoverished nation whose existence was threatened by vengeful enemies from the outside, subversive enemies on the inside, and the loss of its identity under God. He appealed for the recovery of that identity with focus on its religious grounding, and he passionately urged the German *Volk* to subdue its enemies both without and within. His appeal was powerful.

Perhaps an analogy will help us to understand its power. Let us suppose that in the United States the dependence on oil from the Middle East and the preference of the people for products from other countries, for whatever reasons, continues. And let us suppose that the United States fails in its effort to sell enough products abroad to bring about a tolerable balance of payments. Further, let us suppose that other countries, controlling large amounts of our currency, called in our debts, resulting in a dramatic devaluation of the dollar, a higher rate of inflation than the United States has heretofore experienced, and a dramatic drop in the real income of our citizens. Would not a voice that called us once again to think of ourselves above all as a people who must work together for the good of the whole be persuasive? Would not an appeal to recover the finest traits in the "American character," traits we had allowed imperceptibly to fade, find resonance? Would not a proclamation that we can overcome our fate if only we can gain a common mind and spirit and be willing to make sacrifices for the good of the whole win support? Perhaps even a call to reclaim the faith of our forebears would make a good many want to kneel together before the altar.

That response is what Hirsch wanted from the Germans in the postwar years that were so dark and humiliating to him. His conviction that only exceptional leadership could elicit it was compelling to many. He found his leader in Adolf Hitler.

It is tragic that this formidable theologian, who confessed that he had been saved for Christian faith by *critical* theology, made one fateful exception to the principle of criticism. However much that decision may have been a matter of conscience for him, the price was high. He lost thereby any criteria in the Christian tradition on the basis of which the worldview, policies, and tactics

247

of the Third Reich might have been judged to be wrong, and he lost the handle that might have brought his own anti-Semitism under judgment. To borrow an image from Ludwig Wittgenstein, it was as if he had climbed to the roof of the shed and had thrown away the ladder.[7] Such a maneuver is not allowed if one wants to operate in the open forum. Hirsch insisted on his commitment to the open forum, but, as we saw in his controversy with Barth over the Dehn affair, he laid down conditions that guaranteed a provincial, narrowly German forum.

It is ironic that the theologian who most clearly pointed out the source of Hirsch's error in giving himself to Hitler and the Third Reich was the one who by friendship and in mode of thought was closest to him, Paul Tillich. That their modes of thought were so similar is also unsettling. At the beginning of his career, Tillich constructed a theology of culture, and he developed it more fully into a coherent and persuasive comprehensive philosophy and theology of history, which came to a major statement in his book *The Socialist Decision* (1933). It is no wonder that book was thrown on the fire heaps by the Nazis. Similarly and with remarkable structural affinity, at the beginning of his career Hirsch constructed a philosophical theology of history. Over the Weimar years, he developed it more fully and brought it to a high level of coherence and comprehensiveness in his 1934 book *The Present-Day Religious Situation*, in which he hailed the advent of Hitler. These two bodies of thought are not easily distinguishable in their mode and structure of thought.

What distinguishes them and in my judgment accounts for their opposite political conclusions is a pervasive theme in Tillich that is not itself inherent in the mode and structure of thought he shared with Hirsch. I refer to what Tillich called the "prophetic" or "Protestant" principle.

To be sure, Tillich and Hirsch shared a commitment to critical theology, and it can be said of Tillich in much the same way as of Hirsch that critical theology saved him for Christian faith. For Tillich, however, it was not the academic encounter with critical

---

7. Ludwig Wittgenstein, *Tractatus Logico-Philosophicus,* trans. C. K. Ogden (London: Routledge & Kegan Paul, 1949), pp. 188, 189.

theology but an insight that became fundamental to his faith and, at the same time, not only opened the way to critical theology but made it necessary. That insight came in his student days and was ignited by Martin Kähler's interpretation of the classic Protestant doctrine of justification by grace through faith. Following Luther, theologians had understood this doctrine to mean that a person cannot by moral or religious activity win God's favor. The acceptance of a person by God is God's free gift (grace). The graciously accepted person then *wants* to act responsibly in the world under the claim of God. Drawing on Martin Kähler, the breakthrough Tillich made was that thinking is also a mode of acting and that therefore justification by grace apart from works has to do with what we think as well as how we act. The doubter as well as the sinner is justified by God's grace through faith.

> The step I myself made in these years was the insight that the principle of justification through faith refers not only to the religious-ethical but also to the religious-intellectual life. Not only he who is in sin but also he who is in doubt is justified through faith. The situation of doubt, even of doubt about God, need not separate us from God. There is faith in every serious doubt, namely, the faith in the truth as such, even if the only truth we can express is our lack of truth. But if this is experienced in its depth and as an ultimate concern, the divine is present; and he who doubts in such an attitude is "justified" in his thinking.[8]

Tillich named this understanding "the Protestant principle." By that term he meant that at the core of his faith there was a commitment to shrink from no question and to subject everything, including the faith itself and its sources, to radical criticism.

Therefore, when Tillich charged Hirsch with having surrendered the prophetic element in Christian faith, he was not simply pointing to an intellectual flaw, a mistake in method. He was pointing to a perversion of Christian faith itself. His charge was all the more potent because it dealt with the essence of Christian faith. Tillich, indeed, was right. That was "what it's all about."

---

8. Tillich, *The Protestant Era,* trans. Adams, p. xiv.

The theological basis for Althaus's support of Hitler was his adaptation of the doctrine of the Orders of Creation, as that doctrine had developed in conservative Lutheranism, and his conviction, in concert with orthodox and "positive" Lutheranism, that the law continued to have validity under grace. To this theological foundation he coupled his distress over the erosion of traditional values and his sensitivity for the plight of the German *Volk*. Paul Knitter has argued that these factors were formative of Althaus's political ideology and that it was his political ideology rather than his theology that led him to affirm "the great turning point" of 1933.[9] Knitter also attributes Althaus's approval of the Aryan paragraph to his political ideology and insists that Althaus was not theologically anti-Semitic. He reports that he learned from conversations with Althaus's son that Althaus fell silent after 1937 because he saw the evil of the Third Reich. Many people have attested to Althaus's kind and generous spirit, but Knitter's argument makes a distinction that Althaus himself would have disavowed in the years we have considered.

Althaus was not interested in politics on the one side and theology on the other but in political theology. That is, he argued that the primal revelation of the Orders of Creation point us to the importance of our given historical life and that understanding those Orders can and should give us guidance for the conduct of our lives in our specific historical situation. He may not have been anti-Semitic on direct theological grounds, but central to his theology was the *Volk* as an Order of Creation known in the primal revelation, and he understood *Volk* in racial and social terms.

Althaus emphasized the subordination of the primal revelation to the redemptive revelation in Jesus Christ, but his understanding of redemption did not provide him criteria for criticizing what was happening. His appropriation of the doctrine of justification by faith contributed to a measure of caution in his political judgments. This caution is evident, for example, in his overuse of "on the one hand . . . on the other," but this tool was a blunt knife that sliced nothing. Invariably, he stated his reservation, caution, or

---

9. "Die Uroffenbarungslehre von Paul Althaus—Anknüpfungspunkt für den Nationalsozialismus?" *Evangelische Theologie* 33 (1973), 138–163.

critical point first and followed it with his positive and enthusiastic point such that the reader or hearer could have no doubt where the emphasis fell. He or she could easily overlook the reservation.

Althaus has been acknowledged as one of the great Luther scholars of the twentieth century, but until 1937 he did not comprehend what it was that led Luther to say that a good prince is a "rare bird." Even if Knitter's argument were sound, it would not be complimentary to Althaus because it would show that there was nothing decisive in his theology to challenge his "political ideology."

The most troublesome case among the theologians we have considered is Gogarten. When one traces Hirsch, Althaus, and Gogarten from the end of World War I through the Nazi takeover, one notes that only Gogarten underwent a political conversion (not denying that Gogarten defended his politics theologically or that he had some *völkisch* affinities in the twenties). Given his identity with Karl Barth, on the one side of Dialectical Theology, and with Rudolf Bultmann, on the other, one might be able, by a stretch of the imagination, to overlook his short-lived identification with the German Christians in 1933. He distanced himself from that movement when he saw it was fundamentally anti-Semitic. But his dissociation from the German Christians was not accompanied by a criticism of the Third Reich. As a matter of fact, Gogarten continued to support National Socialism through 1937. His sharply critical book against Karl Barth in that year clearly evidences his continuing support of the regime. His position is especially troubling because he was at least as adamant as Barth in proclaiming God's "No" of judgment in the midtwenties, and at the turn of the decade he shared with Bultmann the theological foundation that led Bultmann to understand the ambiguity of everything human.

Along the way, however, Gogarten made two mistakes, one of which relates to his affinity with Barth and one of which relates to his affinity with Bultmann.

For Barth, God was "the Wholly Other" who claims the human being absolutely. A key to Barth's theology is the First Commandment: "You shall have no other gods before me." For Barth, this commandment established the transcendence of God, the abso-

lute distinction between God and human beings, and the consequent judgment of God on all human thinking and acting. For
Barth, this one Wholly Other God was revealed in Jesus Christ as
witnessed in the Bible and proclaimed in the church. Gogarten's
way of saying the same thing was to proclaim the Lordship
(*Herrschaft*) of God and of Jesus Christ. But Gogarten, unlike
Barth, inferred from the Lordship of God and God's total claim on
human beings the analogous necessity of Lordship within the
ordained structures of the world, and he tried to defend this
analogy theologically. To acknowledge the Lordship of God is to
acknowledge that all human beings are at root evil and prone to
self-interest. Left to themselves, they will destroy each other. The
doctrines of Lordship and of human sinfulness became for him
truths from which inferences could be drawn. In this way, he
concluded that the divinely ordained structure of human society is
authoritarian Lordship, that is, a society that coerces people to
live rightly. That structure is providential, because by constraint it
saves human beings from themselves and because it prepares
people, by analogy, for faith, the confession of the Lordship of
God. The church, then, performs a service to the State and the
State to the church.

Although he did not give up his theological authoritarianism, he
moved closer to Bultmann and took up the theme of faith as
relationship, with the consequent correlation of statements about
God and about human being. This development made it possible
for Gogarten to try to make Christian faith comprehensible to
human beings. By describing the corollary and immediate effects
in the human consciousness of faith in the grace of God in Jesus
Christ, he was more able to evoke a "Yes, it is so; now I
understand" from people of faith and even an "I see what you are
talking about" from others if they were willing to use their
imaginations and to think of God and human beings in analogy
with human relationships.

In the early and midtwenties, he could only assert that faith is
the act of God on human beings who, without God's Word, are
helpless. In the analogy of relationship, however, the human
being is grateful to God not simply because the Bible teaches one
to be grateful but because the new life in faith cannot be
understood as an accomplishment of the self. The person of faith

gives thanks to God and thereby attributes his or her faith to God's "act," which is like saying "miracle" or gift.

Further, the development led Gogarten more forthrightly to theological ethics. Justification by grace or redemption turns a person and makes that person want to be turned outward from the self. Because faith does not abstract a person from this world, the consciousness of relationship with God affects one's life in the world by turning one outward to other people. The command to love God and the command to love the neighbor are coherently inseparable. From this connection, which inherently negates the boundaries of "blood and soil," we can see why there was a brake in Gogarten against anti-Semitism.

But in the course of these modifications, Gogarten did not surrender his authoritarian conception of Lordship or the inference he drew from it for the divinely ordained structure of society. He was able to retain and even to intensify these themes because he violated at one crucial point the logic of relationship. Faith in the grace of God through Jesus Christ has its immediate corollary in the human consciousness not only in the sense of new life but also in the acknowledgment of one's own unworthiness of God's gift. That is, faith leads to the confession of sin and, at the same time, to the confession that God is Lord and not oneself. This, in traditional theological language, is what it means to give thanks to God.

It is consistent with the logic of relationship to believe that the conviction of one's own unworthiness applies equally to all human beings, but it is not consistent with that logic to divorce the belief from its basis in self-understanding and then to employ it as a universal truth from which further assertions may be deduced. Because human beings as such are radically evil, it is necessary, he thought, that they be coerced into living civilly with each other and into working together for the good of the *Volk* rather than for what they mistakenly think to be their own gain. Thus—this time from a different base—we must also have Lordship in political life, and this Lordship is a service to faith just as the confession of the Lordship of God in faith is a service to the State.

When Gogarten correlated the Lordship of God and Lordship in political life, he overlooked a fundamental contradiction between the two in their effects. To affirm the Lordship of God is to be given a principle of criticism applicable first to oneself and then to all things human. To affirm Lordship in political life, even when it is not identified with the Lordship of God, is to lose any potential principle of criticism in the political arena. To confess that God is Lord is to acknowledge that neither oneself nor anyone else is God. Yielding to Lordship in the State, however, leads to unquestioning obedience. The two are, on this ground, incompatible; and if one tries to correlate them, the principle of criticism that comes with affirming the Lordship of God is blunted, if not lost. Gogarten committed this conceptual mistake and lost the critical distance from the Third Reich that he might otherwise have had.

The inference Gogarten drew from the Lordship of God was unthinkable to Karl Barth. Like Gogarten, Barth insisted on staying within the framework of what he took to be God's revelation in the Bible, but he maintained that sovereignty or Lordship belongs to God alone. Thus Barth could give theological approbation to no form of the State. In the preface to the second edition of his Romans commentary in 1921, he stated his premise: "If I have a system, it is limited to a recognition of what Kierkegaard called the 'infinite qualitative distinction' between time and eternity."[10] Over the years, Kierkegaard became far less important to him, but he never surrendered or modified the premise. Thus everything human is equidistant from God and falls equally under the judgment of God's "No." Consequently, Barth applied the critical principle to all human institutions and modes of thought, including his own effort rightly to lay hold of and state the truth about God as he believed it to be given in God's revelation.

This premise also substantively affected Barth's view of God's salvific work. He thought it would violate the infinite qualitative distinction between time and eternity if one were to think that faith in Christ yields a transformation of one's life in the world that is theologically significant. Thus he distinguished sharply between reconciliation and redemption. Reconciliation is God's act that removes the alienation between human beings and God. Faith accepts and believes that God has accomplished this reconciliation

10. Barth, *The Epistle to the Romans,* trans. Hoskyns, p. 10.

in Christ. God's objective act is objectively accepted. Redemption, on the other hand, has to do with the new life in Christ. Because of his conviction about the infinite distance between God and human beings, Barth could not speak about redemption as a present reality, not even with dialectical reservations as a having and not having at the same time. Therefore redemption remained for him an eschatological promise and hope. Therefore he found the key to 1 Corinthians in the chapter on the final resurrection in contrast to Bultmann, who located it in the chapter on love.

The perseverance of Barth in this premise accounts theologically for his steadfast opposition to Hirsch, Althaus, and all others who gave their enthusiastic and "happy Yes" to Hitler, for his immediate withdrawal from *Between the Times* when Gogarten sided with the German Christian movement, for his ringing call to do theology "as if nothing had happened" in "Theological Existence Today!," for his tireless work to give firmness of leadership to what became the Confessing Church, and not least for his writing and defense of the Barmen Declaration. A large number of both pastors and lay persons found the strength to stand firm in their faith against the ideological perversion of the church from Barth's steady flow of publications and the decibels of his voice. What many of these persons had to endure during the twelve years of the Third Reich is depressing, maddening, and inspiring. Anyone committed to the God of Jesus Christ rightly and properly celebrates the resistance of Barth. His theological understanding led him to be critical, and in his faith he found the courage to say his "Noes" with exclamation points.

In Karl Barth, we see the strength of commitment to the doctrine of God's revelation in Jesus Christ and to the record of that revelation in the Bible. This theological foundation, however, conceals within it a problem we must explore. Like his theological forebear, John Calvin, Barth exempted the Bible from full participation in the human sphere, where everything is flawed and subject to radical criticism. He was not what we tend today to call a "Fundamentalist" or a "biblical inerrantist." He acknowledged that the Bible is a human word, but that human word as such and in its entirety is the unique bearer of the divinely secured Word of God. It is God by the Holy Spirit who speaks in the Bible, and it is God by the Holy Spirit who inspires the human being to know that it is God by the Holy Spirit who speaks in the Bible. Thus both the Bible as such and the acknowledgment of the Bible as God's Word are the work of God, God's miracle. In this way, what we find in the text of the Bible is not subject to the otherwise universal application of the critical principle.

> The *acceptance* of these incredible testimonies of the Scripture I call *faith*. Here I once again cannot admit that this is a discovery of *my* theology, but ask, aside from sentimentalities, what else faith could be than the obedience which I give, as if it were God's Word, to a human word which it testifies to as God's Word directed to me. Let no one deceive himself here concerning the fact that this is an unheard of occurrence, that the Holy Spirit must now be spoken of. . . . I therefore distinguish between faith as *God's work* on us (for only God can say to us in a way that we will hear it, what *we* can*not* hear, I Cor. 2:9), and all known and unknown human organs and functions, including all our so-called "religious experiences." . . .
> It must be the case that everything that can be said against the possibility of revelation may also be said with the same weight against the possibility of faith. . . . *This* must remain, that the *God* who according to the witness of the Scripture has spoken "the word of Christ" now speaks it *through* the witness of the Scripture through the power of the *testimonium spiritus sancti internum* [internal testimony of the Holy Spirit—Calvin's phrase], also to *me,* that I *hear* it and by hearing it, *believe.* . . . I have no confidence in any other objectivity than the one outlined here or through the correlate concepts of "Scripture" and "Spirit."[11]

The problem with this position is that from any point of view other than its own, it is arbitrary and provincial. The consequences of this problem are hazardous for faith at any time, even in dark times when it seems to serve so well.

First, from any point of view other than its own, the position is arbitrary. From its own point of view, of course, the belief comes

---

11. From Barth's debate with Adolf von Harnack in the pages of *Die christliche Welt,* 1923. In *The Beginnings of Dialectical Theology,* trans. Crim, ed. Robinson, p. 181.

about because of the internal testimony of the Holy Spirit. That is, it is a miracle of God. In the larger forum, however, all events that a person or group claim to be miraculous are ambiguous. Today we tend to offer psychological or scientific (often pseudopsychological and pseudoscientific) explanations as alternatives. In ancient times, when it was common for events to be labeled "miracles," their ambiguity was found in the question about the source of the strange event, as in the repeated claim by Jesus' adversaries that he cast out demons by the power of Beelzebub rather than by the power of God.

The designation of an occurrence, even faith, as a miracle must strike anyone on the outside as arbitrary. Worse, from the inside, from the point of view of the person who claims the miracle, it requires for its affirmation a sacrifice of the intellect. One who makes the claim must know that however much one may insist on the validity of the claim, one cannot make anyone who does not share one's conviction understand it. One is limited to one's own enclave. Perhaps most problematic of all, a good many of those on the outside are quite ready to think that the position is not only arbitrary but that theology as such is necessarily arbitrary. Thereby, because they do not share the premise, they understand themselves to be exempt from the claim of the God to whom the Bible witnesses.

That brings us to the second point. To make the acceptance of the Bible a first act of faith is provincial. By provincialism I mean something more problematic than what we normally mean, as in the statement, "If you want to know how provincial your home town is, travel. If you want to know how provincial your age is, study history."[12] Kurt Tucholsky, whom we met at the beginning of this volume, wrote that aphorism. It takes us a half step beyond provincialism as narrowness by indicating an antidote, namely, stepping outside one's own place and time to see what it looks like from elsewhere. In another aphorism, he is more helpful on the issue before us: "One must read at least four newspapers with a major English daily and a major French one in addition. From the outside everything looks entirely different."[13]

---

12. Tucholsky, *Schnipsel,* p. 28.
13. Ibid., p. 36.

If one recognizes provincialism as narrowness of perspective, and if one knows that things look different from outside one's own province, then it follows that in order not to be provincial one should not claim for oneself or for one's special group something the likes of which one will not grant to those on the outside. Tucholsky illustrated this implication with an imaginative anecdote:

> A Christian[14] and a Jew were discussing religious questions. "One thing I cannot understand," said the Christian. "How is it possible for an educated man to believe that the Jews were led through the Red Sea?" "You may be right," said the Jew. "But how is it possible for a person to believe that Jesus Christ was raised from the dead?" "Oh, that's a different matter," said the Christian. "That's true."[15]

Barth believed it was theologically essential as a first act of faith that one accept the Bible as God's Word and that one assert this belief with no grounding that could be acknowledged from the outside. He could not possibly grant the same claim to a devotee of another religion with respect to another canon of writings, for example, to a Muslim with respect to the Koran. His doctrine of Scripture is inherently provincial.

That judgment, of course, comes from the outside and almost certainly would not have troubled Barth; but coupled with the arbitrariness of the doctrine, it has consequences for the central issue in those dark times. To hold that faith begins with the acceptance of a book or set of books as God's Word requires for the origin of faith a sacrifice of the intellect. That is, one accepts something on grounds different from and contrary to one or another of the ways one understands and talks reasonably about other things. A result is the surrender of the principle of radical criticism of anything pertaining to what has been so accepted.

This sacrifice of the intellect is not formally different from the sacrifice of the intellect theologians who supported Hitler made as

---

14. Tucholsky's text reads "Catholic," a type of Christian he thought was particularly arbitrary in issues of the faith. I have taken the liberty to use the more comprehensive term "Christian."

15. Tucholsky, *Schnipsel,* p. 132.

they gave themselves enthusiastically to his leadership. They, too, climbed the ladder to the roof and then threw the ladder away.

These comments must not be taken as a blurring of the line that sharply separated Barth and his opponents. The difference between Karl Barth and theologians who supported Hitler is enormous. Still, Barth's position, like theirs, rested on an arbitrary premise at one crucial point. This formal similarity is deeply troubling.

There are those who are certain that every religious belief originates in and is upheld by a sacrifice of the intellect. Rudolf Bultmann, however, was convinced that Christian faith does not make such a requirement. His efforts to explain how this is the case help us to understand the shifting ground in the relation between him and Barth and, after 1935, the growing distance between them that led Barth in 1952 to allege that their theological differences were beyond reconciliation.

Barth's title for his 1952 essay on Bultmann was brilliant: "Rudolf Bultmann: An Attempt to Understand Him." The verb "to understand" was used theologically more by Bultmann than by anyone else. It was a key to his case that Christian faith does not require a sacrifice of the intellect, and it was brilliantly appropriate for Bultmann to give the four volumes of his collected essays the title *Faith and Understanding*. He was convinced that the response in faith to the proclamation of the gospel of God in Jesus Christ is understandable not only to those who have faith but also to those who do not, if they can follow the logic of relationship on the human plane.

Christian faith is the consciousness of having been accepted by and set into relationship with the holy God who is beyond all things. In positive response to the proclamation of the crucifixion of Jesus as the decisive act of God, one has the sense of having been transformed by the power of Jesus' death. One is taken out of oneself such that, in Martin Luther's language, the curvature of the self in upon the self is broken. The repeated use of the passive voice is necessary to a proper description. The result is, as Paul put it, the end of boasting, a term Paul used as a synonym for sin.

God's gracious gift of relationship, received in faith, does not lift a person outside of or above the human sphere. One's boundedness and limitations are not removed. Thus faith is never a possession that one holds with unwavering confidence. On the contrary, it must always be received anew. One both has and does not have faith; one both believes and does not believe. Thus, in the interest of faith, one is always questioning the self. One engages in self-criticism of both one's activities and one's understandings.

The distinction between God and self—and consequently all selves—remains firm. It is this sense of difference, coupled with the understanding of one's own boundedness and limitations, that founds self-criticism, which in turn both enables and makes necessary the radical criticism of everything human. The texts of the Bible, as documents written by human beings, are not excluded. One may speak of the Bible as the Word of God, not as a tenet accepted in advance, but because in it one has read and heard what one can only name "the Word of God." That means, however, that the Bible itself, then, must be subjected to criticism on the basis of the word of God or the gospel, just as Paul's writings must be criticized on the basis of Paul's spirit, as Bultmann insisted in his controversy with Barth about 1 Corinthians. In the interest of faith itself and of truth, everything is subject to criticism.

The gospel not only makes radical criticism possible and necessary; it also provides criteria for that criticism. In the conduct of human life in society (recalling Bultmann's essay for Barth's fiftieth birthday in 1935, we might say, in the *polis* [the State]), these criteria emerge directly from the character of the relationship with God and its corollary in the self-understanding. Years before Hitler gained control of Germany, Bultmann argued repeatedly that because the grace of God creates a relationship, it is sharply to be distinguished from a worldview (*Weltanschauung*) or ideology and from a mystical union with God that raises one above the human plane, even if only in occasional ecstatic moments.[16] Readers should not miss the pointedness of these

---

16. Cf. especially Bultmann's 1931 address "Der Crisis des Glaubens" (The Crisis of Faith), which he gave in a series by three members of the Marburg faculty of theology. It is interesting to note that the overarching subject of the three lectures was good citizenship. Under that topic and in that year, Bultmann's sharp distinction of Christian faith from worldviews and mysticism took on special meaning. Bultmann published his address in *Glauben und Verstehen*, vol. 2, pp. 1–19. It has been translated into English under the title "The Crisis in Belief," in *Essays Philosophical and Theological,* trans. Greig, pp. 1–21.

denials. Nazism supported itself by its claim to be a total *Weltanschauung* and by the mystique of elevation that its rites and rhetoric were designed to evoke in people.

If one understands that by God's grace one is put in relationship to God, one's life is determined by gratitude. When gratitude to God is the foundation of one's life, one is drawn out of oneself and wants to be drawn out of oneself while one continues to live one's life in the relativities of this world. Life in the world for one who has been drawn out and wants to be drawn out of the self can be only a life lived in behalf of others (the neighbors). Bultmann not only argued that the chapter on love (13) is the climax of 1 Corinthians but repeatedly referred to the two places where Paul declared that the whole law is contained in the command to love the neighbor (Gal. 5:14 and Rom. 13:8–10). The language is both indicative and imperative, but throughout it tries to be descriptive. What is and what ought to be belong together. Anyone who has a good marriage can understand that.

Life in behalf of the neighbor is guided by the sense for the reality of God. It is the God over the whole world and all peoples whose justice, righteousness, and mercy are the standard by which we measure our hobbling efforts to make things here and now better, more tolerable, and more just. Every violation, one must believe, is an offense against the holy God, and every accomplishment will, in turn, be ambiguous.

There is no guarantee that anyone at any time will be able to recognize the demonic before it shows itself with horns, cleft feet, and trident. Should one see it for what it is, there is no guarantee that one will have the courage and character loudly to say "No!" "Here on earth we have all to go our ways on crutches."

Bultmann did not think that Christian faith eliminated the need for crutches, but he did think it calls one to live this life in the world as a radical critic and on behalf of the justice, righteousness, and mercy of God for all peoples. One can only hope that finding the source of one's life in this God beyond all things will give one sufficient freedom from the world to be courageous in bright as well as dark times. That, Bultmann thought, is what it means to live in the consciousness of the presence of the God of justice and grace.